Class

books by the same author published by Eyre Methuen

JOLLY SUPER
JOLLY SUPER TOO
JOLLY SUPERLATIVE
SUPERJILLY

Magnum Books

SUPER MEN AND SUPER WOMEN
WORK AND WEDLOCK

Fiction (Arlington Books)

EMILY
BELLA
HARRIET
OCTAVIA
PRUDENCE
IMOGEN

Class

Jilly Cooper

A view from middle England

with drawings by
TIMOTHY JAQUES

EYRE METHUEN
LONDON

First published 1979
Reprinted 1979 (twice)
by Eyre Methuen Ltd, 11 New Fetter Lane London EC4P 4EE
Copyright © Jilly Cooper 1979
Illustrations and captions copyright © Timothy Jaques 1979
Printed in Great Britain by
Richard Clay (The Chaucer Press) Ltd,
Bungay, Suffolk

ISBN 0 413 37360 6

Grateful acknowledgements are made to John Murray (Publishers) Ltd for
permission to quote from Collected Poems by John Betjeman; and to Robson
Books Ltd for permission to quote from My Oxford and My Cambridge

My husband, a publisher, claims that it is excruciatingly bad form to dedicate a book to one's publisher. It is therefore entirely in character for me to dedicate this book to my publisher, Geoffrey Strachan, with love and gratitude.

Tracey-Diane Nouveau-Richards in casual clothes

CONTENTS

A member of the telly-stocracy

ACKNOWLEDGEMENTS

I am extremely grateful to the people who have helped me with this book. They include Andrew Batute, formerly manager of the French Revolution Restaurant in London, John Challis, formerly manager of Lloyds Bank, Sloane Square, Michael Davey, funeral director, Mathias of Putney, Brian Edgington, headmaster of Roehampton Church School, Brian Holley, divisional careers officer of ILEA (Putney), Heather Jenner, Auriol Murray, of Nannies (Kensington), Renate Olins, of the Marriage Guidance Council, Charles Plouviez, chairman of Everetts Advertising.

I also owe an eternal debt to my friends, who have entered into the spirit of things, and come up with numerous suggestions, some serious, some less so. They include Brinsley Black, John Braine, Lucinda Bredin, Christopher Brown, Madeleine Carritt, Tony Carritt, Camilla Dempster, Val ffrench-Blake, Jonathan Gathorne-Hardy, Bertie Gratton-Bellew, Caroline Gray, Laura Hesketh, George Humphreys, Sophie Irvin, Jennifer Justice, Susan Kyle, Ronald and Sylvia Lewin, Miles and Juliet McNair, Nicholas Monson, John Parvin, Humphrey Pullar, Elizabeth Steel, Michael Stourton, Antonia Thynne, Guelda Waller, Alexander Weymouth, David Wright, Michael Ward, and Caroline Yardley.

Five other people made it possible for me to complete the book. I would therefore particularly like to thank my agent, George Greenfield, who has always shown such enthusiasm for the project, Beryl Hill, who typed out the manuscript and who miraculously managed to decipher my appalling handwriting, and my resident major domo, Maxine Green, who retyped chunks of the manuscript when I couldn't read my own corrections and kept up my spirits throughout those dark, desperate weeks, before the book was finally handed in. The lion's share of my gratitude, however, must go to my publisher, Geoffrey Strachan, who has been amazingly kind, patient, and encouraging over a long long period, when he must have despaired that the manuscript would ever see the light of day, and finally to my husband, Leo, whose humour and powers of observation have been a constant source of inspiration, and who remained good tempered, even when the whole house, including our bedroom, disappeared under a sea of papers and reference books.

DRAMATIS PERSONAE

The people you will meet in this book are:

HARRY STOW-CRAT, a member of the aristocracy
CAROLINE STOW-CRAT, his wife
GEORGIE STOW-CRAT, his son
FIONA STOW-CRAT, his daughter
and numerous other children, both regularly and irregularly conceived
SNIPE, a black Labrador

GIDEON UPWARD, a member of the upper middle classes
SAMANTHA UPWARD, his wife
ZACHARIAS UPWARD, his son
THALIA UPWARD, his daughter
COLONEL UPWARD, Gideon's father
MRS UPWARD, Gideon's mother

HOWARD WEYBRIDGE, a member of the middle middle classes
EILEEN WEYBRIDGE, his wife

BRYAN TEALE, a member of the lower middle classes
JEN TEALE, his wife
WAYNE TEALE, his son
CHRISTINE TEALE, his daughter

MR DEFINITELY-DISGUSTING, a member of the working classes
MRS DEFINITELY-DISGUSTING, his wife
DIVE DEFINITELY-DISGUSTING, his son

SHARON DEFINITELY-DISGUSTING, his daughter
and numerous other children

MR NOUVEAU-RICHARDS, a millionaire
MRS NOUVEAU-RICHARDS, his wife
JASON NOUVEAU-RICHARDS, his son
TRACEY-DIANE NOUVEAU-RICHARDS, his daughter

INTRODUCTION

About three years ago, when I rather tentatively suggested writing a book about the English class system, people drew away from me in horror.

'But that's all finished,' they said nervously, 'no-one gives a hoot any more. Look at the young.' They sounded as if I were intending to produce a standard work on coprophilia or child-molesting. It was plain that since the egalitarian shake-up of the sixties and early seventies, class as a subject had become the ultimate obscenity.

Three years of research later, I can assure you that the class system is alive and well and living in people's minds in England. There may have been an enormous shift of wealth between rich and poor. Every day Jack may be getting nearer his master financially, but social stratification remains incredibly resistant to change. It takes more than jeans and a taste in pop music to make even the young all one class. In fact after a period of enforced egalitarianism in the sixties when pop culture and socialism were in the ascendant, a whole new generation have appeared, who want the boundaries re-defined. This perhaps explains the popularity of Nigel Dempster's column in the *Daily Mail*, and such books as *The English Gentleman* by Douglas Sutherland and the recently published *U and Non-U Revisited*, edited by Richard Buckle.

Added to this is the colossal success of all those television serials and plays about the higher classes: *Upstairs Downstairs*, *Thomas and Sarah*, *Flambards* and *Rebecca*, not to mention the royal sagas. The fact that they have all been set in the past – because nostalgia excuses everything, enabling people to click their tongues over the out-dated inequalities, yet guiltily enjoy

the sense of hierarchy – must mean a hankering after some kind
of social pecking order.

What struck me, however, as soon as I started the book, was
the enormity of the task I had taken on. It was like trying to
catalogue the sea. For the whole system, despite its
stratification, is constantly forming and re-forming like coral.
'Even a small town like Swansea,' said Wynford Vaughan
Thomas, 'has as many layers as an onion, and each one of them
reduces you to tears.' To me, the system seemed more like a
huge striped rugger shirt that had run in the wash, with each
layer blurring into the next one, and snobbery being the fiercest
at the place where one stripe merged with another.

I found, too, that people were incredibly difficult to pin down
into classes. John went to a more famous boarding school than
Thomas, who has a better job than Charles, who's got smarter
friends than Harry, who lives in an older house with a bigger
garden than David, who's got an uncle who's an earl, but whose
children go to a comprehensive school. Who is then the gentleman?

A social class can perhaps be rather cumbersomely described
as a group of people with certain common traits: descent,
education, accent, similarity of occupation, wealth, moral
attitudes, friends, hobbies, accommodation; and with generally
similar ideas, and forms of behaviour, who meet each other on
equal terms, and regard themselves as belonging to one group.
A single failure to conform would certainly not exclude you
from membership. Your own class tend to be people you feel
comfortable with – 'one of our sort' – as you do when you are
wearing old flat shoes, rather than teetering round on precari-
ous five-inch heels. Aristocrats, for example, feel at home with
aristocrats: 'The nice thing about the House of Lords,'
explained one peer, 'is that you can have incredibly snobbish
conversations without feeling snobbish. Yesterday I admired a
chap's wife's diamonds: he said they came from Napoleon's
sword, and before then from Louis XIV.'

When people consider they are not of the same class it
becomes more complicated. 'Who knows,' wrote Montaigne,
'when I play with my cat, whether I do not make her more sport
than she makes me.' In the same way, quite often you think you
are being terribly democratic talking to some vulgar little
man at a party, while he at the same time is thinking how decent

he is wasting time on some one as socially insignificant as you.

Another charge has been levelled at me. What right, I am asked, have *I* to hold forth on the subject of the English class system? Most people who have tried in the past – Nancy Mitford, Christopher Sykes, Angus Maude – have been members of the upper classes. The answer is no right at all; all I can claim is a passionate interest in the subject, and that, being ashamedly middle class, I am more equidistant from the bottom and the top.

It is perhaps important to point out here, the various definitions of class which have been in use in England over the past twenty-five years. Principally there is the Census: *Classification of Occupations*, which is published every ten years or so (the latest was in 1970), which classifies everyone by the occupation of the head of the household of which they are members, irrespective of all other circumstances. This arbitrary categorisation is used as 'gospel' in most social surveys. Secondly there is 'U and Non-U,' a distinction invented by Professor Alan S. C. Ross in an essay first published in a learned Finnish periodical in 1954, which divided English people into 'U' (upper class) and 'Non-U' (non-upper class), mostly by the way they spoke and by the vocabulary they used. And finally comes the classification: 'A, B, C1 and C2, D and E', which is used by the media and by advertising, but which is basically the same as that of the Census.

What follows is the idiosyncratic view of someone bred in Yorkshire who has lived most of her life in London. If it reveals an obsessive interest in the classes nearest to the one in which I put myself, showing envy of those just above me in the hierarchy, scorn of those just below, and a slightly romanticized fantasy of those most far from my own experience, this will surely only confirm what is most typical of attitudes to class. An interest in social mobility and an obsession with class are, after all, thoroughly middle-class characteristics.

It might therefore be appropriate here to digress a little to explain what my own origins are. My paternal grandfather was a wool-merchant, but my maternal grandmother's family were a bit grander. They owned newspapers, and were distinguished Whig M.P.s for Leeds during the nineteenth century. My mother's side were mostly in the church, her father being

Canon of Heaton near Bradford. Her mother was a beauty.
Both sides had lived in the West Riding of Yorkshire for generations. They were very very strait-laced; to this day there has
never been a divorce in the family.

My father went to Rugby, then to Cambridge, where he got a
first in two years, and then into the army. After getting married,
he found he wasn't making enough money, and joined Fords,
and he and my mother moved somewhat reluctantly to Hornchurch, where I was born. At the beginning of the second world
war he was called up, and became one of the army's youngest
brigadiers. After the war, we moved back to Yorkshire, living
first in a large Victorian house. I was eight, and I think for the
first time became aware of class distinction. Our next-door
neighbour was a newly rich and very ostentatious wool manufacturer, of whose sybaritic existence my parents disapproved.
One morning he asked me over to his house. I had a heavenly
time, spending all morning playing the pianola, of which my
mother also disapproved – too much pleasure for too little effort
– and eating a whole eight-ounce bar of black market milk
chocolate, which, just after the war, seemed like stumbling on
Aladdin's cave. When I got home I was sick. I was aware that it
served me right both for slumming and for over-indulgence.

Soon after that we moved into the Hall at Ilkley, a splendid
Georgian house with a long drive, seven acres of fields for my
ponies, a swimming pool, and tennis and squash courts. From
then on we lived an élitist existence: tennis parties with
cucumber sandwiches, large dances, and fêtes in the garden. I
enjoyed playing little Miss Muck tremendously. I had a photograph of the house taken from the bottom of the drive on my
dressing-table at school, and all my little school friends, and
later my boy-friends, were very impressed when they came to
stay.

My brother, however, still had doubts about our life-style: it
was too bourgeois, too predictable and restricted, he thought.
One wet afternoon, I remember him striding up and down the
drawing-room, going on and on and on about our boring
middle-class existence.

Suddenly my mother, who'd been trying to read a detective
story, looked over her spectacles, and said with very gentle
reproof: 'Upper middle-class, darling.'

Occasionally we were taken down a peg by a socialist aunt

who thought we'd all got too big for our boots. One day my mother was describing some people who lived near York as being a very 'old' family.

'Whadja mean old?' snorted my aunt. 'All families are old.' On another occasion when my mother was grumbling about her char not turning up, my aunt suddenly snapped: 'And who are you to demand service?' Both became family catch-phrases.

There were very few eligible young men for me in Ilkley. The glamorous hard-drinking wool merchants' sons with their fast cars, teddy-bear coats, and broad Yorkshire accents were as above me sexually as they were below me, I felt, socially. But when I was about eighteen, two Old Etonians came to live for a year in the district. They were learning farming before going back to run their estates. They were both very attractive and easy-going, and were consequently asked everywhere, every mum with a marriageable daughter competing for their attention. I was terribly disconcerted when, after a couple of visits to our house and one of them taking me out once, they became complete habitués of the house of a jumped-up steel merchant across the valley. Soon they were both fighting for the hand of his not particularly good-looking daughter. But she's so much commoner than me – I remember thinking in bewilderment, why don't they prefer my company and our house? I realise now that they far preferred the easy-going atmosphere of the steel merchant's house, with its lush hospitality, ever-flowing drink, and poker sessions long into the night, to one glass of sherry and self-consciously intelligent conversation in ours. I had yet to learn, too, that people invariably dislike and shun the class just below them, and much prefer the class below that, or even the one below that.

I was further bewildered when, later in the year, I went to Oxford to learn to type, and shared a room with an 'Hon.' who said 'handbag'. This seemed like a blasphemy. Nancy Mitford's *The Pursuit of Love* had been my bible as a teenager. I knew peers' daughters, whom she immortalised as 'Hons', said 'bag' rather than 'handbag'. At that time, aware, too, of a slowly emerging sexuality and away for once from parental and educational restraint, I evolved a new way of dressing: five-inch high-heeled shoes, tight straight skirts, very very tight cheap sweaters, and masses of make-up to cover a still rather bad skin. I looked just like a tart. People obviously took me for one too.

For when the room-mate who was an Hon. introduced me to all her smart friends at Christchurch, one young blood promptly betted another young blood a tenner he couldn't get me into bed by the end of the week. Before he had time to lay siege, the story was repeated back to me. I was shattered: shocked and horrified to my virginal middle-class core; I cried for twenty-four hours. My would-be-seducer, who had a good heart, on hearing of my misery, turned up at my digs, apologised handsomely, and suggested, by way of making amends, rather than me, that he take me to the cinema. On the way there, he stopped at a sweet shop and bought a bar of chocolate. Breaking it, he gave me half, and started to eat the other half himself.

'But you can't eat sweets in the street,' I gasped, almost more shocked than I had been by his intended seduction.

'I,' he answered, with the centuries of disdain in his voice, 'Can do anything I like.'

Hons that talked about handbags, lords who ate chocolate in the streets like the working classes, aristocrats who preferred the jumped-up to the solidly middle class: I was slowly learning that the class system was infinitely more complicated than I had ever dreamed.

It takes many years, writes Jonathan Gathorne Hardy in *The Rise and Fall of the British Nanny*, for the outsider to master those complex, subtle distinctions, the nuances of accent, attitudes and behaviour that went, indeed which go, into that living, changing thing – English upper-class snobbery. He might have added that this is true of any class's snobbery.

The whole thing is relative. Freddie Trueman, who was certainly born working-class, defined a gentleman as someone who gets out of his bath 'to go t' toilet.' George IV said you could recognise the people who weren't gentlemen by the way they divide their coats when they sit down. The Queen Mother used to listen to *Mrs Dale's Diary* to find out how life went on in a 'middle-class' family. But most people who consider themselves middle-class, would regard Mrs Dale's life-style as flagrantly 'lower middle'.

When I went on Yorkshire Television with Jean Rook of the *Daily Express* a few years ago, the interviewer began most embarrassingly by saying: 'Now here you are, two columnists from Yorkshire, but from very different backgrounds. You're working-class, aren't you Jean, and, Jilly, you're upper-class.'

We both shrieked with horror.

'I'm middle, not upper,' I muttered, going scarlet.

'I'm upper middle,' said Miss Rook witheringly. 'I know lots of duchesses.'

Conversely when I go to very grand parties, my hostess invariably excuses my commonness and polyester cleavages by saying: 'D'you know Jilly? She's rather famous.'

Every court, I suppose, needs its jester.

But even in an egalitarian age, when it's no longer done to despise someone of a different class – (although the chippy working classes don't make much effort not to) it's very difficult not to adjust your behaviour according to the company you are in.

Shopping in Harrods with a peer's daughter recently, I actually found myself buying a little white dress with blue snowdrops for a boy baby rather than a Baby-Gro, because I'd read the week before in *Harper's* that the upper classes thought Baby-Gros were common. Next day I was lunching in a restaurant with a working-class writer and I found myself, who never touch pudding, saying I'd love some because he was, and I didn't want to appear snooty.

I heard also of a psychiatrist who was treating an aristocrat for depression. A month went by, and they seemed to be making little progress.

'I want you to be completely honest,' said the psychiatrist at the next session, 'And tell me exactly what's in your mind at the moment.'

'I was thinking,' said the aristocrat apologetically, 'What a vulgar little man you were.'

It was their final session. The psychiatrist was unable to go on, because he'd completely lost any feeling of ascendancy.

'And so,' as John Coleman once wrote in the *Sunday Times*, 'the old movements of social advance and recoil go on, just as much as they always did. It is the perpetual inaccuracy of imitation that makes up the English social comedy and tragedy.'

But there is plenty of comedy. As a small boy at my son's last school pointed out in an essay, 'All people should be gentlemen except ladies, but it puts a bit of variety into life if some are not.'

I am very aware of the inadequacies of this book. The subject is so vast and so complex that I have only touched on a few aspects, which seemed important to me. I have made many sweeping generalisations, which I hope people won't take too seriously, because other classes are not better or worse than one's own, they are merely different. I have also tried to show that there have certainly been changes in vocabulary and attitude in the past twenty-five years.

One need look no further for an example than Miss Barbara Cartland, being interviewed by Sandra Harris on the *Today* programme, and being asked whether she thought the class barriers had broken down.

'Of course they have,' said Miss Cartland, 'Or I wouldn't be sitting here talking to someone like you.'

Putney, May 1979

1　THE CLASSES

The aristocracy

All the world loves a titled person.

According to sociologists, the aristocracy is such a tiny minority – about 0.2 per cent of the population – as to be statistically negligible. The ones that do not work or who run their own estates are not even listed in the Census. They are like the scattering of herbs and garlic on top of a bowl of dripping or, more poetically, like water lilies who float, beautiful and some would say useless, on the surface of a pond. Being a lord, of course, doesn't make you an aristocrat. Only about half the nobility are aristocracy, the rest being life peers. These are commoners elevated to the peerage so that they may sit in the House of Lords, but their titles die with them. And only about a third of the aristocracy are ennobled, the rest being families of younger sons or country squires, some of whom have had money and influence far longer and can trace their families back much farther than many a duke or earl.

In fact so many of the aristocracy don't have titles that they regard *Burke's Peerage*, which covers the landed gentry as well, as a far more important source book than *Debrett's Peerage and Baronetage*. One peer told his secretary she must get an up-to-date copy of *Burke's* 'so you'll know all the people I'm talking about.' The point about the aristocracy is they all know each other.

Traditionally, as will be shown in later chapters, they didn't work for their living, and although many of them have jobs to-day, they find difficulty in applying the same dedication and materialism as the middle classes.

They used, of course, to be terribly rich. At the turn of the century, if you were asked to stay at Woburn, one chauffeur and a footman would take you as far as Hendon, where another chauffeur and a footman would be waiting to take you to Woburn. As a gentleman never travelled with his luggage, another two cars were needed to carry this. So it meant two chauffeurs and two footmen to get you and your luggage as far as Hendon, and two more chauffeurs and footmen to take you to Woburn. Eight men to transport one guest, in heaven knows how large a house party, down to the country. Then there was the Marquess of Hertford, who had a house in Wales he'd never been to, but where every night a huge dinner was cooked by a fleet of servants in case he *did* turn up.

The late Duke of Westminster's family in 1978 owned 300 acres in Belgravia and Oxford Street, 12,000 acres around Eaton, 14,000 acres in North Wales, 1,000 acres in Kent, 400 acres in Shropshire, 800 acres in North Wales and 1,000 acres in British Columbia, Hawaii and Australia. The heir, Earl Grosvenor, inherited sixteen million pounds on his twenty-first birthday. Hardly the bread line.

Today, as a result of death duties and capital transfer tax, however, most aristocrats are desperately broke, certainly by comparison with their grandfathers, and are reduced to renting off wings as apartments, selling paintings, turning their gardens into zoos and amusement parks, and letting the public see over their houses. Anyone who has experienced the nightmare of showing a handful of people over their own house when they put it up for sale, will understand the horror of having a million visitors a year peering into every nook and cranny.

Although they have considerable influence in the Tory party, the aristocracy no longer run the country as they did in the eighteenth and nineteenth centuries. But, despite the erosion of his privileges, the aristocrat's view of his responsibilities remains the same; responsibilities to the tenants, the community (the good aristocrat always had a strong sense of public duty), and to the house he lives in, often so beautiful as to be a national monument, but to which the nation pays no contribution.

One of the characteristics of the aristocrat is the extreme sentiment he feels towards his house, and his inheritance. His wife is expected to feel the same. Because our own aristocracy were so anxious to preserve their inheritance, they tended only to marry their own kind. The middle classes married for love. The upper classes married to preserve their rank. All twenty-six dukes are, as at present, related to one another. And as long as rank was protected, and money obtained in sufficient quantities to support this rank, infidelity after marriage, as Brian Masters points out in *The Dukes*, was taken for granted:

'A painter,' screamed the Duchess, 'What painter? Sylvia Roehampton's daughter to marry a painter, but of course she won't. You marry Tony Wexford, and we'll see what can be done about the painter later.'

As they weren't expected to be faithful, unlike the middle classes they didn't feel guilty if they wandered, which explains the over-active libido of the aristocrat. He expected to exercise his *droit du seigneur* over his tenants but he also saw himself as a Knight Errant like Don Quixote, living in a world of romantic adventure. When your ancestors have been fighting battles and seducing women for thousands of years, one German nobleman told me recently, it's terribly difficult to settle down to one wife and an office job.

As a result of all this infidelity, a high proportion of the aristocracy is irregularly conceived, but, as they all know each other, they're still pretty dotty with inbreeding. When my uncle was Lord Spencer's agent, my aunt said she met all the local aristocracy, many of them as mad as hatters. When they talked about one of their friends 'coming out', you never knew if they were doing the season, or being discharged from a loony bin.

Colossal self-confidence is perhaps the hallmark of the aristocrat. Like the *chevalier* 'without fear and without self-reproach' he goes through life unafraid, and doesn't question his own motives, or feel guilty about his actions. One summer when I went shooting in Northumberland I noticed a beautiful blond young man in a red sweater at the next butt. Why didn't he have to wear green camouflage like the rest of us, I asked.

'Because he's a duke's son,' said my host. 'He can do what he likes.'

Not answerable to other people, the aristocrat is often unimaginative, spoilt, easily irritated and doesn't flinch from showing it. If he wants to eat his peas with his knife he does so.

'Dear Kate,' said Henry V, 'You and I cannot be confined

within the weak list of a country's fashion; we are the makers of manners, Kate; and the liberty that follows our places stops the mouth of all find-faults.'

As the makers of manners, many of the aristocracy, while feeling they have a duty towards the community as Sheriffs and Lord Lieutenants, are indifferent to public opinion.

'One doesn't care what the press say,' said the Marquess of Anglesey, at a dinner party. 'One's friends know what one's like and that's all that matters.' The only thing he minded, he went on, was that the National Trust film on television had said he was very rich. The hostess then asked him if he'd like moussaka or cold turkey.

'I'd like both,' he said.

Not caring a stuff what people think leads also to a rich vein of eccentricity: the Marquess of Londonderry throwing soup at a fly that was irritating him in a restaurant, and Sir Anthony Eden's father hurling a barometer out of the window into the pouring rain, yelling: 'See for yourself, you bloody thing!'

Or there was the imperious peer who, when he missed a train, ordered the station-master to get him another one.

Professor A. S. C. Ross has said that above a certain level, all 'U' people are equal. With respect, I think few upper-class people would agree with him. The ancient aristocracy consider it's very vulgar to have been founded after the Tudors, which puts most of our present dukes beyond the pale. In fact, in the nineteenth century most of the aristocracy were so worried about the comparative youthfulness of their families that they all employed genealogists to try and trace their ancestors back to the Conqueror. Brian Masters tells a story of the Duchesses of Buccleugh and of Westminster sidling through a door together in their determination not to give precedence.

Between aristocrats and other classes there is certainly a barrier of rank. My mother and father used to live near Hampton Court Palace, where widows of distinguished men, some of them aristocrats, have apartments. My mother met a peer's widow at a drinks party, and they got on so well that my mother wrote to her next day asking her to dine. Back came a letter of acceptance, but with a P.S. 'I hope you don't mind my pointing out, Elaine dear, that the palace should be the first to issue invitations.'

It has been suggested that this obsession with rank probably

Harry Stow-Crat, Caroline and Snipe

had something to do with boredom. Without a career, the aristocrat had to fill his days. He was not a great intellectual: Jane Austen's Sir Walter Eliot, whose reading consisted of his own entry in *Burke's Peerage*, is fairly near the mark. He preferred more exciting entertainment, hence his addiction to blood sports, and to gambling. I shall never forget watching an aristocrat and a television newsreader playing backgammon one evening. The newsreader's wife, who was ravishingly beautiful, and bored by the lack of attention, suddenly came in with no clothes on and danced round and round them. Neither of them took any notice.

The aristocrat, when he wants to, has very good manners, The Scottish upper classes, in particular, have that shell-shocked look that probably comes from banging their heads on low beams leaping to their feet whenever a woman comes into the room. Aristocrats are also deeply male chauvinist, and, although you get left-wing extremists like Lord Weymouth who sends his children to a comprehensive school and has revolutionary ideas, on the whole they tend to be reactionary.

While writing this book I found there were very much two strands in the character of the aristocracy: first the wild, delinquent, arrogant, capricious, rather more glamorous element; and second the stuffy 'county', public-spirited, but publicity-shy element, epitomised by the old baronet whose family were described 'as old as the hills and infinitely more respectable'.

Or, as a small boy, writing in my son's school magazine, pointed out: 'Gentlemen are of two types: the nose-uppish and the secluded'.

In order to write this book, I have dealt in archetypes. The aristocracy and upper classes are represented by the HON. HARRY STOW-CRAT. Son of the fifth Baron Egliston, educated at Eton, he served in the Coldstream. He now runs his diminishing estate, selling the odd Van Dyck to make ends meet, but does more or less what he pleases. He lives in a large decaying house in the North Riding of Yorkshire, and has a flat in Chelsea. He has a long-suffering wife, CAROLINE, who does a great deal for charity, an eldest son, GEORGIE, a daughter called FIONA, and several other children. He has numerous mistresses, but none to whom he is as devoted as to his black labrador, SNIPE. He has had many moments of frustration and boredom in his life, but never any of self-doubt.

The middle classes

*Would you come round the world next year in
the France with me? I got a letter from Gerry
Wellesley on a cruise saying he'd never met
middle-class people before, and they are quite
different from us. Isn't he awful.*

Nancy Mitford

The middle classes are in fact *quite* different – being riddled with
self-doubt, which is hardly surprising after all the flak they've
received over the years. The upper classes despised them for
their pre-occupation with money, and because they suspected it
was middle-class malcontents rather than the rabble who had
plotted and set alight the French Revolution. 'How beastly the
bourgeois is,' mocked the working-class Lawrence, and in fact
épater le bourgeois has always been a favourite sport of both high
and low. Even their own ranks have attacked them: 'The People
in Between,' wrote Hilaire Belloc, 'Looked underdone and
harassed,/And out of place, and mean/And horribly embarrassed.'

And they have even been blamed for the evils of the class
system. It is the middle classes, wrote one sociologist, with their
passion for order and reason, who have sought to impose a kind
of stratification on what is in fact an eternally malleable and
bubbling class system. Which is rubbish because, as we have
already seen, the aristocracy is just as obsessed with rank.

Occasionally they have their defenders. 'I come from the
middle classes,' said Neville Chamberlain, 'and I am proud of
their ability, the shrewdness, the industry and providence, the
thrift by which they are distinguished.'

But even Chamberlain's finest hour, returning from Munich
proclaiming 'Peace with Honour', was witheringly described
by some aristocrat at the time, as 'Retreat with Boasting'.

In a way, the middle classes seem to suffer as the middle child
does. Everyone make a huge fuss over the firstborn (just as all
the world loves a lord). And everyone adores and pets and
coddles the baby (who is like the working classes, shored up by
a great feather bed of the welfare state). But the child in the
middle gets the most opprobrium, often left to fend for itself,
and ganged up on by the other two. It is doubly significant that

in the English Civil War, the rabble joined up with the King, against the Puritan middle classes. If Marx was the champion of the working classes, Calvin was the prophet of the middle classes. They believed implicitly in the Puritan Ethic, in the cultivation of such virtues as diligence, frugality, propriety and fidelity. Work to keep sin at bay, feel guilty if you slack. Shame is a bourgeois notion.

Although there is a world of difference between the top of the middle classes and the bottom, between the great merchant banker, and the small shopkeeper, they are united in their desire to get on, not just to survive. Unlike the upper classes and the working classes, the middle classes thought careers were important. They started little businesses. They worked to pass exams after they'd left school. They believed in the law of the jungle and not the welfare state – if you got on in life, good luck to you.

For this reason they believed in the importance of education long before the other classes. They believed in deferred satisfaction. They saved in order to send their children to private schools, or to buy their own houses. If the upper classes hand on the estates they have inherited to their children, the middle classes hand on the small businesses they have built up to theirs. To the working classes the most important criterion of middle-class membership, after money or income, is owning a small business or being self-employed.

Although they don't 'know everyone' like the upper classes, the upper middles, and many of the middles, having been to boarding school, and probably their parents or even grandparents having been too, have a much wider spread circle of friends than the working classes. They are also able to keep in touch with them by telephone, or by their ability to write letters. Many of them have a spare room where friends can come and stay.

They therefore tend to know many more people outside the district where they live than the working classes, and don't need to depend on the street and their immediate neighbours for help or for their identity. They can afford to keep themselves to themselves. Aloofness, reserve, and a certain self-righteousness are also middle-class qualities.

To illustrate the three main strands of the middle classes we again fall into archetypes, with SAMANTHA and GIDEON UPWARD

The Upwards

as the upper middle-class couple, HOWARD and EILEEN
WEYBRIDGE, as the middle middles, and BRYAN and JEN TEALE
as the lower middles.

Gideon and Samantha Upward: the merry-tocracy

The upper middle classes are the most intelligent and highly
educated of all the classes, and therefore the silliest and the
most receptive to every new trend: radical chic, health foods,
ethnic clothes, bra-lessness, gifted children, French cooking.
Gideon Upward gave his mother-in-law a garlic crusher for
Christmas. The upper middles tend to read *The Guardian* at
least as much as *The Times* and are proud of their liberal and
enlightened attitudes. They are also the most role-reversed of
the classes: Gideon does a great deal of cooking and housework.
Samantha longs to be a good mother and have an Int'risting Job
at the same time. To save petrol, she often rides round on a
sit-up-and-beg bicycle, with wholemeal bread in the front basket, and a bawling child in the back. Sometimes her long dirndl
skirt catches in the pedals. She has a second in history and a
fourth in life.

Gideon and Samantha both went to 'good schools', Gideon
probably to Winchester or to Sherborne. He might be an
architect or work in the City. He wears a signet ring with a crest
on the little finger of his left hand, in an attempt to proclaim
near-aristocratic status, just as the middle middles would wear
an old school tie, to show they'd been to boarding school; the
lower middles would give their house a name instead of a
number, to prove it wasn't council but bought; and the working
class bring back plastic bulls from Majorca to show they've
travelled.

Gideon and Samantha have two children called ZACHARIAS
and THALIA, whom they might start off liberally sending to state
school, and trying not to wince at the first 'pardon', but would
be more likely to send to a private school. They love their
English setter, BLUCHER, and feel frightfully guilty loving it
almost more than their children. Harry Stow-Crat would have
no such scruples. Gideon plays tennis and rugger for a club, but
he wouldn't use the club to make friends, and he and Samantha
wouldn't touch a Country Club, as reeking of suburbia. They
prefer to entertain in their own house, which is large and old,

and being restored to its original state rather faster than they'd like. Samantha is into good works with a slightly self-interested motive: anti-pollution, conservation, the Parent Teachers Association.

In the past fifteen years, the upper middles have aimed for a standard of living they can't afford, taking on many of the pastimes of the upper classes. Gideon goes shooting quite often. They have two cars, which are falling to pieces and for which they have to pay a fortune every time they take their M.O.T. They once had a country cottage, holidays abroad, and a boat. Now they have two children at boarding school, and since the advent of the permissive society, Gideon has been playing at adultery almost like Harry Stow-Crat. As a result, he spends a fortune on lunches, and a fortune on guilt presents for Samantha afterwards. They are both so worried about trying to make ends meet, they're drinking themselves absolutely silly which is why I call them the 'Merry-tocracy'.

Virginia Woolf wrote a novel called *The Years* about an upper middle-class family called the Pargeters. 'Parget' is an English dialect word meaning to smooth over the cracks and plastered surfaces. The Pargeters whitewash and gloss over the deep sexual and emotional fissures of life. In the same way Samantha doesn't particularly like her mother-in-law, or later, her daughter-in-law, or several of her neighbours; but she tries to get on with them, because she feels guilty about her dislike. If Samantha hired a gardener even for two hours, she wouldn't flaunt him as a status symbol, she'd keep quiet, because she feels it's more 'creative' to do all the garden herself.

She and Gideon call each other 'darling', rather than 'dear', and try to remember to say 'orf'. Gideon's parents, Colonel and Mrs Upward, living on a fast dwindling fixed income, are much more thrifty than Samantha and Gideon. As they're not drinking themselves silly, they don't smash everything and still have the same glasses and china as they did when they were first married.

Howard and Eileen Weybridge: the middle middles

Howard Weybridge lives in Surrey or some smart dormitory town. He works as an accountant, stockbroker, surveyor or higher technician. He probably went to a minor public school

The Weybridges

or a grammar school. He never misses the nine o'clock news and says 'Cheerio'. He wears paisley scarves with scarf rings and no bottoms to his spectacles. He calls his wife 'Eileen, dear', and when you ask him how he is, says: 'Very fit, thank you'. He is very straight and very patriotic. His haw-haw voice is a synthetic approximation to the uppers; he talks about 'Ham-shar'. His children join the young *Con*-servatives and the tennis club to meet people. He buys a modern house, and ages it up. It has a big garden with a perfect lawn and lots of shrubs. He despises anyone who hasn't been to 'public school', and often goes into local government, or politics for social advancement. He is a first generation pony buyer, and would also use the pony club to meet the right sort of people. His wife Eileen shops at Bentalls in Kingston, and thinks the upper middles are terribly scruffy. They are both keen golfers, and pull strings to get their road made private. Their favourite programmes are *Any Answers*, *These You have Loved*, and *Disgusted Tunbridge Wells*. They are much smugger than the upper middles.

Howard Weybridge's father hasn't a bill in the world, and is on the golf club committee, he found bridge to be one of the most wonderful things in life, it's a very easy way of entertaining. He has a sneaking liking for Enoch Powell. ('We should have stopped sambos coming here in the first place.')

Bryan and Jen Teale: the lower middles

The Teales are probably the most pushy, the most frugal, and most respectable of all the classes, because they are so anxious to escape from the working class. The successful ones iron out their accents and become middle like Mr Heath and Mrs Thatcher, the rest stay put, as bank and insurance clerks, door-to-door salesmen, toast-masters, lower management, police sergeants and sergeant majors. In the old days, the lower middles rose with the small business or the little shop, but the rise in rates, social security benefits and postage has scuppered all that.

The lower middles never had any servants, but as they are obsessed with cleanliness, and like everything nice, they buy a small modern house, and fill it with modern units which are

Bryan and Jen Teale

easy to keep clean. Jen and Bryan have two children, WAYNE
and CHRISTINE, and a very clean car.

As Jen and Bryan didn't go to boarding school, didn't make
friends outside the district, and don't mix with the street, they
have very few friends, keeping themselves to themselves. They
tend to be very inner-directed, doing everything together,
decorating the house, furnishing the car, and coaching and
playing football with the children. Jen reads knitting patterns,
Woman's Own, and *Reader's Digest* condensed books. To avoid
any working-class stigma, she puts up defensive barriers: privet
hedges, net curtains, talks in a 'refained' accent, raises her little
finger when she drinks and runs with her hands turned out, as
though she were drying her nail polish. Her aim is to be dainty,
and wear six pairs of knickers. She admires Mary Whitehouse
enormously, disapproves of long hair and puts money in the
Woolwich every week. She sees herself as the 'Woolwich girl'.
The children are always being pulled up for some real or
imagined coarseness of speech. The Teales don't entertain
much, only Bryan's colleagues who might be useful, and
occasionally Bryan's boss.

The Working Classes

One of the great class divides has always been 'Them' and 'Us'.
This, as a result of the egalitarian, working-class-is-beautiful
revolution of the sixties and early seventies, has polarised into
the Guilty and the Cross. On the one side are the middle and
upper classes, feeling guilty and riddled with social concern
although they often earn far less money than the workers. On
the other are the working classes, who have been totally brain-
washed by television and magazine images of the good life, and
feel cross because they aren't getting a big enough slice of the
cake.

In a time of economic prosperity, everyone tends to do well,
wages rise. The middle classes can afford perhaps a new boat,
or central heating, the working-class man buys a new car and a
fridge for the missus. Man's envy and rivalry is turned towards
his immediate neighbour (keeping up with the Joneses) rather
than towards the classes above and below. But in times of
economic stress, when people suddenly can't get the things they

want, and prices and the cost of living outstrip wages, they start turning their envy against other classes. Antagonism against a neighbour feathering his nest tends to be replaced by an awareness of class inequalities.

In a time of economic security, society therefore tends to look fairly cohesive, which is probably why in the early seventies, a lot of people genuinely believed that class barriers had finally broken down. But as the decade advanced, the working-class people who'd bought their houses and were up to the necks in hire purchase suddenly found they couldn't keep up their payments. Their expectations had been raised, and their security was being threatened by the additional calamity of mass unemployment. This discontent, fanned by the militants, resulted in the rash of strikes in the winter of 1978.

For although the middle classes often think of the working-class man earning huge sums on overtime, the rewards of his job are in fact much less. The manual worker doesn't have job satisfaction or a proper pension, he doesn't have fringe benefits, all the perks of cars, trips abroad, expense account lunches, and longer holidays. He has to clock in, and his earning span is much shorter. Once his physical strength goes, he can look forward to an old age of comparative poverty and deprivation. This all results in workers avoiding any kind of moral commitment to the management. We cheat the foreman, is the attitude, he cheats the manager, and the manager cheats the customer.

Richard Hoggart in *The Uses of Literacy* brilliantly summed up the workers' attitude to Them; (i.e. the establishment and the management):

'They are the people at the top, the highers up, the people who give you your dole, call you up tell you to go to work, fine you, make you split up the family in the thirties (to avoid a reduction in the means test allowance) get yer in the end, aren't really to be trusted, talk posh, are all twisters really, never tell yer owt (e.g. about a relative in hospital), clap yer in the clink, will do y'down if they can, summons yer, are all in a click together, treat y'like muck.'

Because they dislike the management, the working classes don't like people saving their money or getting on through hard work. They put a premium on enjoying pleasure now, drinking their wages, for example, or blowing the whole lot on a new colour telly. Traditionally the only legitimate way to make a lot of money was to win it. Hence the addiction to gambling, football pools, racing, bingo and the dogs.

Living from hand to mouth, they can't manage their money like the lower middles. When the army started paying guardsmen by cheque recently, my bank manager said they got into the most frightful muddles. If he wrote and told one of them he was overdrawn, say by £30, the guardsman promptly sent in a cheque for that amount.

Traditionally working-class virtues are friendliness, co-operation, warmth, spontaneity, a ready sense of humour, and neighbourliness. 'We're all in the same boat', is the attitude. That 'love' is still the most common form of address really means something. They have been defined as people who belong to the same Christmas club, characteristically saving up not for something permanent, like the deposit on a house but for a good blow-out. They have a great capacity for enjoyment.

Because they didn't have cars, or telephones, and couldn't afford train fares, and the men tended to walk to work nearby, working-class life tended to centre round the street and the neighbourhood. 'Everyone knowing your business', said one working-class man, 'it's no good putting on airs, because you earned more. The neighbours remember you as a boy, knew your Aunt Lil, who's no better than she should be, and took you down a peg. The network acts as a constant check.'

Girls seldom moved away from their mothers when they married. Sons often came home for lunch every day, or lived at home, even after marriage. The working-class family is much closer and more possessive than most. They seldom invite friends into the house. 'I've never had a stranger [meaning non-family] in here since the day I moved in,' said one woman. 'I don't hold with that sort of thing.'

Being so dependent on the locality, the working classes are often lost and desperately lonely if the council suddenly moves them to housing estates, or shuts them up in little boxes, in some high-rise block. Working-class men have also lost much of the satisfaction that came from the old skills and crafts. Many of these have been taken away from them during the past twenty-five years and their traditional occupations destroyed by machines. In the old days the husband gained respect as a working man in the community.

Women's Lib hasn't helped his self-respect much either. The working classes are the most reactionary of all the classes. (You only have to look at those Brylcreemed short backs and sides, and wide trousers flapping like sails in the breeze at the T.U.C. Conference at Brighton or Blackpool.) But despite this, the working-class housewife now reads about Women's Lib in the paper, and soon she's fretting to go back to work full time and make some extra cash, rather than act as a servant to the family, and have her husband's dinner on the table every night when he gets home. She starts questioning his superiority, and, having less autonomy at home, and never having had any at work, he feels even more insecure.

Leaving school at sixteen, he feels inadequate because he is inarticulate. He is thought of as being so bloody-minded and lazy by the middle classes (because he can't express himself) that 'Definitely, disgusting', in answer to any question put to him, is the only way he can show his disapproval.

Among their other rankings, the working classes divide themselves firmly into the Rough and the Respectable. The Rough get drunk fairly often, make a great deal of noise at night, often engage in prostitution, have public fights, neglect their children, swear in front of children and women, and don't give a stuff about anything – just like the upper classes in fact. The Respectables chunter over such behaviour, and in Wales sing in Male Voice Choirs; they are pretty near the Teales. They also look down on people on the dole, the criminal classes and sometimes black people, whom they refer to as 'soap-dodgers'.

Mr and Mrs Definitely-Disgusting

Our archetypal working-class couple are MR and MRS DEFINITELY-DISGUSTING. They have two children, SHARON and DIVE, and live in a council house with walls so thin you can hear the budgie pecking its seed next door. Mr Definitely-Disgusting is your manual worker, he might be a miner in the North, a car worker in the Midlands, or a casual labourer in the South. He married young, and lived for a while with his wife's parents; after a year or two he went back to going to the pub, football, and the dogs with the blokes. He detests his mother-in-law. But

The Definitely-Disgustings

despite his propensity to foul language, he is extremely modest, always undressing with his back to Mrs D-D and even peeing in a different way from the other classes, splaying out his fingers in a fan, so they conceal his member. He often does something slightly illegal, nicking a car, or knocking off a telly. He is terrified of the police, who, being lower middle, and the class just above, reserve their special venom for him. Mrs Definitely-Disgusting wears her curlers and pinny to the local shop, and spends a lot of the day with a cigarette hanging from her bottom lip gossiping and grumbling.

Mr and Mrs Nouveau-Richards

The other couple you will meet are the NOUVEAU-RICHARDS, of working-class origin, who've made a colossal amount of money. Boasting and ostentation are their salient characteristics. At coffee mornings Mrs Nouveau-Richards, who lives in lurex, asks anyone if they've got 'any idea whether gold plate will spoil in the dishwasher.' She has a huge house, and lots of servants, whom she bullies unmercifully. She is very rude to waiters and very pushy with her children, TRACEY-DIANE and JASON, who have several hours after school coaching every day. Mr Nouveau-Richards gets on the committee of every charity ball in London. The upper classes call him by his Christian name and appreciate his salty humour, but don't invite him to their houses. Jason goes to Stowe and Oxford, and ends up a member of the Telly-stocracy, who are the real powers in the land, the people in communications who appear on television. They always talk about 'my show'.

The Nouveau-Richards

2 CHILDREN

The kiddy is the dad of the guy . . .

At the beginning of the seventies, the small-is-beautiful brigade mounted a campaign to bring down the birthrate. Family Planning Association supporters brandished condoms outside the Commons, and sidled bossily up to women who'd just had babies at parties saying: 'Two's yer ration'. Middle-class lefties were rumoured to be concealing third babies in attics rather than display evidence of such social irresponsibility. Disapproving ads appeared in the cinema showing defeated slatterns in curlers trailing herds of whining children along the street. 'Superdad or Scrounger?', howled the *Daily Mirror* when a man on social security proudly produced his twenty-first child.

In the face of economic gloom, a rocketing dole queue and mothers wanting to get back to work, people probably thought twice about bringing more children into the world. Whatever the cause, the campaign worked. The birth rate in the U.K. dropped by 30 per cent. The working classes in particular, having discovered the Pill, curbed production dramatically and at the last count were only producing 2.16 children per family while the upper middles were down to 1.7. The higher you go up the social scale, in fact, the smaller the family, although the aristocracy tend to run unpatriotically riot, probably because, as Evelyn Waugh pointed out: 'Impotence and sodomy are socially O.K., but birth control is flagrantly middle-class.' One can't imagine an aristocrat having a vasectomy.

With the working classes on the Pill, the middle classes, particularly the wholemeal bread brigade, started panicking about long-term effects, and switched to the coil or sterilisation.

The respectable working class still favour the sheath, described by Mrs Definitely-Disgusting, as 'my hubby always using something'.

The birth

Caroline Stow-Crat gives up work with relief the moment she gets pregnant. The office is relieved too, they're fed up with the endless telephone calls, the Thursday to Tuesday weekends, and falling over the labrador everytime they go to the filing cabinet. Samantha Upward tends to work till the last possible minute, ticking away like a time bomb, and terrifying all the men in the office.

Our Queen was born by Caesarian, feet first. When Prince Charles was born, the Duke of Edinburgh was playing squash. Today he would probably have been squashed into the maternity ward of St Mary's, Paddington. The trend now for the higher socio-economic classes is to have epidurals, which makes the whole thing less harrowing, and for the husband, albeit very reluctantly, to be present at the birth. 'They do rather get in the way,' said my G.P. 'It's best if they stand at the head of the bed to give their wife moral support, but they keep creeping down the bed to have a look' (probably the first they've had in months).

Despite working-class prudishness, this trend will no doubt also filter down the social scale, since those two sacred cows, Anthea Redfern and Esther Rantzen recently calved with husbands Bruce Forsyth and Desmond Wilcox in attendance, and beaming with besotted middle-aged joy afterwards. The labour wards will soon be as crowded out with nail-biting males as Twickenham during an England–Welsh International.

When the wife of Superdad-or-Scrounger produced their twenty-first child, four of the children were allowed to watch. Perhaps the television had broken down. 'It was very exciting,' said the eight-year-old afterwards.

The upper classes are not wild about new-born babies. Nancy Mitford once described one as a 'howling orange in a black wig'. But they are delighted to have their double-barrelled names carried on by sons.

A few years ago *Harper's* published a brilliant piece on the

'Sloane Ranger', the girl who has a flat in Kensington and
parents in the country, who lives in headscarves and went to a
'good' girls' boarding-school. She epitomizes the strand where
the more traditional upper middles merge into the lower rungs
of the upper classes. The Sloane Ranger husband is very chuf-
fed whatever sex child he has. If he has a boy he goes straight off
to his club and writes two letters, one to 'my housemaster at
Eton, one to Mrs Ingham at Eaton House'. Then he opens a
bottle of champagne.

Harry Stow-Crat, who certainly wasn't present at the birth,
doesn't bother to write letters to anyone, perfectly confident he
can get his son in anywhere. He might ring up his mother and
his old nanny, have a large whiskey and soda, then go off and
see his mistress.

Poor Gideon Upward is having a horrid time. He now knows
exactly why it's called a 'con-finement' – he's being conned
rotten forking out for a private room, and it's not very *fine* the
way Samantha, who insisted on natural childbirth, disapproving of epidurals, is now yelling her head off. Still he's delighted
when little Zacharias (Samantha went right through the Bible
to find a name no one else had used) appears. It's so nice to have
a boy first so he can take little 0.7 to dances when they grow up.

While Samantha was in hospital, Gideon was planning to
have a crack at his secretary, but ever-thoughtful Samantha has
arranged for married friends to ask him out every night. Gideon
gets drunk out of frustration, and the prospect of his mother-in-
law coming to stay next week, and makes sodden passes at the
wives while their role-reversed husbands are doing the washing
up. The passes are tactfully forgotten about afterwards.

Mr Definitely-Disgusting finds it difficult to visit his wife in
hospital because of shift work, and National Health visiting
hours. When he does, the conversations are usually mono-
syllabic and inhibited by groans from the labour ward next
door.

Aristocrats often get married just before the birth to legitim-
ise the child in case it's a boy. I attended one such wedding
where the bride was actually in the last stages of labour. The
hospital had thoughtfully provided an altar with a brass cross
and two plastic orchids in a mauve vase. The bridegroom
hadn't bothered to brush his hair but looked so impossibly
handsome that the screaming queen of a hospital chaplain got

thoroughly over-excited; and spent so long holding his hand, he almost forgot to join it to that of the bride, who was manfully carrying on with: 'To have ... *(groan)* ... and to hold, from this ... *(groan)*.'

The announcement

If you are very grand *The Times* reports the birth on the social pages free of charge. The rest of the upper classes put it in the birth column as briefly as possible.

'To Caroline, wife of Harry Stow-Crat – a son.'

Harry wouldn't have bothered, but Caroline thinks Mummy's friends would like to know. The Upwards' announcement might include the name of the baby, 'Zacharias Daniel', and a 'née Garland-Watson' to remind people of Samantha's former up-market connections. Jen and Bryan Teale might include the name of the hospital and mention earlier children: 'a brother for Christine and Wayne.' Less smart but more reactionary members of the middle classes use the *Daily Telegraph*. The left-wing middles, conveniently combining parsimony with a flouting of convention, don't bother, which explains why *The Guardian* seldom has any birth announcements.

Mrs Definitely-Disgusting who gets her children's names from the *TV Times*, tend to put the announcement of Sharon Esther, a sister for Dive Darren, in the local paper, with a special thanks to the midwifery department of the hospital. It is a working-class characteristic to be touchingly grateful for any kind of hospital care, enjoying the rare treat of a rest and three free meals a day cooked by someone else.

Sometimes the Teales, who like a dainty word for every thing, and the Definitely-Disgustings, who have difficulty in expressing themselves, will send out cards to friends and relations, entitled, 'Baby's Announcement', with a picture of a stork on the front. Inside they fill in: 'My name is Sharon Esther, I weigh 10 lbs, my happy Mum and Dad are...'

Receiving one of these cards, Auntie might send off a nylon quilted pram set in canary yellow with the words: 'A gift for baby from...' printed on the box. Other alternatives might be a fluffy brushed nylon stuffed rabbit or a teddy bear, referred to by everyone from the lower middle classes downwards as a 'cuddly toy'.

The upper and upper middle classes, particularly the slightly retarded Sloane Ranger belt, have a tendency to add 'y' or 'ie' onto everything. In the twenties they did it with names: 'Bertie', 'Diney,' 'Jakey', 'Piggy'. Today they have 'choccy cake', 'presies'; 'cheesey things', which children like so much better, don't you agree; 'araby', which the private wards are getting awfully; and their 'gyny', whom they always fall in love with. The Queen's gynaecologist is called Mr Pinker, the colour he goes, perhaps, when he examines the royal person.

The upper classes don't mix socially with their doctors, but Caroline Stow-Crat makes an exception by asking her 'gyny' to come to her first dinner party after the birth. (Esther Rantzen had hers to hers, too, so no doubt the entire working classes will follow suit.) Fantasising about one's 'gyny' is the only thing that makes those agonising post-natal screwings possible. (Samantha Upward knows Gideon must not be denied sex longer than six weeks after the birth.) The crush on the 'gyny' usually lasts about six months.

On return from hospital, the upper classes often get their old nanny out of mothballs to come and help with the baby. She usually leaves after a few days in high dudgeon because things are being done the wrong way. With the middle classes, Granny often forks out for a maternity nurse for a month, or else the wife's mother comes to stay, and husbands have to remember to put on a dressing-gown when they go to the loo in the middle of the night. The working classes are often living with, or near, their parents anyway, or haven't got a spare room for anyone to stay in. The middle-class career mother, avid to get back to work, is praying that the new *au pair*, who isn't being very good about waking up in the night, is going to work out all right.

Clothes: the wages of synthetic fibres is social death

The upper classes, as was pointed out in the introduction, think Baby-Gros are common. Consequently, Caroline Stow-Crat prefers to dress babies of both sexes in long white dresses in wool or cotton, which probably explains little Lord Fondle-Roy and the strong strain of sexual ambiguity about the aristocracy.

'Leggings and cardigans nubbly from being knitted by old Nannies', say *Harper's*, are also all right. So is the matinée jacket, which always sounds like some moulting musquash cape worn by old ladies to afternoon performances of *The Mousetrap*. Anything nylon, polyester or made from any kind of synthetic fibre is definitely out.

Convenience however is a great leveller. Ironing long smocked dresses and washing eight Harrington squares and nappy liners a day was fine in the old days when there was Nanny to do it. Today when there aren't many servants, and upper-class mothers often have to cook dinner for returning husbands, they may resort to Baby-Gros and disposable nappies when no one is looking, their babies only going into regulation white dresses for tea parties or when grandparents come to stay.

Little Zacharias Upward lives in Baby-Gros, in whatever colour *Vogue* is promoting for grown-ups. He only goes into pink and yellow nubbly cardigans knitted by Samantha's mother's Mrs G, when the family go and stay with Samantha's mother, and Mrs G comes in to wash up on Saturday night.

The Nouveau-Richards having denuded the Toddler's Layette at Harrods, have also acquired the biggest shiniest Silver Cross pram for Tracey-Diane. They have furnished it like their car, with nodding Snoopies, hanging dolls, parasols and frilled canopies to keep off the sun. Tracey-Diane rises from a foam of nylon frills and lace like Venus from the waves. Mrs Nouveau-Richards and the *Daily Mirror* think the word 'pram' is common and refer to it as a 'baby carriage'.

Samantha Upward, conscious how important it is for children to be brought up with animals, nevertheless invests in a cat net. She also knows how jealous husbands get with new babies around and is paying particular attention to Gideon. In Harry Stow-Crat's house, the only member of the family who suffers from post-natal depression is Snipe the labrador. One maternity nurse said half her day in upper-class houses was spent boosting the dogs' morale.

Breast-feeding is also coming back into fashion. In the old days the upper classes had their babies suckled by wet nurses, or fed from bottles at once. Jonathan Gathorne-Hardy in *The Rise and Fall of the British Nanny*, quotes one nanny as saying her mistress was 'remarkable, in fact as far as breast feeding goes

'Bad dog Snipe – I told you not to play with the village children.'

she was well nigh incredible.' It turned out she'd fed the baby for one month. Today, as a backlash against working mothers abandoning their babies to the bottle and rushing back to the office, Caroline Stow-Crat and certainly Samantha Upward are tending to breast-feed for several months.

Breast-feeding in public is indulged in by left-wing trendies, and surprisingly by Jen Teale who (probably thinking it's uninhibited upper-class behaviour), will even whip out a tit in the middle of a christening, sending uncles, grandfathers and male godparents fainting into the garden. Mrs Definitely-Disgusting feeds Dive whenever he's hungry. The left-wing middle-class mother, too, feeds her baby on demand, and it's been demanding ever since.

Old-fashioned nannies, who came from the working classes, tended to get their children on the pot and out of nappies very early – quite understandable as they had no washing machines or Napisan in those days. Geoffrey Gorer in his book *Exploring English Character* suggests that the obsessive desire for privacy of the upper-class male is the result of being watched-over on the pot. 'Immersed in clubs, behind ramparts of newspapers, silent in the corner of first class carriages, at last he is free of Nanny.'

Caroline Stow-Crat talks about 'toilet trining' with a cockney accent to excuse the use of the word 'toilet'.

It is very Jen Teale to use the word 'diapers'. (Caroline says 'nappies'.)

Let us now digress slightly onto nomenclature. While the upper classes, spurning euphemisms, will tend to say someone is 'pregnant', the middle classes describe it as 'expecting a baby', or 'starting a family'. The working-class mother, however, will say: 'Three months after I had Dive, I fell for Sharon,' which doesn't mean that due to post-natal gloom she developed Lesbian tendencies, merely that she got pregnant again.

Upper- and middle-class children call their parents 'Mummy' and 'Daddy', although the boy might call his father 'Dad' as he gets older, or refer to him as 'my father'. The lower middles and working classes call them 'Mum' and 'Dad'. Socially aspirant lower middles, like Sandra in *The Liver Birds*, also call their mothers 'Mummy'. Trendy lefties and women who are reluctant to grow old insist their children call them by their Christian names. Jen and Bryan Teale call each other 'Mummy' and 'Daddy'.

A lot of confusion is caused by the word 'nanny'. To the upper and middle classes it means someone who looks after children for money, although Samantha Upward would prefer to call her 'my girl', or 'the *au pair*'. To the working classes 'Nanny', 'Nana' or 'Nan' is one's grandmother who, as all the mothers are rushing back to work, probably also looks after the children – but is not paid for it. To the upper classes 'Nana' means a large dog in *Peter Pan*.

The upper classes call their aunts 'Aunt Mary', the middle classes, 'Auntie Mary'. Lower middle and working-class children are often expected to call any friend of their parents, 'Auntie' or 'Uncle'. Two working-class expressions that seem to be creeping upwards are: 'Baby needs changing', as though you were fed up with her already, and 'I've potted Sharon', as though she were a shiny red billiard ball. Confusion is also caused by the word 'putting down'. The upper classes 'put down' sick or senile dogs. Jen Teale tends to 'put them to sleep' or 'send them to the Happy Hunting Ground'. The middle classes 'put down' children for schools, but when the working classes say: 'I've put Sharon down', it means they've put her to bed. When they say: 'I mind children', it doesn't mean they dislike them, but that they look after them.

The sociologist refers to the child as 'The Third Estate of the nuclear family'. The lower middles and working classes call him a 'kiddy', the middle classes a 'kid'. The upper middles and uppers talk about 'the children'. But upper-class people, trying to be democratic, have started to call them 'kids'. This unnerves Samantha Upward.

It is also an aristocratic trait to refer to members of one's family by name, assuming automatically that other people will know who they mean. Caroline Stow-Crat would say: 'Harry's shooting, can I bring Fiona and Georgie?' (i.e. the children). She would also say 'the baby', rather than 'my baby' or 'Baby' or the American-influenced 'my little girl' which is very Jen Teale. Harry, on the other hand, if asking a friend how his son was getting on, might easily say: 'How's your boy?'

One of the first events in the baby's life is a trip to the clinic. On rainy days the place is deserted, because the Mrs Definitely-Disgustings who always dress up to wheel their prams to the clinic, don't like getting their best clothes wet. You can tell the middle-class mothers because they are much more scruffy and have smaller prams (to fit into the Volvo). On a recent visit I made to a clinic in Putney, there were naturally no upper-class mothers, because they don't live South of the River, and they never go to clinics. Several working-class mothers in mini-skirts, leather coats, and high-heeled shoes with very done-up babies, were capping each other's crawling and teething stories. Two left-wing middle-class mothers with eager, unpainted faces, ragged hair and dirndl skirts were talking about an anti-aircraft noise meeting that night. Behind them a pretty Samantha Upward appeared to be carrying on a very enunciated conversation with another upper middle-class mum, to which no one could help listening. Suddenly I realised she was addressing a non-stop monologue to her own six-month-old baby, having obviously read somewhere that the more you talk to your baby, the sooner it talks back. The ratlet race had begun.

The christening

The next big event in a child's life is the Christening. The Queen was christened in a private chapel at Buckingham Palace at five weeks, baptised with water from the Jordan, and was dressed in christening robes of cream Brussels lace, worn by every baby in the royal family since Victoria's children.

The aristocracy tend to be christened in their own thirteenth-century churches, wearing slightly yellowing christening robes embroidered with the family crest. *The Times* will report it on the social page. A London christening takes place at the Guards Chapel or the Crypt at the House of Commons, with lunch at Boodles afterwards.

Sloane Ranger christenings tend to have Earl Grey tea, not enough champagne, and if they're short of cash, the top layer of their wedding cake re-iced. Christening presents include silver mugs with at least four initials to take in the double barrels, and premium bonds, but not napkin rings or building society shares, which are very middle-class.

As the trendy upper middles are fast reaching a state when they can't open their mouths without a glass in their hand, their christenings are tending to get later and later, with champagne, chicken drumsticks and leprous quiche at 5.30.

The suburbs and Jen and Bryan Teale tend to go in for multiple christenings with each couple looking beadily at everyone else's baby, and thinking how much more 'well spoken' their own godparent is when she names this child. The vicar looks in at all the parties afterwards, and has difficulty not shlurring his wordsh at Evenshong.

The left-wing middles, combining parsimony with agnostic puritanism, don't have their 'kids' christened.

Mr Definitely-Disgusting goes out mini-cabbing to pay for the party and a new costume for Mrs Definitely-Disgusting, who makes all the food, which includes pork pie, apple pie with pastry leaves, sponge cakes and fruit punch. The godparents probably keep the local pub.

Social climbers choose famous or successful godparents who might advance their careers or improve their status. They've dropped all their childhood friends. Sloane Rangers' mothers advise them not to ask that awfully nice girl from next door in Fulham, because you probably won't see her after you move to the country. Jean Cocteau once acted as a godparent, then promptly forgot about the child. Some while later he met the father who reproached him for neglecting his duties. Mortified, Cocteau at once sent his godson a large teddy bear.

'Was he pleased?' he asked next time he met the father.

'Not awfully,' came the reply. 'He's a colonel now.'

The christening, like the wedding, is frequently an occasion when two different classes meet head-on. The baby's mother for example may be lower middle and determined not to put a foot wrong, while the baby's father's family may be upper middle and equally determined to patronise. Less smart relations are kept in the background or ruthlessly excluded. Examples of this can be found in Colin Bell's fascinating book, *Middle Class Families*, in which he devotes a chapter to describing three Welsh christenings.

The first involved a lower middle-class couple, who asked a hundred guests to the church. Of these only six were manual workers and their wives. The baby's mother was awfully pleased that her cousin (the sole member of the family who'd been to a public school) had bothered to come. Only one manual worker and his wife however were asked back to the party at home after the service. The husband worked on the railways, and they lived in a council house. 'But she's my auntie,' said the baby's mother, 'And they're the salt of the earth' (an expression used by all classes to excuse those of lower station). As a first grandchild, the baby was given a staggering £1,000 by his grandparents, and enough clothes to keep Dr Barnado for a year.

The second christening involved a slightly less smart family. The father was described as a 'geographically mobile plant superintendent', which actually meant he'd moved around the country in his career, upping his salary each time. On this occasion their daily woman came to the church to keep the older children quiet, but was not invited back to the house for tea afterwards, even to help – a classic example of the *nouveau-riche* not knowing how to treat servants – and presumably because she was embarrassingly close enough to the family in class to be mistaken for a more common relation. In spite of this she sent the baby a cuddly toy. Unsmart relations also weren't asked, even though they lived nearby. 'Not because I'm a snob,' said the mother untruthfully, 'But he's a porter or something.'

In the final christening, the parents were both bright children of working-class parents, who'd met at university and promptly moved to another part of the country, away from any embarrassing roots. The relations were mercifully too poor to come to the christening. Godparents were friends from work. The grandparents didn't send any presents, only vastly elaborate christening cards.

Another example of the clash between the two classes occurred at a recent middle-class christening I went to. One of the godfathers, a working-class actor who'd done very well for himself but who had never been to a christening before, missed the church service, and rolled up in time for tea armed with a christening cake, complete with primrose yellow icing, the baby's name in mauve, and a stork and a baby made out of a sugared almond with its features slipping. Alas, the baby's grandmother had also provided a large white christening cake complete with stork and slipping-featured sugared almond. The cakes were placed side by side – with Storky and Co gazing sourly at one another.

And while we're on the subject of cakes, Caroline Stow-Crat would never call marzipan, 'almond paste'.

The ratlet race

The christening over, the ratlet race starts in earnest. The battle is particularly vicious among the middle classes, where if you can't boast an 'int'risting' career, you justify your existence by rearing a little genius. This is another part of the backlash against women going out to work. Newspapers and women's magazines are constantly stressing the importance of the child being mentally stimulated during the first five years of its life. Journalists like Mary Kenny recant on women's lib principles, and expound the joys of motherhood. This is very easy for lady journalists, who can always write at home *and* see their babies when they want to. Society is teeming with women having nervous breakdowns because they feel so inadequate about only being a wife and mother.

At plonk-and-pâté-tasting-of-old-socks-parties beloved by the upper middle classes, you can hear the battle raging. Samantha Upward, who, in spite of having a degree, believes ''is teacher says 'e's gifted at writing.'

in staying at home to creatively raise little Zacharias is talking
to a career mum.

SAMANTHA (*who knows one is never regarded as a cabbage if one's
    interested in other people*): How's the job?

CAREER MUM: Oh, exhausting. I had to lunch George Best on
    Monday, look after Graham Greene all week, then we had a
    press party for Isherwood last night.' (*Fifteen-love to Career
    Mum*).

SAMANTHA: And how's Damian?

CAREER MUM: All right I think, how's the baby? (*Not being round
    much she doesn't even know Zacharias's name*).

SAMANTHA: Oh he's just finished *Alice in Wonderland*, simply
    couldn't put it down, I do recommend flash cards, and he can
    already beat Gideon at chess. We're a bit worried he's a
    Gifted Child, but you can't really tell at two. (*Fifteen-thirty to
    Samantha*).

Harry Stow-Crat doesn't believe in wives working (or husbands, for that matter) – it would interfere with the shooting
and fishing. After all, someone's got to provide luncheon.

The upper classes have 'nurseries' upstairs. The upper middles call them 'playrooms', and tend to have them downstairs so the children won't miss any cultural pearls dropped by their parents. In the kitchen, a cork board groans with Zacharias's first scrawlings. Jen Teale, who is determined that little Wayne shall get on in life, has settled for the lounge, with model soldiers on the mantelpiece and children's posters on the wall. The garden will be filled with wendy huts and social climbing frames.

Dive Definitely-Disgusting will have no room set aside for him, and often sleeps in the same room, or even bed, as all his brothers and sisters. The reason they go to bed so late is because Mrs Definitely-Disgusting has to ensure one child is soundly asleep before she can put the next one to bed, and so on. The cot will often be bought with Embassy coupons.

The upper classes send their children to bed early, at six-thirty so they'll be out of the way before their father comes back from shooting, or the city. The role-reversed upper middle classes, who believe contact with the father is essential, tend to keep them up slightly later, so they'll have half an hour with Daddy before going to sleep. Gideon Upward, knackered after a hard day, is corrected by little Zacharias every time he tries to skip a page of Paddington Bear and longs for a little bit of upper-class peace downstairs with a large gin and tonic.

Sleeping alone, the middle-class child is often frightened of the dark, but his parents can afford to leave a light on all night outside his room. The middle classes have always given a lot of parental authority to the father. The upper and working classes tended to leave disciplining to the mother, nanny or grandmother. But with shorter working hours, and less shift work the working-class father is tending to be at home more, take more interest in his children, and no longer be ashamed to be seen pushing the pram. 'Vic takes baby up the park on the weekend, while I get the dinner on,' says Mrs Definitely-Disgusting.

Equally, as the upper classes get poorer, and can't afford servants, the fathers are forced to pay more attention to the children.

'I used to shove the baby into his arms,' said one maternity nurse 'And walk out of the room. He'd hold it like a rattlesnake, but by the time I left, he was pushing the pram and changing nappies.' One upper-class husband she said, refused to push the pram, but he'd walk behind his wife when she was pushing it, pushing her.

By the time the middle-class child is a year old, say the statisticians, he will be less likely to have a tantrum than the working-class child, have had a much better diet and be off the bottle (as though he'd been on an alcoholic binge for the first twelve months). Baby Georgie Stow-Crat will have had a grille put in the back of the estate car to stop him bothering Snipe, the labrador, and had his first children's party, which he won't remember, but which was a great show-off occasion for his nanny. Wayne Teale will now be referred to as a 'toddler' or a 'tiny tot'. Samantha Upward will now be out on the culture beat, hawking little Zacharias round museums and art galleries to stop herself becoming a cabbage. The Hayward gallery won't allow prams inside but provides baby slings to help Mummy appreciate Dada.

Children's clothes

Little Georgie Stow-Crat will be out of long dresses now and into romper suits with Peter Pan collars, or short trousers which he will wear until he's half-way through prep-school. Occasionally in Hyde Park on cold days one sees the camp sight of little upper-class boys wearing tights under their shorts. He might occasionally be allowed to wear jeans like the middle classes but never ones that fit, in case their tightness stops him carrying on the line. Upper-class little girls are smock-marked.

The middle classes dress their children like small adults – in the hope that they'll grow brighter and more adult earlier. In the same way that the upper classes force boy babies into little dresses, the middle classes force little girls into jeans. Jen Teale's daughter Christine wears her dresses slightly too short, to display hen's bum knickers.

All little girls in fact are lower middle by inclination. If allowed, they would permanently dress like Christine Teale in frilly party dresses with matching pochettes, or peasant blouses with elasticated waists and sleeves, their hair in bunches, sticking out above the ears. Or like Tracey-Diane Nouveau-Richards in earrings, painted toenails, huge nylon bows in the hair, pink plastic butterfly slides, and white slingback or even high-heeled shoes. The Teales and the Nouveau-Richards encourage such prissiness by saying 'always try to be a little lady,' or 'isn't Tracey-Diane a little flirt.' Mrs Nouveau-Richards, who believes in getting her pound of flesh from the nanny, insists that all Tracey's clothes are 'hand-washed' as she calls it. Mrs Definitely-Disgusting dresses her children in polyester and acrylic in very bright colours; shocking pink, mauve, royal blue and turquoise being the most popular. They also wear very shiny tee-shirts with 'Arsenal' on them and mock suède coats with nylon fur collars. The upper classes used only to allow their children to wear anoraks on the ski slopes, but have now given in.

Hair is also a class indicator. Upper-class little boys have their curls brushed flat, and cut in the shape of a pudding basin. The middle classes have their hair tapered like Cliff Richard. Upper-class little girls either wear their fringes on the eyebrows like Shetland ponies, or drawn off their foreheads (pronounced 'forrids') with a small velvet bow at the side or the crown of their head. They sometimes wear Alice bands, but sewn and with proper velvet, not made out of stretch material. Jen Teale cuts Christine's fringe half-way down the forehead, so there is no danger she won't be able to see out. She cuts Wayne's hair short at the back so that half an inch or two of neck shows. The working classes no longer Brylcreem their kiddies' hair into tight curls, too much like 'the darkies' – but they do brush Baby's hair upwards like a Sioux Indian's.

Until recently, it was much easier to tell a child's background from its clothes than its mother's. But since the entire nation's youth is now clad in spin-offs from whatever film is fashionable and Mary Quant (who staged the great sixties revolution, making duchesses interchangeable with shopgirls) has gone into children's clothes, all children will soon look alike.

The régime

Upper-class mothers believe in fresh air and walks to feed the ducks in the afternoon. Ducks in Kensington Gardens ought to be members of Weight Watchers, so stuffed are they with bread (but never sliced, because the upper classes think it's common). Ducks that live near the Round Pond in Hampstead get wholewheat crusts. As soon as Georgie Stow-Crat can walk he's put on a pony. From Monday to Friday upper-class London children have to make do with the rocking horse at Harrods.

Conventional upper-class children have cake, sandwiches and perhaps as a treat an ice at four o'clock – what the working classes would describe as 'afternoon tea'. Middle-class children have 'high tea' about six consisting of baked beans, beefburgers or fish fingers and yoghurt. The working classes tend to have the same, but if any of the food is cooked, the meal is called a 'dinner', i.e. 'Karen has a dinner at lunchtime and a dinner in the evening.' The working classes might also say, 'I gave Baby juice and cereal at three.' The upper classes would specify '*orange* juice', and 'cornflakes' or 'Weetabix'. The lower you get down the social scale the more likely people are to use convenience words like 'teacher' as opposed to 'schoolmaster' or 'mistress'. The lower working classes eat chip butties and sweets all day – they don't have meals.

Upper-class children tend to have other children over to tea at four as a social occasion. Middle-class children come over to play at any time. When the middle classes send their children to state schools, they ask their working-class school mates home to tea and then feel hurt because they never get asked back. It never occurs to Zacharias Upward that Dive Definitely-Disgusting might feel ashamed of the smallness of his house or flat and the fact that he doesn't have a nursery.

The working classes tend to cram their children with sweets, cheap placebos like 'Mollteasers', 'Croonchy' and 'Cadbury's Fruit and Not'. Samantha Upward having read about nutrition, tends to restrict Zacharias's sweet-eating, although career mums, conscious of being away too much, bombard their children with guilt presents every time they're late home. Little Zacharias who is only allowed two sweets after lunch and is fed up with museums, wishes Samantha would get a part-time job, so he could get guilt presents too.

Upper-class children are taught nursery rhymes by their nannies and know them all by the time they're eighteen months, which gives them a vocabulary of about 500 words. Traditionally a lot of nursery rhymes chronicle the activities of their forbears anyway. Little Jack Horner pulling out a plum and presumably putting it in his mouth, for example, refers to the fat pickings culled by the Horner family during the dissolution of the monasteries.

Sharon Definitely-Disgusting only knows television jingles. In a recent quiz at a state school, none of the eleven-year-olds could say what Little Miss Muffet sat on.

Staying with granny

Working-class children, as has been said before, often live with or near their grandmothers, and the working-class Nan is much the best with children, because she's had the most practice. Since Georgie Stow-Crat's grandparents often live in the country, they have more room and servants to take the children off the mother's hands. Zacharias Upward's grandparents live on their nerves and ever-dwindling fixed incomes. They move into smaller and smaller houses, but hang onto all the ornaments, which are double-parked on every piece of furniture. The place looks like an antique shop. All the china is moved up a shelf when grandchildren come and stay, but eventually they break the place up, because they're fed up with not being allowed to touch anything, and with playing the same old brought-out game of bagatelle. A terrible family row develops because one ball bearing disappears. Both daughters and daughters-in-law feel on trial all the time; the tension is transmitted to the children. If they're let out into the garden, footballs snap the regalia lilies. Mealtimes are a nightmare because the middle classes are obsessively hot on table manners.

'Why do all my grandchildren eat as though they're gardening?' said one middle-class granny recently.

Children invariably let the side down saying: 'Why can't we have baked beans in front of the telly like we do at home.'

Upper middle-class grannies invariably had nannies to bring up their own children, and cannot understand why their grandchildren should be so exhausting, or so much more badly behaved than they remember their own children were. They forget they only saw them when they were presented newly washed for an hour after tea.

Samantha drives her mother-in-law crackers. Every time little Zacharias interrupts, she stops whatever adult conversation she is having to answer his question.

The middle classes tend to reason.

The working classes tend to clout.

The working classes have dummies. Middle-class children are more likely to suck their thumbs.

Growing up

Sexual modesty is also a good index of social class. The majority of the working classes never see their parents naked, which must be quite an achievement as they often sleep in the same room – rather like undressing on the beach.

Social Class I (which according to the Census includes scientists, doctors and structural engineers) are much more likely to let their children see them with no clothes on. Pretty horrifying really, and enough to put one off sex for life, having a hairy scientist streaking round the house.

The upper middles are less likely to worry about masturbation, and more likely to tell their children the facts of life. They are aided in this by Althea, of Dinosaur Books fame, who has written a very explicit children's book about having a baby. Known locally, as the 'rude' book, it is a great favourite to read aloud when Granny comes to stay.

To Jen Teale, the word 'rude' means slightly smutty. To the upper classes it means 'impertinent'. Similarly the uppers use 'cheeky' to mean impertinent, to Jen Teale it means a bit risqué, or near the knuckle.

The working classes are incapable of explaining anything, so you get their children coming into the public library asking: 'I want a book about life.'

'Whose life?' says the librarian. 'Biographies over there.'

'Facts a life, miss.'

Georgie Stow-Crat doesn't need to be told about sex because he's seen plenty of farm animals copulating and procreating. As a result upper-class men often take their wives from behind.

My husband heard about sex for the first time when he was walking in a prep school crocodile along the beach.

'I say chaps,' said a boy called the Hon. James Stewart, 'I know how babies are made.'

Whereupon they all gathered round saying, 'Go on, Stewart, tell us.'

'The man lies on top of the woman,' said Stewart portentously, 'And is excused into her.'

The middle classes will start taking their children to the dentist almost before they've got teeth, the working classes tend only to go when their teeth ache. 'You can tell what class a person is the moment he opens his mouth,' said John Braine, 'by the state of his teeth.'

The upper classes give their children 10p from the fairies when a tooth comes out. Inflation and indulgence have pushed the middle classes up to 50p. Among the upper middle merrytocracy the fairies often get drunk and forget to put the money under the pillow and have to compensate with twice as much the next day. When the local funfair arrives every year, children have been known to tug teeth out with forceps untimely for more money to spend on the fruit machines.

People are gradually realising that illiteracy in schools today is nothing to do with the teaching, but simply because children have been turned into a race of zombies watching television. Soon the middle classes will start banning television altogether, and illicit watch-easys will be set up in darkened dives round the country. Samantha Upward tries not to let little Zacharias read comics or watch more than an hour's television a day. Upper-class children go into the kitchen and read the housekeeper's children's comics. Samantha reads out loud to Zacharias in a clear voice, altering words she thinks are common, and remembering to say 'orf'.

By the age of two, little Georgie Stow-Crat will be looking out on life with a clear blue gaze, frightened of no one, totally self-confident. He will also have a frightful accent from playing in the stables but no one is in the least bit worried. Working-class children always hold their noses in the country.

The lower middle-class child will already be shell-shocked with instructions. Don't tread in Doggie's duty. Put your hand over your mouth when you cough. Don't turn your fork over to eat peas. It's rude to whisper. It's rude to shout. Talk in a low, clear voice like Anna Ford or Mrs Thatcher. Class is beginning to creep in. Samantha has great difficulty explaining to little Zacharias why he may sprinkle his pepper but not his salt. Jen Teale's children will be constantly pulled up for some real or imagined coarseness of speech or enunciation. It's so important to be 'well-spoken'.

Middle-class children put cherry stones on the side of their plate with their spoon and chant: 'Tinker, tailor, soldier, sailor, rich man, poor man, beggerman, thief.' The upper classes put them on the side of their plates, concealing the journey from mouth to plate with a curled fist, and saying: 'Army, Navy, Law, Divinity, Independent, Medicine, Trade.'

The working classes only eat cherries out of tins of fruit salad, with the stones removed already.

3 THE NANNY

*The daughters of tradespeople however
well educated must necessarily be underbred,
and as such unfit to be the inmates of our
dwellings or guardians of our children's minds,
and persons.*   Charlotte Brontë.
With a hey ho, and Hey Nanny No.

Anyone studying the English Class system will have noticed
certain similarities between the extreme upper and lower
classes; their toughness, xenophobia, their indifference to
public opinion, their passion for racing and gambling, and their
fondness for plain speaking and plain untampered food.
Jonathan Gathorne-Hardy in *The Rise and Fall of the British
Nanny*, says the reason is that the ruling classes for the last two
hundred years, have been brought up almost entirely by
working-class nannies, their parents abdicating all responsibility.

'With maternity nurses, nannies, prep school and public
school,' admitted one mother, 'It's almost as though we put
them in care.'

Certainly one of the reasons the aristocracy has always
notched up so many marriages was because they never had any
boring middle-class worries about how it might affect the children. Nanny would always be there to look after them, and
provide continuity.

Working for the great, nannies took on their own snobbisms,
not unlike suburban crones working in Knightsbridge dress
shops for £50 a week who make you feel bitterly ashamed of
your scuffed heels and the fact you can't afford £500 for a little
black dress.

There was a group of Nannies who ruled Hyde Park.

'Are you a titled mummy's nanny,' said one gorgon, when a newly employed nanny tried to sit down beside her.

The new nanny shook her head.

'Well I'm afraid,' said the gorgon, 'This bench is reserved for titled mummies' nannies.'

Until a few years ago, Nanny was a fixture in the upper-class house, taking on the surname of the family, and often staying with them until she died, when an announcement would appear in *The Times*, stating the family's gratitude at her length of service. When her charges grew up, there were always grand-children. Sometimes she regained her ascendancy when the master became senile, and needed looking after, or when Miss Caroline became an alcoholic. One friend of mine spends £6000 a year keeping a large house in Sussex going simply as a base for his old nanny and her dog. Another nanny when her children grew up, took over the care of the three family dogs, keeping them in baskets upstairs, and giving them the same nursery routine of brushing, walks, mealtimes and early beds. While yet another old nanny keeps an eye on visiting dogs. When a friend's golden retriever had been cavorting in the loch for an hour, she sidled up and said: 'I think Porridge has been in for long enough.'

In the old days, upper to upper middle-class husbands used traditionally to knock off the nanny. Today far more often, you find husbands getting jealous of the mutually sycophantic, love–hate relationship that exists between the wife and the nanny, particularly since the advent of the permissive society, when nanny often covers up for the wife's sexual peccadillos, and therefore has even more power over her.

Samantha Upward only works part-time and doesn't feel this justifies a nanny so she gets foreign *au pairs* to help Zacharias with his French and says: 'Go and do your Devoir, darling', when he gets home from school. Gideon hopes every time for someone like Brigitte Bardot, but Samantha has so much middle-class guilt about employing anyone, and spends so much time scurrying round doing all the work, that the various Claudines and Marie Josés soon become au pear-shapes.

No such scruples overcome Mrs Nouveau-Richards, who, as a first generation employer, is determined to get several pounds of flesh off the nannies. She expects them to work six days a

'Gideon, you'll have to ask for a rise of at least fifteen thousand a year just to pay for Nanny.'

week for only £12, to wear uniform, to keep the children upstairs, and to call her 'Mrs Nouveau-Richards'.

One of the professional nanny's least enviable tasks is helping with the playgroup. The rich send their children to nursery schools, where trained nursery nannies take them over for three hours a day, and teach them the rudiments of reading, writing and making castles out of the insides of lavatory paper rolls. The less rich have to make do with playgroups, where different mothers take it in turns in threes to supervise the children. Here the lower middle Jen Teales are *far* more bossy than the upper middle mums, and if a working mother sends her nanny or her *au pair* instead of herself, the Jen Teales, probably feeling themselves perilously close to the status of the nanny, refuse to talk to her, except for making her do all the dirty work. When my own nanny used to do it, she was the only adult who wasn't offered a cup of coffee.

Many people who didn't have nannies themselves regard them as a status symbol. One *nouveau riche* family who employed a girl, insisted she wear a uniform, but gave her a nervous breakdown by never allowing her near the baby. In 1978 Esther Rantzen devoted a whole column in the *Evening News* to her daughter's 'lovely Nanny, who even likes the mucky bits', but who only has to wear uniform when she goes to official B.B.C. events like *Miss United Kingdom*. A Birmingham journalist, who had a baby at 42, had a daily nanny 'a lovely lady, who we call Auntie Margaret'. Being described as 'lovely' in the national or provincial press is worth at least £10 a week. Although many permanent nannies today act as managing director for the whole household, for some reasons they feel they will be looked down on socially if they admit what their job is. I had one girl, who instead of saying she was a nanny used to tell her boy-friends that she was on the dole and only staying with me. Another girl was just getting her employers and the children off for a weekend, when some man rang up: 'Hang on,' her employers heard her saying, 'I'm just saying goodbye to some friends.'

On another occasion when a commercial was being made in her boss's house, she asked him to carry his newly-ironed shirts upstairs, because she didn't want the film crew to realise she was a nanny. If asked what she does she says she's a P.A.

The nanny–employer relationship is interesting because it is one of the few occasions when the classes meet head on, not just during the day, as people do in the office, but at all times, and the nanny has to adjust to a completely different life style.

Nannies divide households into 'upstairs' and 'downstairs' families. The Upstairs families keep the children upstairs, and allow the nanny complete, if lonely, autonomy. Downstairs families are usually middle-class, where the nanny and the mother muddle along, both looking after the children in uneasy complicity.

Differing taste of course is often a bone of contention in the nanny–employer relationship. There's often a problem when a member of the Serviette Union goes into a family which says 'napkin'. Children suss out areas of discord all too soon. Samantha Upward's *au pair* comes in very red in the face saying: 'Zacharias refuses to say "pardon".'

Whereupon Samantha goes even redder and stands on one leg, saying: 'Well actually we always say "What?" I don't know why.'

Jonathan Gathorne-Hardy claims that there was never any

strain between the upper-class 'What?' the lower middle 'Pardon?', or the working-class 'Eh?' Nannies simply became bilingual, and said 'lounge' to their friends, and 'drawing room' to their employers.

Nannies in the past, however, did make up their own little snobbish rules ... 'Nanny Ellis said it was common to stare, common to play with children whose friends were in trade, however rich, common to play in the front garden, or to eat jelly with anything but a fork. Vulgar children say, "Hip Hip Hoorray", and eat Fry's chocolate. We say, "Hip Hip Hurrah", and eat Cadbury's.'

4 EDUCATION

After three years at a private day school, the upper classes pack their children off to prep school at eight because they're too stupid to do the homework any more, because they can't cope with the complications of getting them to school and because even though they're not all afraid of the school staff, they have no desire to mix with them socially at the string of fund-raising events laid on by day schools. Even at eight, little Georgie Stow-Crat misses home less than a middle-class child because his affection is divided between his mother and nanny. He misses Snipe the labrador most of all and calls Caroline Stow-Crat 'sir' in the holidays. Any boisterousness or subversive tendencies are ironed out of him at school, and everyone, particularly his grandmother, says how much he is improved. No one, on the other hand, can explain why the housekeeper's cat has been strangled.

Samantha Upward, trying to be enlightened, starts Zacharias off at a state primary which she refers to as 'the village school', but even with his head start little Zacharias doesn't do as well as expected, and develops a frightful accent, which makes his grandmother wince, and his cousins at Summerfields take the mickey out of him. After a lot of heart-searching and Gideon Upward having to give up smoking and drink wine instead of whiskey, Zacharias is sent to the local day prep school at eight, only to find that all the other upper middles by now have been sent off to boarding school, and the place is crawling with pushy lower middles, and Nouveau-Richards. Against such competition Zacharias does less and less well. He's called 'Zacharine' and beaten up in the playground by Jason Nouveau-Richards and his gang and is eventually sent off to a cramming boarding school at eleven, because the head-master has suggested the horrible possibility that he might not pass Common Entrance (required to get to a public school), and because Gideon and Samantha can't get him to do two hours' homework a night against a background of *The Sweeney*.

Left-wing intellectuals pack their children off to the local comprehensive, rejoicing in the spare cash, and the first glottal stop. Actually their children are bright enough to waltz through any system; if not, they have them coached. Six years later the parents shriek like hell when they have to fork out for university.

The middle classes, of course, always work the system. They have cars to take their children to the better state schools, and they deliberately buy houses in the right area. The Oxford local papers, for example, advertise houses with swimming pools, four bedrooms and location in the catchment area for a fashionable state school.

Often a group of middle-class parents picks on a school and enforces its own standards, until it's so oversubscribed the head can pick and choose. There is a primary school in Berkshire known as 'the Trojan horse of the state system', where the headmaster only takes children whose parents have been to boarding school or a university, or whose mothers are extremely pretty. The result is scholarships to all the top public schools, and speech days full of headscarves and labradors, not unlike The Fourth of June at Eton. The only difference between this and the local day prep school is that the mothers picking up their children from the state school are better dressed because they have more cash to spend.

'Hooray, now we can afford a Volvo,' said one mother when she heard her child had got a place.

Meanwhile Jen Teale is tearing her hair because she can't get Wayne or Christine in, and has to fork out for a day prep. Having forked out she is extremely pushy. She always goes along to open day to see what she's paying for, and says she's 'very satisfied' because little Wayne is bound to get qualifications later, and that's all that matters. Wayne has also brought home some very nice boys, which could never have happened at the local primary where the hazard of him chumming up with the local dustman's son was always a thunderous

'Oh Gideon – do you think he's having his first breakdown?'

possibility. In conversation with friends who have children at
state schools she often mentions Wayne's French, or asks them
if they've got a Latin dictionary.

The Nouveau-Richards dispatch little Jason to a day prep,
and then to one of the top boarding schools, paying extortionate
fees to buy a little upper middle-class child on the never never.

The Tory press recently reported that a docker, a
warehouseman and a gasmeter reader were sending their children to private schools while a vast number of middle class
parents couldn't afford it any more. How ironic, the report went
on, if the working classes commandeered private education, as
it moved further and further out of the reach of the middle
classes. I think this is unlikely. Traditionally the financial
situation of working-class parents makes them accept the state
system as normal. Both in streamed and unstreamed schools,
the middle classes receive different and longer education, and
are educationally more successful. The chances of the child of
an unskilled worker being a poor reader at seven are six times
greater than in the case of the upper middle-class child, who

arrives at school tuned in to educational demands, and who, when he gets home, has someone to help him with his homework, and somewhere quiet to do it.

While half the children in the Census Social Class I (the upper middles) reach higher education, either at university or polytechnic, only one in a thousand of Class V (unskilled workers) stays on at school after sixteen.

The middle-class child is realistic about prospects and sees success in terms of steady progress and cumulative success, while the working-class child sees it in terms of a quiet life, or sudden fame as a pop star or a footballer. Those who leave school early often regret that they can't get a particular job because they haven't got any qualifications, or that lack of education makes the job difficult.

Parental involvement

The National Foundation for Educational Research, who ought to be collectively shot, is convinced that the greater the parental involvement the more Able (Abel as opposed to Cain) the child will be. Parental involvement is the main hobby of the non-working mother, it's an extension of justifying your existence by creative child-rearing. The frightfully lower middle expression a 'caring and concerned parent' is bandied around a great deal both by the press and the teaching profession. If a child isn't doing well at school, you ring up the parents and rocket them that the home back-up isn't 'caring' enough, and do spot checks by asking the children to write essays entitled 'My Mummy' or 'My Daddy'. If Zacharias Upward writes: 'My Daddy drinks whicksy all day, and my mother looks like a princess, but never comes to kiss me goodnight,' Samantha and Gideon get a black mark.

A daunting idea put forward by all schools today is that parents should educate themselves in order to help their children – father education – my husband calls it. Samantha Upward is taking an Open University course in absolutely everything in an attempt to push Zacharias. Jen Teale has gone back to part-time teaching, to catch up on the latest techniques.

Parents are advised to join the Parent Teachers Association and bully for their own maths workshops. In the same way that

Communists monopolise union meetings, so the middle classes, even in a comprehensive school, tend to take over the P.T.A., leading to a serious distortion of influence. Mrs Definitely-Disgusting doesn't speak the same language as the staff, and is often frightened of them.

About once a week, a note with a perforated section about forthcoming events arrives full of lower middle-class words like 'refreshments', 'pleasant' and 'enjoyable'. 'If you can be of service as a helper', it concludes rather wildly, 'please tear off your slip and send it to one of the committee.'

At Christmas there's a nativity play, which at state schools is often held in the morning. This means lots of working-class fathers on shift work, and Gideon Upward looking at his watch and wondering how late he dare be at the office. The Virgin Mary's parents are invariably divorced and acrimonious. They turn up and sit glaring from opposite ends of a school bench, but in the end are forced to sit next to one another through lack of space. No one can hear the kiddies tunelessly chanting 'Ark the 'erald' or 'Once in Royal Divid' because of all the baby brothers and sisters squawking their heads off.

At fee-paying schools, there are no babies, because the parents pay someone to look after them for the afternoon. The following announcement was once sent out by my son's old day prep school: 'We hope you will all come to our informal Carol Service on December 15. This year we shall be having kindergarten boys for the first time, I'm sure we shall all enjoy them.'

School meals

When my son first went to a primary school five years ago, faced with the utter impossibility of having the right dinner money every day, I asked if I could pay by cheque for the whole term. The school was extremely shocked; it was good for discipline they said, for the children to bring the right money each day, and was I too insensitive to realise that it was beyond most working-class budgets to fork out all at once for a whole term? Now I notice that most state schools allow parents to pay by cheque. Private schools call it 'lunch' and put it on the bill. State school dinners are supervised by someone grandiosely called a 'dinner lady'.

The 'milk run'

The routine of taking children to school by car on a rota shared between parents, often known as the 'milk run', causes more aggravation than any other part of the day school curriculum, particularly when mothers are trying to shunt three children to three different schools all coming out at different times. Where the children are concerned it's one of the last bastions of snobbery – the bigger and shinier the car you're picked up in the better. On the whole, mothers dress more scruffily the higher-class they are. Caroline Stow-Crat turns up in jeans in a filthy Range Rover, and is admonished by Georgie who thinks she ought to wear smarter trousers, and clean the car more often. Why can't she be more like Mrs Nouveau-Richards who is always dressed up to the nines and takes the 'show-*fur*' and the Rolls?

Jen Teale who is terrified her children may miss a second of school that's being paid for, gets quite hysterical when Samantha's French *au pair* oversleeps and picks up the Teale children ten minutes late.

Caroline Stow-Crat is always getting stuck in someone else's house at weekends and ringing up at midnight saying she's snowed up and can Samantha do the milk run. Samantha is furious, but doesn't say so. 'A lady never lets herself go.' Nor can she get any sympathy out of Mrs Nouveau-Richards, who is only too glad to put her 'show-*fur*' at Caroline's disposal at any time. Jen Teale, who cleans the Volkswagen herself, thinks Caroline's Range Rover is much too draughty, and she's fed up with having Snipe's hairs all over little Wayne's newly brushed blazer.

Georgie Stow-Crat complicates matters on Samantha's milk run by telling everyone that he's being allowed to stay up till midnight tonight, because his mother is giving a party for eighty people – to which none of the milk run mothers have been asked.

A friend's child went to a pre-school open day, at one of the most fashionable London high schools. All the little new girls were told: 'At the end of the afternoon, you stand in the hall, and the moment you see your Mummy's car coming up the drive, you can tell your form mistress, and go and meet

'Dad, why can't you pick *me* up from school on a motor bike?'

Mummy.' It was automatically assumed that all the parents had cars.

In state schools, many of the children walk or go by bus. When Samantha suggested Zacharias might go by bus, so she could take a little part-time job, Zacharias refused, he didn't want his cap knocked off by 'Comprehensile' boys.

The most relentless upstaging goes on between children on the school runs.

'My mother went to Princess Anne's wedding,' said one child.

After a long pause, the second child replied.

'My parents were asked, but they didn't want to go.'

The attitude towards chauffeurs is interesting too. One working-class boy whose father had made good, made the chauffeur drop him off a quarter of a mile from his primary school, and walked the rest of the way to his state school, so the other boys wouldn't mob him up.

But two teenagers at a private day school had different ideas. The younger sister hated the chauffeur wearing his cap because the other girls would think it so snobbish. The older girl on the other hand hated him not wearing his cap: 'It would be so awful, if anyone thought he was Daddy.'

Accent

> *Primary Mary, teacher wary*
> *How does your accent grow*
> *With cockney vowels, and Mummy's scowls*
> *And glottal stops all in a row.*

An English upper-class accent is often called a 'public school accent'. But as Johnathan Gathorne-Hardy has pointed out, in his book, *The Public School Phenomenon*, accent became a distinguishing characteristic socially with the emergence of the court and the capital of London long before the founding of the public schools. This dialect of London, Cambridge and Oxford was originally South East Midlands but as it became the social speech of a class, it developed apart from the regional variety. William the Conqueror spoke Norman French but by the sixteenth century, London English (hence the King's English) was regarded as the only language for a literary man or a gentleman, and remained so throughout the seventeenth and eighteenth centuries. The public schools only intensified this.

In the nineteen-sixties during the hippy egalitarian revolution against materialism and never-having-it-so-good, the upper and middle classes identified profoundly with the new culture and became devotees of long hair and pop music. Working class became beautiful and everyone from Princess Unne downwards spat the plums out of their mouths, embraced the flat 'a' and talked with a working-class accent. Even today you can invariably age twenty-two to thirty-year-olds by their voices. Prince Charles preceded the revolution and speaks his mother's English, Prince Andrew came after it. Nicholas Monson, who is one of the more enlightened and intelligent of the new wave of right-wing writers, said that during that period he got very embarrassed with being at Eton and having a smart background, so by listening carefully to the housemaid and watching 'Rossel Harty', he began to talk with a modulated regional accent.

'After Eton,' he went on, 'I put off trucking to Katmandu and discovering Zen. Instead I went to Kingston Polytechnic. As I was mixing with "real" people, I put on sweaty T-shirts and dirty jeans, let my hair collapse in rat-tails over my shoulders and affected an accent that owed its origins to Cilla Black, California and the East End of London ... I was uncomfortable with this voice, so I said little, but nodded vigorously and tried to look tough ... We also sneered at a certain lecturer ... who wore a pinstriped suit and talked posh. It was at such an airing of bigotry ... I realised to my acute embarrassment, that I was guilty of the same crime as before. I was a snob.'

It must have been about this time in the seventies, that many other people were undergoing the same realisation. The prosperity ran out, and the working class, the simple life, and dropping out became less attractive – because there were no jobs to drop back into when you'd had enough. Upper- and middle-class schoolchildren became more conventional again – more right-wing, and shed a good deal of their working-class accent. As my niece said: 'It simply isn't cool to talk like a yobbo any more.'

The result is a different kind of speech, much more clipped, 'awf'ly' and 'frightf'ly', 'ya' or 'yp', instead of 'yer', or 'yeah'. Georgie Stow-Crat might say 'funtustic', and 'whole' to rhyme with 'doll', but he wouldn't say 'amizing' like the cockney child. He is often bi-lingual and will lapse into mid-atlantic or disc-jockey when he's with his friends. And when he wants to irritate Caroline in the holidays, he cultivates a glottal stop and asks her to pass the 'bu-er'. To the middle classes, although they won't admit it, a fee-paying school means 'no more ghastly accent'. Or, as a headmaster said euphemistically, 'We try to get rid of accents, they're a lazy way of speaking.'

Alas for the Nouveau-Richards, the effect often isn't lasting. When I lived in Yorkshire, the rich manufacturers all sent their sons to Oopingham and Roogby to iron out their accents, but a few years after they left, they were speaking broad Yorkshire again.

'It's extraordinary,' said a don at Radley, 'How bucolic some of the old boys sound when they come back after a few years.'

Quite often you get marked class discrepancies in a family because a father has made his pile while his children were growing up, and been able to send only the younger children to

boarding school – or alternatively gone bankrupt in the middle
and been forced to send the youngest child to a comprehensive.

The left-wing trendies who send their children off to the local
state school, go into ecstasies at the first flat 'a'. She has not
failed us, she has not failed us. Accent makes the heart grow
fonder.

The Jen Teales often regard moving from place to place as an
advantage. Not only does Bryan up his salary, but there is more
likelihood of Wayne and Christine being well spoken and not
picking up a regional accent.

Class consciousness

> *A gentleman has good table manners and should*
> *not make wild gestures when speaking at banquets,*
> *so that he sweeps a bowl of semolina into his*
> *neighbour's lap.*
>
> Kings House School Richmond, magazine

There is no worse snob than the prep school boy, but he is
usually a possession snob, status being dependent on the size of
his parents' car, how many rooms his house has, whether they
have a swimming pool, where he went on holidays, and the
intricacies of his digital watch.

The dawnings of true class consciousness vary. A duke's
daughter said she was aware of her position for the first time
when she was four; she was playing in the garden and a particularly oily butler said: 'Would my lady like some luncheon?' She
was very clever, however. And she said at school her intellect
was much more of an embarrassment than her title.

My son, at ten, is beginning to come out with remarks like,
'How many lords do we know?'

'My family used to own most of Bath,' announced one of his
school friends, 'But unfortunately they lost it in a game of
cards.'

Most snobbery, in fact, is instilled by the parents. For a brief
period an earl's son was sent to my son's previous day school,
and it was horrifying the way the mothers urged their sons to
ask him to tea, and birthday parties. He must have seen *Star
Wars* about fifteen times.

There is another beautiful story of a very aristocratic child, going away to prep school for the first time, who got hauled up before the headmaster because he insisted on calling his form master 'Mr Brown' instead of 'Sir'.

'I suppose,' said the headmaster with infinite sarcasm, 'You expected Mr Brown to call *you* "Sir".'

'Yes I did,' said the boy simply.

I also spoke to a girl who had just left a London fee-paying school in the city.

'No one ever talked about class,' she said, 'But one day a friend whispered, "You and I are upper middle, but the rest of the class are incredibly lower middle." Most of them come from Romford and Loughton, their parents have scraped the money together to send them. Another girl's father is the head of a primary school, he won't let her out in the evening, she has to work. If you ask her where she lives, she always says "the back of beyond", actually it's somewhere like East Ham. . . . Because they tend to be alderman class, they're very job conscious and materialistic. They have no desire to do good for other people, only themselves. They talk a lot about losing their virginity but are more interested in whether it will ruin the relationship, than the moral aspect.'

Warfare – or the Eton–Jarrow match

> *I am conscious, moreover, of a marked distaste*
> *for those who have not benefited from a public school*
> *education, this distaste is based on no superficial*
> *prejudice, it is founded on experience. People who*
> *have not endured the restrictive shaping of an English*
> *public school are apt in after life to be egocentric,*
> *formless and inconsiderate. These are irritating*
> *faults. They are inclined also to show off. This*
> *objectionable form of vanity is in its turn destructive*
> *of the more creative forms of intelligence.*
>
> Harold Nicolson

Whenever people attack the English class system they start slinging mud at the public schools. I say 'English' specifically because there aren't any famous public schools in Wales, and because education in Scotland is far more democratic. Anyone wanting to explore the splendours and miseries of the system should read Jonathan Gathorne-Hardy's excellent book on the subject, *The Public School Phenomenon*.

In it he points out that in the nineteenth century, the difference between the old landed gentry and the manufacturing classes was that the first inherited their money, the second earned it. And, paradoxically, although the ambitious merchant or industrialist exalted work, once his son went to a boarding school and then on to Oxford or Cambridge, and mixed with the upper classes and espoused country house life (probably the most seductive of all life styles), he had to value idleness as the supreme mark of status. The point of the aristocrat was that he does not need to work for his living. This, Jonathan Gathorne-Hardy goes on to explain, is *crucial* to the understanding of English class attitudes. It underpins the idealisation of the amateur, it explains why money went on the houses, horses and beautiful things, rather than back into the business. It explains the horror of trade, and why the English, unlike the French, Americans and Germans, have always regarded 'intellectual' as a dirty word.

The public schools were not required to educate: they taught strength of character, leadership, and self-reliance. This, in turn, explains why until a few years ago the upper and upper middle classes took little interest in education. 'The English gentleman,' wrote Douglas Sutherland, as recently as the middle seventies, 'regards any child who comes more than half way up the class with extreme suspicion.'

Things have been changing during the last twenty-five years however. Capital transfer tax has made it harder to leave much money. The only inheritance one could be sure of giving one's child was a good education.

In the nick of time, most public schools have subordinated their earlier aim of building 'character' and acting as a gentleman factory, to the achievement of academic excellence. The Old Boy Notwork is a thing of the past.

This obsession with education has spread down the classes, resulting in a complete rate-race – with nine-year-old day school children working ten hours a day with no Arthur Scargill to protect them; with teenagers being offered holidays in Bermuda if they pass A levels; and whole families, including the cat, going on tranquillisers before O Dear Levels.

'Your father is making *every* sacrifice to pay for your education!'

Last year sixty-seven per cent of middle-class children interviewed said they would rather work for an exam than go to a
party, and one working-class family knifed their father collectively, because he pushed them so hard to go to a university.
Even the upper classes are infected and in August the beaches
at Bembridge and the grouse moors echo with Caroline Stow-
Crat and her friends upstaging each other over how many A
levels Fiona got.

In the middle seventies the products of public schools, which
took about a sixth of the school-going population, were still
bagging the top jobs: eighty per cent of judges, sixty-seven per
cent of bishops, eighty per cent of directors of clearing banks,
sixty-eight per cent of directors of major industries.

In *The New Anatomy of Britain* (written in 1972) Anthony
Sampson doubted whether the public schools could maintain a
dominant position in the 'eighties. The middle classes would no
longer be able to afford them and the great lower middle-class
movement, the growth of the grammar schools, was acting as a
bridge between the lower classes and the corridors of power.

Getting into a grammar school was the crucial step for upward mobility, since this facilitated entry into the middle classes and the professions. University re-inforced the upward climb. In 1975, however, with the abolition of the grammar schools, the bridge was smashed. The direct grant schools joined the public schools in becoming financially independent, as did several of the old maintained grammar schools. With this scrapping of the grammar schools, the old social schism was intensified. The comprehensive schools and fee-paying schools glare at each other across the abyss – Us against Them again – the result is well and truly a class war.

Traditionally the public schools look down on the grammar schools, and equally the boarders at public schools looked down on the day boys because they pay less for their education. Etonians look down on everyone, and the smartest Catholic school, Ampleforth, looks down on Eton. The big London public schools tended to be superior academically, but it wasn't smart to be academic, and most of the St Pauls and Westminster intake lived in and around London, and no gentleman lived in London. And so it goes on. The great public schools, Eton, Harrow, Winchester, Rugby and Marlborough look down on the minor public schools. And the boarding prep looks down on the day prep, who looks down on state school boys who, in return for such contumely, duff prep school boys up on the way home. Finally the good comprehensives despise the 'sink' schools, where the brighter children despise the dumber ones, and the dumber ones actually refer, according to one schoolmistress, to the bright ones as 'snobs'.

Harry Stow-Crat thinks streaming has something to do with trout.

Eton

As the lower middles drop Latin into the conversation the middle classes drop Eton. One parvenu always boasts that his wife had a second cousin there. Girls will casually mention a brother who went.

Eton is also a very large school, which means there are a lot of Old Etonians about. They have long had a tradition of political dominance, stemming from the days when power lay in the

hands of the landowning aristocracy who automatically sent
their sons to Eton. They still hold considerable sway in the Tory
Party. Six were members of Mrs Thatcher's first Cabinet.
Coutts' only branch outside London stands in the High Street
at Windsor.

Eton is also a prime example of self-perpetuating selectivity.
Seventy per cent of the boys are sons of Old Etonians.

It is very vulgar to wear an Old Etonian tie except with a
morning coat. Frank Harris, who started as an American cow-
boy, when later living in France used to get his biographer
Hesketh Pearson to send him out six at a time. All gentlemen go
to Eton, but not necessarily all Etonians are gentlemen. There
is also a belief that Eton is secure enough to assimilate all types,
that the Nouveau-Richards will be less pilloried there than at
other schools, that intellectuals and eccentrics are more toler-
ated. Recently, however, a boy who said he supported Labour,
had his study covered in red paint.

To muddle *les autres*, Etonians often refer to the school as
'Slough Comprehensive'. Like most public schools they have a
private language. They call masters, 'beaks', the matron, the
'dame', terms 'halves', and use quaint expressions like 'Lower
Boy Pulling' or one's brother having been in 'Pop', which
means he was one of the élite, not a fizzy drinks manufacturer.
In the school list, Hons are called 'Mr', while those without any
title are listed just by their Christian and surnames.

Eton's activities are closely reported by the *Daily Mail*, which
regularly quotes the *Eton Chronicle*, as though it were gospel for
upper-class behaviour.

The Press also regard Harrow as very up-market.

'Harrow boys may all come from the upper classes,' a
housemaster's wife is quoted as saying a year ago, 'But they are
not rich, some of the boys even do their own laundry, and we've
even got two Punk Rockers' (rather like token blacks).

One is reminded of the Winchester headmaster, chided in the
nineteenth century by the authorities for only taking rich boys,
who somewhat irreverently replied: 'The boys are not rich, in
fact most of them are extremely poor, it's their parents who are
rich.'

Sports day

The upper classes regarding the word 'sports' as vulgar, call sports day things like 'the Fourth of June' or 'Gaudy'. At Eton it is rather like a race meeting without the horses, but the deficiency is more than made up by the braying voices. Everyone knows everyone so the din is tremendous. As picnics of megalomaniac lavishness are unpacked, a dog bowl is always laid on the long grass. The place in fact is stiff with Snipe Stow-Crat and other dogs, barking with delight to see their young masters again. The year I went other pets included a parrot, a white rat, a hamster and several guinea pigs.

The horseplay among the young was unbelievable, one old boy charged about carrying a bearskin aloft, and was finally brought down by a rugger tackle. In the tea tent a lot of the boys and their girl friends were openly necking and yelling at each other.

'Wouldn't see behaviour like this at a comprehensive school,' said one grandmother.

'Everything's gone to the dogs', said her friend, 'They've even got tea bags instead of proper tea now.'

The captain of the eleven who'd made a lot of runs came in. No one took any notice of him so, he went out again. Some one let off a stink bomb, and we all went off to watch the procession of boats.

The crews wore boating jackets (evidently the word 'blazer' is common), white flannels, and straw boaters fantastically garlanded with flowers: roses, peonies, trailing laburnum, lupins, syringa. It's probably part of the gilt-edged security of being a member of the upper classes, that none of them appeared at all self-conscious.

In the middle-class sector, sports day used to be a great hassle, but now that parents are far more interested in academic than athletic achievement, they are very relaxed occasions. At prep schools, a lot of little boys run round a daisied lawn for 'silver' cups. Every time the starting pistol goes off, all the labradors look up, expecting a large duck to fall out of the sky, rather like Chekhov with fairy cakes. There are a lot of masters in lovat green tweed jackets and baggy grey flannels swaying from one leg to another. At state school sports days, the masters wear off-the-peg suits, or tee shirts and track suits. At state schools, the children all wave back at their parents. At prep schools they insist you turn up and then ignore you, it is the beginning of middle-class inhibition.

What is amazing at middle-class sports days which are usually held during the week is the number of fathers present. Are they all 'concerned and caring parents,' or just skiving or on the dole?

The pattern is always the same. Harassed working mothers talking about *au pairs*: and non-working mothers, having grisly heartburn that Simpkins minor might not make Oxbridge. There's always a sprinkling of bra-less earth mothers, with John Innes compost and wholemeal flour under their finger nails, wearing long skirts because they've been caught on a hot day with unshaven legs, who wobble in the mothers' race. Perhaps that's why all the fathers go.

At comprehensive schools, masters have great difficulty making any of the children turn up at sports day. In 1978 one headmaster suspended the whole sixth form a week before A levels, because none of them had bothered to put in an appearance. They said they preferred working for their exams.

Vocabulary

Both the upper and upper middle classes consider it is very vulgar to use the word 'teacher'. In ordinary adult conversation the upper classes say 'schoolmaster' or 'schoolmistress'. At school they will say 'master' or 'mistress'. Jen Teale resists the word, 'mistress', because it has sexual connotations, and says 'schoolteacher'.

It is all right to describe someone as a 'good teacher' if you mean he is good at teaching, but very common if you mean he is a morally irreproachable schoolmaster.

'Teacher' without an article (e.g. 'Teacher says . . .') is even worse.

'Youngster' is another very lower-class word, employed by Shirley Williams and Tony Benn (i.e. Anthony Wedgwood Benn) when they're trying to be democratic. So are 'lad' and 'lass'; e.g. 'I've got two fine lads at College'. Harry Stow-Crat would say 'Georgie is up at Oxford'. 'Youth' and 'teenager' (perhaps because it's American) are somehow more O.K.

Other unacceptable expressions include 'plimsolls' for 'gym shoes'; 'P.E. for 'gym'; and 'bathing costume' or 'swimsuit' for 'bathing dress', or 'swimming suit'. 'Scholar' should not be used as a synonym for 'pupil'. It means a child who's won a scholarship.

Here is an example of lower middle-class journalism. It is a report on Prince Andrew's girl friend:

'A scholar at exclusive Gordonstoun School, Scotland, she penned an excited note to her Gran on Palace notepaper. Among the Xmas cards gathered on the mantelpiece, above a coal fire was a card from Prince Andrew.

"We are not particularly wealthy," enthused her Gran, "At the moment she is studying for an examination, she's very keen on sports."'

There are at least nineteen expressions here which Caroline Stow-Crat would regard as socially dubious.

Journalists invariably use the words 'exclusive' and 'select', as a euphemism for 'rich' or 'upper class'.

It is very bad form to ask someone where they went to school. The expression 'public school' is also very lower middle in the sentence, 'Wayne is going to public school next term.' Among the upper classes it would be assumed a child was going to one anyway.

Girls' schools

Be good sweet Maid, and let who can be clever.

Animosity against the public schools is aimed far more at boys' schools than girls', because it is still the men, rather than the girls, who are bagging the top jobs, because girls schools are far less snobbish, and because among the upper echelons it matters far less where girls went to school, a lot of people still believing it's nice for a girl to stay at home.

The upper and middle classes traditionally spend far less on their daughters' education than their sons'. A feeling still persists that it doesn't matter so much for girls, as long as they learn French, and nice manners, get a few O levels, and make some jolly nice 'gairl' friends.

A classic example of this was the diplomat quoted in *Harper's* who sent his secretary to find a boarding school for his daughter, adding that if she had been a boy, 'I'd have had to do it myself.'

Girls at boarding schools are seldom taught any domestic science beyond making cod in cheese sauce and rhubarb crumble, nor do they ever learn how to clean a room. This is a hangover from the old days when it was assumed they would always have servants when they grew up.

Comprehensive schools have home economics sections, often grander than those of any finishing school, but the girls get so good at housework, that this often leads to conflict at home.

Some girls' schools pretend the class barriers are breaking down, but the old prejudices remain. Gathorne-Hardy quotes one headmistress as saying she would love her girls to go to dances with neighbouring boys' schools, but alas there were none in the area. Actually there were several comprehensives: what she meant was no public schools.

English vice

> *You can't expect a boy to be vicious until he's been to a good school.*
>
> Saki

In the debating society of one of the most famous schools recently, a master rather rashly asked one of the more glamorously decadent of the senior boys, how widespread homosexuality was.

'Well,' drawled the boy, echoing Mrs Patrick Campbell, 'At least we don't do it in the passages.'

The deliberate segregation and mutual dependence of English public school life has led, Gathorne-Hardy suggests, not only to the Old Boy Network, but also to a strong strain of homosexuality (and I would add mysogyny) in upper- and upper middle-class men. It is interesting too that only in England – home of *le vice anglais* – does the word 'stroke' mean both a caress and the lash of the cane. The fact, too, that prostitutes say a high proportion of their clients who want to be beaten or to watch beatings, come from the upper and upper middle classes must be something to do with older boys being allowed to cane younger boys, and also be present at beatings to see the cane doesn't go higher than the head.

In the old days the only glimpse school boys got of naked women were from smuggled-in copies of *Health and Efficiency*, or of black ladies in *The National Geographic*. Now instead of sporting prints on the study walls, they have posters of near-nude Bardots and Jacqueline Bissetts. The latter with her small-breasted androgynous figure, is a significant choice, because as John Mortimer, an old Harrovian, points out in *My Oxford*:

'When emerging from the chrysalis of schoolboy homosexuality, the girls we preferred were notably boyish. Veronica Lake rather than Betty Grable, and Katherine Hepburn in *Philadelphia Story*, described by Frank Hauser, as the natural bridge into the heterosexual world.

'The only women, we saw at school', he goes on, 'were elderly and fierce matrons. We were waited on at table by footmen in blue tailed coats, and settled down for the night by a butler called George. Our homosexuality was therefore dictated by necessity rather than choice. We were like a generation of diners condemned to cold cuts of beef because the steak and kidney was off.'

One of the great panics of upper and middle-class mothers, is that their sons may turn out homosexual. Samantha Upward feels a Becher's Brook has been cleared, when Zacharias surreptitiously spends some pocket money on *The Daily Star*, and equally surreptitiously tears out the coloured page with the nude, and pins it over the poster of John Travolta above his bed. Mrs Nouveau-Richards, however, who is too working-class to be on the lookout for homosexuality is enchanted that Jason has a photograph of his school friend, little Lord X, by his bed in the holidays.

The latest generation of public school children, reacting presumably against their parents' idiocies during the permissive age, are much calmer and straighter than their predecessors. The drug problem which haunted the sixties is supposed to have been cured by inflation and fashion, although a Harrovian was recently caught buying cocaine by mail order. Drink has now taken its place. Every public schoolboy worth his salt has a bottle of Southern Comfort hidden under the floor boards, and gout has become the fashionable disease among teenagers.

5 UNIVERSITY

I'm afraid the fellows in Putney rather wish they had
The Social ease and manners of a varsity undergrad.
For though they're awfully decent and up to a lark as a rule.
You want to have the varsity touch after a public school.

John Betjeman.

The expression 'an Oxford accent' (like 'a public school accent') was once used synonymously for an upper-class English accent. And certainly among the lower and lower middle classes, going to a university gives one social cachet.

I remember a Jen Teale in one office in which I worked who fell for one of the more degenerate copywriters, saying she knew that her mother would approve of him because he was 'a graduate and nicely spoken'. Mr Definitely-Disgusting thinks his sons have 'gone up in the world, because they've both got letters after their names'. Howard Weybridge and the more entrenched right wing of the middle classes, however, might disapprove of undergraduates. To him 'intellectual' means wishy-washy lefty – and why should young layabouts looking exactly like trainee Old Testament prophets spend three years at some fun palace at the taxpayer's expense?

Mrs Nouveau-Richards is frightfully excited about Oxford and gets everything wrong. She tells all her friends Jason is going to 'New'. Harry Stow-Crat didn't go to a university, he'd acquired quite enough character at Eton by the time he was eighteen, but his great-great grandfather, being a nobleman, was allowed to graduate after two years, and Georgie Stow-Crat – now the upper classes are beginning to take education seriously – worked hard at Eton and managed to scrape a place

at 'The House' (Christchurch College, Oxford). In John Betjeman's time the House, was the home of the aristocracy and
this is certainly true today.

'Christchurch undergraduates,' writes Sir John, 'gave the impression of dropping in at Oxford on the way to a seat in the
House of Lords... They hunted, fished and shot, but I never
heard of any of them playing football or hockey or even cricket,
although cricket was played on the grounds of country houses
within motoring distance of Oxford, and men from the House
might have been called in to swell a village team.'

The House was also the mecca of the socially ambitious in the
fifties, when I was at an Oxford typing school. I had one or two
boy friends at Christchurch, and went to several parties there.
I'd never encountered people so noisy, wild and totally self-
assured. They always seemed to be drinking champagne, whiz-
zing up to London in fast cars to go to nightclubs, or breaking
up the rooms of luckless grammar school boys. One of them was
sent down for shooting a don through the foot with a twelve
bore. All of them ran up the most frightful debts.

Fortunately for them, they were surrounded by a galaxy of
witty Nouveau-Richards who were always ready to pick up the
bill. None of them appeared to do any work or go to any
lectures. I was totally intoxicated by their sophistication and
their ancient names: Mowbray, Bathurst, Ashton, Stormonth
Darling. But for me it was a time of great insecurity. Not only
did I feel intellectually inferior because I wasn't an undergraduate, but also socially inferior because I was middle-class.
It was the first time I'd met the upper classes *en masse*.

If school, with its private and state sectors is the great
divider, university should be the great bringer-together. For
many undergraduates it's the first time they meet people of
different classes. My thrill at Oxford was that I met the aristocracy, but for Angus Wilson, the thrill was rubbing shoulders
and goodness knows what else, with the working classes:

'There had, of course, been my London sexual encounters,
many of them with cockney working-class young men, but the
glory of Merton was I found myself meeting for the first time
working-class men who came from the Midlands and the
North.'

This and the earlier extract by John Betjeman comes from *My Oxford*. Recently published together with *My Cambridge*, this is a book in which very successful people each wrote a chapter describing their experiences as undergraduates. What is remarkable – apart from the high standard of writing – is what incredibly class-conscious documents they all are. One feels that the authors wrote with an honesty about their origins they would never have displayed if they hadn't been so successful.

Eleanor Bron, for example, found herself mixing with an upper middle-class intellectual élite, which made her unable to communicate with her own family (working-class Jewish), when she went home:

'I was too clever, like Alice I had grown and couldn't fit in the door any more.'

Alan Coren arrived at Oxford at the beginning of the 'Flat A working class is beautiful Era':

'This was in the post Angry days, when people referred to themselves as "one", blushed and started referring to themselves as "you", and tall willowy lads with inbred conks and hyphens stood before mirrors abbreviating their drawl, dropping aitches, and justifying a family that went back to the 14th century by saying they were all solidly behind Wat Tyler.'

Piers Paul Reid, upper middle-class, and second generation intellectual, arrived a few years later at Cambridge when the egalitarian movement had reached its height, and the middle classes actually sought out working-class company. One of his friends recounted with delighted frisson that there was actually a miner's son with rooms in the same building.

By 1968 the 'working class is beautiful' movement was coming to a head with student power joining forces with militant workers (a far cry from the undergraduates who rallied in 1926 to break the General Strike). But from then on things began to change, the austerity years arrived, and instead of power, undergraduates started worrying about survival, about fast diminishing grants and getting a job when one went down. The possibility of actually joining the working classes on the dole queue suddenly made them seem less attractive. People no longer wanted to get a job helping people or burned to do something in the third world. Instead they wanted to amass a fortune in the middle east.

'Apart from medics and Indians', said one Oxford undergraduate, 'all anyone wants to do when they leave here is to make a fast buck.' According to the *Sunday Telegraph*, in recent years the main scramble has been into those twin middle-class fields of indispensability: law and accountancy. The proportion has doubled in the last two years. Soon, no doubt, the market will be flooded, and there'll be hundreds of out-of-work accountants working as waiters (at least they'll be better at adding up the bill than out-of-work actresses).

'A few years ago,' confirmed a don, 'I spent my time convincing people that Marx hadn't said the last word on everything. Now I spend the same amount of time persuading them everything he said wasn't complete rubbish.'

The universities in fact have become bourgeois. How then have the classes re-aligned?

'One does generally mix with people of one's own type [i.e. class]' said an upper middle-class undergraduate from Oriel, 'Though this is by no means a conscious or rigid principle – but it does seem that many comprehensive and grammar school types are not very interesting people, or at least seem to have less in common with one because of their background.'

'At teacher training college,' said a working-class boy, 'We found our own level, and stuck together. Particularly in evidence was a stuck-up group we called "the semis" [lower middle, Jen Teale again], who got engaged in the first year. All they talked about was houses and cars. The only aggro I got was at Christmas dinner, when the principal told me to leave the table for not wearing a tie.'

'You don't notice people's backgrounds,' said an Old Harrovian now at Reading, 'until someone almost beats you up for asking his name. Yobbos are less tolerant of having the piss taken out of them, and tend to over-react, which public school boys don't understand. When they get a bit of confidence, yobbos who've been up for three or four years, take a delight in mimicking one's accent, which can get very offensive.

'I went out with a grammar school girl,' he went on 'and I shared a flat with a boy from a comprehensive school. Apart from his talking about "lounge", "settee" and "toilet", we got on very well, although communal eating was a problem. He wanted to eat early, I wanted to eat late.

'One thing I did learn was that if I got drunk, I broke up

public schoolboys' rooms, and they always broke up mine. It's much easier to break up rooms of those who don't mind so much about possessions and who you know will take it well.'

Today at university the classes seem principally to be re-aligning into upper- and middle-class guilty; the lower middle materialistic; and the working-class, cross. And although the middle and upper classes are no longer assiduously courting the working classes, a terrible inverted snobbery has now developed. The young, reports Ann Thwaite in the introduction to *My Oxford*, 'tend to avoid Oxford and Cambridge for egalitarian reasons, opting for Sussex, York or East Anglia, as somehow being more mysteriously like real life.'

Then there was the don at a university redbrick who said he would never dare write a book about the middle classes, because he couldn't possibly justify it to his students.

Very much the sign of the times, Nicholas Monson, the journalist, wrote about overhearing two sociology students having a passionate row over which of them was more working-class.

'One said his father was a miner in Darlington, while the other countered victoriously that, although his father had worked as an insurance clerk, his grandfather had gone on the Jarrow march. The first refused to concede his superior origins because his opponent's origins had been particularly diluted by the capitalist occupation of his petty bourgeois father.'

'They clearly needed the assistance of a recognised authority,' added Mr Monson drily, 'perhaps next year we might see the first edition of *Burke's Peasantry*.'

An interesting statistic is that English women graduates as a whole tend to be grander socially than men. Most of them come from Social Class I in the Census, which means they are daughters of all those upper middle-class lawyers, doctors, engineers and accountants. This is probably because the upper middles are the least male chauvinist of all the classes, and therefore unlike the aristocracy and the lower middles and working classes wouldn't be so resistant to women educating themselves.

The exception to the upper-class rule is, of course, the Pakenham family, who were all expected to get a first. Evidently when Lady Antonia Fraser broke the terrible news to

Lord Longford, her father, that she'd only got a second, there was a long pause; then he said with characteristic charity, 'Never mind, darling, I expect you'll get married.'

Social style

At Oxbridge wearing college scarves and blazers is traditionally considered vulgar. But Dive Definitely-Disgusting is so proud of getting to a university he wants to advertise the fact by wearing college scarves, and blazers with badges, at the same time dissociating himself from the plebs in the street, showing that he's 'ge-own', not 'te-own'.

In the conventional late seventies, sales of college scarves have gone up sevenfold in Oxford, and sales of blazers with badges fourfold, this may be because the 'campus look' is fashionable; because in a time of uncertainty people search for identity; or because they're all being bought by Zacharias Upwards trying desperately to look like yobbos.

Georgie Stow-Crat imports crumpet from London, spends about thee hours a week reading geography (a traditionally thick Yock-Yock's subject) and runs the college beagles.

Jason Nouveau-Richards gave his college scarf and blazer with a badge to a jumble sale, after one acid comment from Georgie, and now wears cavalry twill trousers, a tweed coat and fine green check shirt, and looks more straight than Georgie, all of whose gambling debts he paid off. Mrs Nouveau-Richards has learned that 'Magdelene' should be pronounced 'Maudlin' and the High Street is known as 'the High' but she makes Jason wince by talking about the 'varsity' and 'freshers' and 'undergrads' which is almost as common a word as 'students'.

Zacharias Upward wishes Georgie would ask him to his parties. With seven men to one girl, he never even gets a fumble. Where Stow-Crats rush in, Upwards fear to tread.

When Samantha and Gideon take their daughter Thalia back to Sussex, Samantha in her ethnic and Gideon in his jeans, it looks as though Birnam Wood has arrived at Dunsinane, the car is so thick with potted plants for her room. Samantha was certain she would be miles the youngest and trendiest mother, and was disappointed to find the entire campus swarming with identical middle-aged Bolivian peasant ladies.

'But Wayne, dear – are you *sure* that's the sort of tails they meant?'

Dive Definitely-Disgusting feels horribly disorientated, and homesick his first year. He's never been away from home before, and this is his introduction to 'adollt' life, and his college doesn't even look 'ollde'. Mrs Definitely-Disgusting has had a telephone installed for the first time since her latest baby, Joanne, was taken on by a modelling agency, so Dive rings her every night, holding the telephone miles away because Mrs D-D talks so loudly. Dive is reading maths or science. Used to being a big fish in a small comprehensive pool, he finds no one takes much notice of him here, they all seem to be in clicks. No wonder he eats in hall every night, and sticks to his rooms. He doesn't meet any girls and in desperation imports his steady girl-friend from home, but is so broke on his grant, he has to smuggle marmalade rolls out for her from hall. Mrs Definitely-Disgusting doesn't quite appreciate the glory of having a son at Oxford, until she sees him on University Challenge, and hears that Bambi Gaskett, telling him, 'Well interrupted, St Cats.'

Games, it seems, are the one great social mixing ground. Social divisions are genuinely forgotten and genuine friends are made between people of different classes. The smart set would never bother to know anyone who didn't go to a public school if it weren't for rowing or cricket.

Rowing used to be élitist, but although Old Etonians have gained 640 Blues since the boat race began, (schools such as Radley and Shrewsbury failing to get within 500 of the score), times are changing. Over the past ten years, Eton still leads with 22 Blues, but Hampton Grammar is now third.

In 1978 there were three undergraduates in the Oxford boat who would have been formerly dismissed as 'colonials', four grammar school boys, and three public schoolboys. 'The class thing is going fast,' said one of the crew, 'Last year there was a touch of class feeling, a sort of "them" and "us" in the boat, but not this year, perhaps it's something to do with the whole sport opening up. All along the river are clubs who want good rowers, and don't care where they went to school.'

In the national eight, there are now more dockers and lightermen than people who went to a university.

6 OCCUPATIONS

Oh let us love our occupations.
Bless the squire and his relations.
And always know our proper stations.

According to the sociologists the two most important factors affecting upward mobility are your job and marriage. But this may be partly due to the fact that the Census, upon which most government and sociological statistics are based, judges a person's class entirely by the occupation of the 'head of the household' in which they live. In all societies, there is a division of labour and consequently a hierarchy of prestige, but such arbitrary distinctions as the Census makes, lead to a gross over-simplification of the complexities of the class system. Photographers, for example are rated Class III, which puts Patrick Lichfield, Anthony Armstrong-Jones and Christopher Thynne in the same social bracket as David Bailey and Terry Donavon. Brewers, including, presumably the Guinesses and the Cobbolds, are even lower in Class IV. Athletes all rate Class III which puts Princess Anne on a level with Kevin Keegan. While the Marquis of Anglesey as a writer (Class II) is rated lower than all the dentists, chemists and opticians in Class I. The deb, working as a waitress (Class IV) and having *nostalgie de la boue* fantasies about lorry drivers, is actually bettering herself because they're rated Social Class III. Peers of the realm don't get a rating at all, unless they have a profession, and are lumped together with the disabled, undergraduates, ex-convicts and the chronically sick, which should mean that Lady Chatterley, as a peer's wife, pulled herself up like mad when she embarked on an affair with a (Class III) gamekeeper.

PERCENTAGE OF ECONOMICALLY ACTIVE AND RETIRED
PEOPLE IN EACH SOCIAL CLASS IN GREAT BRITAIN
DEVISED FROM CENSUS, 1971

SOCIAL CLASS I — Professional – 4%

Accountants, chemists, university dons, lawyers, vets, opticians, ornithologists, scientists, vicars, engineers, architects, dentists.

SOCIAL CLASS II — Intermediate occupations – 18%

Airline pilots, chiropodists, farmers, members of parliament, schoolmasters, police inspectors, artists, nurses, publicans, journalists, sculptors, diplomats, chicken sexers, actors, company directors.

SOCIAL CLASS III(N) – Skilled occupations – Non Manual – 21%

Sales reps, secretaries, shop girls, bank clerks, photographers, restaurateurs, policemen, cashiers, models, undertakers.

SOCIAL CLASS III (M) – Skilled occupations – Manual – 28%

Bus drivers, cooks, miners, guards in trains, upholsterers, butchers, all athletes including horseback riders and footballers, plumbers, shoemakers, printers, brewers.

SOCIAL CLASS IV – Partly skilled – 21%

Farm labourers, barmen, bus conductors, fishermen, postmen, telephonists, milkmen, gardeners, hawkers, ambulance men, barmaids, brewers, waiters and waitresses.

SOCIAL CLASS V – Unskilled – 8%

Office cleaners, porters, builders' labourers, messenger boys, lorry drivers' mates, stevedores, window cleaners, chimney sweeps, ticket collectors, charwomen.

Cabinet Ministers, M.P.s and diplomats are only graded Class II which figures. Once upon a time diplomats used to be all Old Etonians with firsts, now they're parvenus like Peter Jay and all the British embassies, according to a recent observer, ring with flat 'a's and regional accents.

When you marry, according to the Census, you automatically take on the class of your husband, which means that the day a duke's daughter (even if she's qualified as a Class I barrister) marries a chimney sweep she is promptly assessed with him as Social Class V.

What one does on the other hand, can be used as a class indicator. One thinks of solicitors as being middle-class, and lorry drivers working-class – but then again I know of a peer of impeccable and ancient lineage whose daughter has been a long distance lorry driver for the last five years. Repeatedly however, one is struck by the relativity of the whole system. The aristocrat regards barristers and solicitors as 'middle-class'. The Census rates them as 'Class I' and to the working class, equally, they seem not middle- but upper-class. A solicitor told me that lower-class women invariably put on a hat when they come and see him, and in *Family and Class in a London Suburb* Michael Young quotes a man in Woodford Green saying: 'We have a very dear friend who's a practising barrister, and it amazed us that people might want to know us because we knew him and called him by his Christian name.'

The other day I met a woman at a party who said her daughter had just got engaged to a dustman. Uncertain of her political affiliations, I was wondering whether to compose my features into a 'How Splendid!' or a 'How Awful!' expression, when she went on complacently: 'But it's quite all right, because his father's a general.' (But then again, a general who'd started his career in the cavalry would probably be a very different class to one who had begun in the Royal Corps of Transport.)

One poll conducted among the working classes showed that being a footballer was regarded as the most prestigious career, followed by that of a chauffeur. My daily woman was grumbling one day that her daughter didn't speak to her any more since she'd married into the professional classes. What did her son-in-law do, I asked.

'Oh,' said my daily woman, 'He's an undertaker.'

One notices too that occupations that have a slightly comical image acquire new, more euphemistic and therefore more Jen Teale titles: 'dental surgeon' instead of 'dentist'; 'rodent operative' for 'rat catcher'; 'public health inspector' for 'sanitary inspector'; and, worst of all, 'refuse collector' (presumably because they refuse to collect) for 'dustman'.

The position of the doctor is also ambiguous. The working classes think of him as upper-class. He has even usurped the lord as the most popular hero in romantic fiction. But a publisher I know was driving down the village street with a very grand old woman, when he saw a man on the pavement waving at her.

'Some friend's trying to attract your attention,' he said.

'That's not a friend,' snorted the old lady, 'he's a doctor.'

I recently heard a very upper-class girl say she must go home to Lancashire, because 'I've got to help Mummy with a horror party for the doctor, the dentist, the solicitor, and the agent.' Medicine, except in the private sector, is fast dropping caste, along with teaching, nursing and the army, because they are all dependent on state pay, and are generally too ethical to go on strike.

The upper-class attitude to farmers is curious, too. Many aristocrats have land run by farm managers, with whom they enjoy talking shop, and whom they far prefer to businessmen or people in the professions who don't know their place – 'more genuine' is the phrase used. Harry Stow-Crat also has to suck up to neighbouring farmers in case he should want to hunt, shoot or fish over their land. Upper-class young often go and work on farms as apprentices, before going home to manage their own estates, and say 'How sooper the farm blokes are', although they don't drink in the same pubs as them.

The preference of the upper classes for the working class because they are far enough away socially, is exquisitely summed up by Jane Austen's Emma (who I suppose could be described as 'landed gentry'):

'A young farmer whether on horseback or on foot is the very last sort of person to raise my curiosity. The Yeomanry are precisely the order of people with whom I feel I can have nothing to do. A degree or two lower and a creditable appearance might interest me, I might hope to be useful to their

families in some way. But a farmer can need none of my help
and is therefore in one sense above my notice, as in every other
sense he is below it.'

Emma, believing her young friend Harriet to be the illegiti-
mate daughter of a *gentleman*, firmly discourages her from marrying this particular young farmer as being far beneath her.
When, however, Emma discovers Harriet is only the daughter
of a rich *tradesman*, she changes her mind, and finds the farmer a
perfectly suitable match.

Which brings us to the upper-class horror of trade. A gentleman didn't have to earn his living, as has been pointed out in
chapter four. 'The acceptance of high living and leisure,' wrote
Evelyn Waugh, 'as part of the natural order, is a prerequisite of
the aristocratic qualities and achievement. The aristocrat who
goes into business and sticks to it and makes good is soon
indistinguishable from his neighbour in Sunningdale. You
should not have said that aristocrats can't make money in
commerce, but that when they do they become middle-class.'

In fact, if one looks back on most of the great families they
started off in trade. Many of them got rich lending money to
both sides in the wars of the Roses, and then bought land.
(William Greville, the flower of the wool merchants, who died in
Chipping Campden in the fifteenth century was the forbear of
the famous and ancient family of Greville.) But once their pile
was made, the life of leisure was espoused and their origins
rejected, which explains the parlous state of British industry
today.

Trade seems less despised if one is flogging works of art, and
somehow shipping or oil seem to be more respectable.

'Wouldn't it be heaven if Hamish got a job in Shell at £600 a
year,' wrote Nancy Mitford in the thirties, and the Onassis and
Niarchos family seem to have been accepted totally by the
English and French aristocracy, if not by the Greeks, which is
often the case. One's social deficiencies always seem more
glaring to one's fellow countrymen than they do abroad.
Onassis and Niarchos have been brilliantly described as 'para-
chutists', people who drop out of nowhere into a new class.

Social advancement is also dependent on access.
Businessmen tend not to meet the upper classes. But members
of the 'professions' – architects, doctors, dentists, estate agents,

solicitors – encounter all classes, and so do West End tailors, interior decorators, dress-makers and journalists, while chauffeurs, nannies, and masters at boarding schools have long-term access. All these people not only see the upper classes at close range and have the opportunity to observe them and ape their manners, but also, if they have charm and a certain deference, often get 'taken up'. When Michael Fish was invited to some frightfully smart house, the keeper was overhead saying to the butler: 'Things have come to a pretty pass when they ask the shirt-maker to stay.'

In Germany and America the businessman is of a far higher caste, and at the same time more democratic. In America, even though the men on the shop floor call the Managing Director by his Christian name, no one looks down on him socially. Advertising is also much smarter in America because ad men get paid such vast sums of money.

'Advertising is still not considered a fit occupation for a gentleman,' David Ogilvy, the celebrated English advertising tycoon observed recently. 'If I were top of another profession such as law, I would be in the House of Lords today. If I were an actor or even a jockey I would have been knighted, as it is I get the C.B.E. When the Queen heard what I did her expression was a mixture of amazement and amusement.'

On the other hand, the laid-back, lotus-eating entrepreneurial atmosphere of advertising must be very well suited to the upper classes.

'What do you do?'

'Nothing.'

'In which agency?'

Jobs for nobs

> *Lord Finchley tried to mend the electric light.*
> *It struck him dead, and serve him right.*
> *It is the business of the wealthy man*
> *To give employment to the artisan.*

Hilaire Belloc

Nobility of birth commonly abateth industry, said Bacon, but during the twentieth century, the gospel of work has been spreading to the upper classes. What career, then, is open to

Georgie Stow-Crat. He has obviously got to start making a living, since the money won't last much longer – two more generations at a pinch. He's unlikely to go into any of the professions (Lord Colwyn as a trumpeter and a dentist being a rare exception), because he lacks the application to train for six years and he'd find the people too stuffy. One aristocrat who actually managed to pass his bar finals, left the legal profession after a year: 'I couldn't stand the other barristers, they were so pompous and middle-class, and only interested in shop.'

Georgie wouldn't like the bar because he couldn't take Snipe into court. He might temporarily become a stockbroker, like the Marquess of Tavistock, or dabble in accountancy, like Lord Greenock. This would help him to run his estate later and learn the rudiments of tax evasion. Others take up 'head-hunting' or go into property where they do very well because they know all the right people and get hot tips about whose land is coming onto the market. Georgie might also run a restaurant or add kudos to a smart nightclub, acting as bait to rich upper-class friends, and even richer nouveaus.

Some aristocrats try photography because it gives them the chance to get at pretty girls, others flatten their 'a's and go into the pop music business or produce films. They are very good as front men in P.R. because they know the right people, but they are better at charming the press and clients, than dealing with all the follow-up work.

A lot of them are going into Sothebys, or Christies, or art galleries, because being surrounded with beautiful things at home, they're supposed to know something about furniture and pictures. They don't, of course.

Then there are the whore lords, who get their names on to as many firms' writing paper as possible. Kind hearts may mean more than coronets, but a lord on the board means business and impresses customers, particularly Americans.

Georgie is most likely to go and farm his own land. If he were a younger son he might go into the army. Cirencester Agricultural College takes heirs to prepare them for the duties of managing their estates, and currently (in 1979) boasts three sons of earls, three sons of viscounts, two barons' sons, a peer and, much to the joy of the popular press, a bewildered-looking Mark Phillips. Sandhurst takes more second and subsequent

'I don't mind you working at Christies, Georgie, but why on earth do
they want to come and look over the place?'

sons for training in the martial arts. All that shooting is such
good practice for the grouse moors later.

There is also a strong correlation between the aristocracy
and the arts. Genius, being unbridled, is certainly patrician. In
the old days Sir Philip Sidney said look in your heart and write
but don't get paid for it. No one worries about that today. Lord
Kilbracken and Lord Oaksey are journalists, the Marquess of
Anglesey is writing a four-volume history of the British
Cavalry. Dukes and earls burst joyously into print publishing
their memoirs, or extolling the merits of their ancient houses.
Lord Weymouth paints murals and writes thrillers.

In the same way, there's nothing unsmart about science as
long as it's not applied. It is perfectly all right for his Lordship
to potter around in the West Wing letting off stink bombs, and
making hot air balloons. It should be pointed out that in the
arts and among academics social snobbery is invariably suspended in favour of intellectual snobbery. This works both
ways between the two cultures.

'When I find myself among scientists,' said Auden, with

unusual silliness, 'I feel like a shabby curate who has strayed by mistake into a drawing room full of dukes.'

Or as John Betjeman gently taking the mickey out of donnish attitudes put it: 'Objectively our common room; Is like a small Athenian state./ Except for Lewis, he's all right,/ But do you think he's quite first rate?'

That tentative, fusty 'quite first rate' seems to sum up the whole world of academic snobbism. The egghead is mightier than the strawberry leaf.

Compute, compete and commute

To the middle classes, wrote Dahrendorf, the career is the supreme reality. Fear of failing is almost as strong as the urge to succeed, the fittest survive and escape to another rung up the ladder, the unsuccessful are ostracised. The historical origin of the middle classes lies in trade. They can be traced back to the bourgeoisie in the chartered towns where they grouped together, to demand their rights, and govern the towns, terrifying the aristocracy in much the same way as the Unions scare the middle classes today. (Samantha Upward's mother thinks T.U.C. stands for 'Terribly Unkind Communists'.)

The middle classes didn't become really powerful until the Industrial Revolution, when the development of industry brought the need for new types of work: insurance, banking, accounting, engineering, and science. Many of the people who entered these professions were successful craftsmen or farmers who had left the land. The penalty of failure was to sink back into the working-class ranks, so a gulf grew between the classes. As the big towns developed, the ranks of the middle classes swelled. They moved out of the towns and made suburbs and dormitory towns, and this seclusion enabled them to copy the way of life of the upper classes. Their children, as has been pointed out in Chapter Four were sent to the new boarding schools, and developed refinements of dress and speech, and, like all newly risen classes, walked through life gingerly as though they were treading on eggs. Their distinctive characteristic was that their work was non-manual and, like the working class they had numerous rankings between themselves. They included manufacturers above the grade of foreman, most farmers, the majority of civil servants, professional people, businessmen, and shopkeepers who owned their own shops, as well as independent craftsmen.

Ever since the middle ages the 'professions' have considered themselves superior to bankers and businessmen, and as the middle class emerged they became almost a class of their own; medicine, law, and the church were more suitable occupations for a gentlemen: they did not dull the brain like manual work, nor corrupt the soul like commerce, they did not advertise. Some sort of qualification was needed, so they formed professional associations and became members of closely knit and protective groups. The smartness of the various professions is subject to change. Architects are considered smart today because there is something creative about their work. There would never be any stigma attached to a young man going into the church, because the upper classes have to believe in God. Indeed a country parish was traditionally the destiny of younger sons of the aristocracy with small private incomes. Medicine, as we have pointed out, is on the way down, except in the private sector. Dentists, on the other hand, are on the up. They tend to make much more money than doctors, because they've escaped the clutches of the National Health, and because the desire for perfectly capped teeth has spread from America. Vets are also on the way up, aided by a little touch of Herriot in the night, because they make so much money and because the profession is getting so popular.

Schoolmasters could be described as middle-class, but again there is a vast difference socially between the headmaster of one of the great public schools or fashionable prep schools, and the junior master in an urban 'sink' school. On the whole schoolmasters within the private sector feel guilty about not being part of the comprehensive sector but look down on state teachers socially. On the other hand they make exceptions. I was talking about the headmaster of a fashionable state primary school the other day.

'Oh yes,' said the head of my son's former prep school, 'He's obviously a coming man, *I've met him at a dinner party.*'

Engineering has always been an unsmart profession, partly because no one knows what it involves. Harry Stow-Crat thinks it is something to do with driving a train. But once again things are changing. For the last few years, engineering has been far away the most popular career for public school leavers. This year also, according to the Public Schools Appointments Board, law and accountancy are both down, probably due to the difficulty newly qualified lawyers and accountants are having in finding work. Medicine and teaching are also down, and the civil service has halved since 1967. Industry, on the other hand, is up, along with farming, forestry, geology and biology.

Amongst the great variety of middle class-occupations there are three main strands which are particularly in evidence: The 'burgesses', the 'spiralists' and the lower middle class. The terms 'burgess' and 'spiralist' were coined by W. Watson in his article 'Social Mobility and Social Class in Industrial Communities' (1964). The *burgess* tends to stay put in the neighbourhood where he was brought up or started work, and establish prestige in the community. The burgess is often the country solicitor, accountant or local businessman, who takes an interest in the community and often gets into local government to further his business interests.

In *Middle Class Families* Colin Bell quotes a burgess describing his life. He is a typical Howard Weybridge. The Weybridge expressions are italicised.

'*My people* have always been *comfortably off*. After going into the *forces*, I went into *Dad's* business. We have several *representatives*, who have come up from the shop floor ... I am a very keen member of *Rotary* [on a par with Teacher and Doctor]. I belong to many clubs and associations because I think it's a good thing other Swansea *folk* see me at the right *functions*, and realise we are not just tradesmen. I also belong to several *social clubs* as a duty so that I meet the important Swansea people.'

This is typical middle-class behaviour, the careerist socialising, the pomposity of expression, the desire to be a power in the community, a big fish in a small pool, and the joining of clubs, which would all be unthinkable to the working or upper classes.

The second category in Watson's brilliant description, the *spiralist* moves from job to job, and place to place, upping his salary and his status as he goes. Colin Bell quotes a chemist from a working-class background, who is far more upper-class and direct in his language than the burgess.

'I went to a grammar school and then to a university, very red-brick and provincial, I worked like hell and got a first, then did a Ph.D in chemistry to avoid going out in the world. Meantime I got married and had several children, after that I moved from firm to firm, upping my salary every time, then I was promoted to Holland' [where class and accent didn't matter].

He then left the research side, because if he didn't, he realised he wouldn't get on, and went into the middle-class admin. side, which was far more cut throat, but which counted more. Now as the head of a large industrial plant he had to decide whether to move up to head office in London to up his salary, or to change jobs. His only friends were people he worked with, his wife's only friends were their wives. The only way to get on he felt, was to move. He hoped it didn't interfere too much with the children's education. 'If I get a couple of notches further up,' he concluded. 'I'll send them to boarding school. Not that I really approve of it, but it will make moving about easier.'

Here you have a man, sometimes working-class, sometimes lower middle in origins, who is prepared to sacrifice friends, children, and principles to his career – in fact he's happy to leave his family and the friends of his childhood, because they might be a social embarrassment. Later the spiralists often jettison their wives, and trade them in for a Mark II model that goes with a new life-style.

Interesting, too, that this particular spiralist showed working-class shyness by taking a Ph.D and cocooning himself against the world a bit longer; made a typically working-class early marriage to combat the loneliness; but then made a deliberate decision to move over to the middle-class admin side because it would further his career.

In a survey of managers' wives, it was shown that they all wanted their daughters to marry a *burgess* in the professions. All believed that this would provide more effortless security than a marriage to someone in industry, higher status, and enough money so one didn't have to keep on moving. They could not see how many young barristers have to tramp the streets for months after qualifying before they get any work. Nor could they appreciate the status props that go with the spiralist's job: the houses, the company cars, trips for the wife, gardeners and chauffeurs, the source of which can all be concealed from the neighbours.

The salient characteristic of the spiralist, whether he is from the working classes or the lower middles, is his adaptability and his total ruthlessness. He is the cog in the wheel, the corporation man who can charm his colleagues, while tramping them underfoot with his slip-on Guccis. His mecca is the conference.

'I've come a long way,' said one spiralist. 'My parents were working in the North East, my expectations were at best tradesman. When I'm at conferences I feel how far I've come.' On the other hand, because his social mecca is Sunningdale or East Horsley he often ends up sounding exactly like Howard Weybridge.

I went to a conference on direct mail recently, where the spiralists were rampant. The 'venue' as they would call it was the Café Royal, and it was all firm handshakes, and announcing their names: 'Vic Taylor. Pleased to meet you Ji-ell' (always two syllables), accompanied by a card pressed into one's hand.

Another favourite gesture on seeing an acquaintance was the thumbs-up sign, or jerking their heads on one side and winking simultaneously. (The middle classes, particularly schoolmasters, tend to raise one arm at about twenty degrees to the ground.) The smell of *Brut* fought frantically with that of deodorant. Most of the spiralists had goalpost moustaches, and brushed forward thatch-cottage hair, with that flattened lack of sheen from being washed every day under the shower, rather than in the bath. They all wore natty lightweight suits in very light colours as being more American in style.

On the spiralists' lapels, are unfaded circles which have always been protected by conference badges. One can hear the rattle of Valium as they take off their lightweight long-vented jackets to reveal belted trousers. Their accent is mid-atlantic: justified by the fact that they've spent a lot of time in 'the States' (spiral-speak for America) which usually means a brief business trip or a cheap weekend on a Thomson flight.

Their vocabulary (i.e. spiral-speak) is peppered with expressions like 'product attributes', 'growth potential', 'viability', and 'good thinking'. Perhaps it is some unconscious search for roots, but whenever they meet, they start tracing advertising

'It's great, Angela! I've been promoted to Patagonia!'

genealogies: (That's Les Brace, he used to be Saatchi and Saatchi, Garland Compton, before they became....) with the same intensity with which Caroline Stow-Crat and her group of jolly nice girl friends are always saying: 'Sukie Stafford-Cross, she was....'

Conscious of their seemingly effortless mobility, Spiralists always have razors, toothbrushes, Gold Spot, pyjamas and a drip-dry shirt in their briefcases.

Our third strand is the lower middles who don't rise, whom Orwell called 'that shivering army of clerks and shopwalkers. You scare them by talking about Class war, so they forget their incomes, remember their accents, and fly to the defence of the class that's exploiting them.' They are also the sergeant majors, the police sergeants, the toastmasters, Prufrockian, neatly dressed, cautious, thrifty. 'In the old days,' as Len Murray pointed out, 'they had an affinity with the boss, who saw them as people who could be confided in and trusted. They haven't the bargaining power, now there's more education about. The nineteenth-century entrepreneur has gone, and in his place have come huge management empires, where the smooth pegs thrive in round holes.'

If the ex-working-class spiralist's mecca is the conference, the lower middle's mecca is the 'function', where in hired tails or dinner jackets they play at gracious living and the 'Ollde Days.' Howard Weybridge goes to lots of such events and rather takes them for granted. But Bryan Teale's ambition is to be president of the Stationery Trade Representatives' Association for one year, and stand with a chain round his neck, beside Jen Teale, who has a little chain and a maidenhair corsage, graciously welcoming new arrivals, and being stood up for and politely applauded when they come into the dining room. Throughout the five-course dinner which starts at 6.30 they will 'take wane' with each other and various dignitaries and past presidents and their ladies down the table. As this is a Ladies Night, each Lady will get a gift of a manicure set or an evening pochette in uncut moquette by her plate. Later there will be Ollde Time dancing interspersed with popular favourites. Bryan will 'partner' Jen in the valeta. They both enjoy 'ballroom dancing.' The conference gang on the other hand would bop until their thatched hair nearly falls off. The difference between the lower middle 'function' set and the spiralists is that the former crave the 'dignity' of a bygone age, while the latter are geared towards America and the future.

But the real battleground in the late 1970s is between Bryan Teal's 'function' brigade of clerks and insurance salesmen, and the skilled manual workers one rung below them. For a long time the skilled worker has been earning far more money than most clerical workers, and because the former tend to live in rented council flats, rather than paying commercial rents or buying houses on mortgages, and have all the kiddies at state schools, they have far more money to play around with.

One notices, too, that, in the light of extra cash people tend to think themselves far higher class than the sociologist considers them to be. The financially disadvantaged lower middle class may feel not only envy but under social threat from the skilled working class, men who tend to consider that class depends not so much on education and income as on production and consumption. Large number of miners interviewed for a recent survey called themselves 'upper middle-class' whereas the Census would have placed them at upper working-class.

Barriers

Although the barriers are slowly breaking down, there are still jobs from which you will be excluded if you come from a particular class. Many firms in the City – stockbrokers, insurance and shipping brokers, commodity dealers – still appreciate what they call 'polish and mixability' (which is a euphemism for 'upper and upper middle-class background') beyond academic qualification.

The discrimination, however, is now going both ways. A company director recently said if he interviewed two equally well qualified graduates, one working-class, and one from a public school, he took the working-class boy, because he'd had to fight harder to get there. Nicholas Monson, an old Etonian, was sacked from his provincial newspaper, because of what was loosely called his 'background'. A fortnight later he was told by a London advertising agency that his credentials were fine, but he couldn't have the job because the staff objected to old Etonians.

You can't get a job as a disc jockey if you're upper-class, nor as a television reporter. This is particularly so if you're an upper-class woman. You may look glamorous but you mustn't sound it. Time and again, one hears the terrible flat 'a's and dreary characterless midlands accents of the reporter, which conjure up a picture of some folk-weave goon, then suddenly the camera pans onto a ravishing creature in a trench coat, tawny mane blowing. Jison Richards, having dropped the 'Nouveau' and lost the 'a' in 'Jason', and by dint of dragging his mother round with him to all the interviews, has got a job interviewing on ITN. Georgie Crat on the other hand, despite brushing his hair forward and taking elocution lessons from the gardener, forgot to say 'As-cot' and 'Sollisbury' at the interview and was turned down.

Many people, particularly rock stars, find they can only get into high society if they go abroad. Vital Sassoon went to America, which he described as 'a society where there are no class barriers, where the cop's son can become president of a great corporation and where profit isn't a dirty word.' Mr Sassoon was wrong, there are plenty of class barriers in America but he, as a foreigner, wouldn't be aware of them nor feel self-conscious if he transgressed them. No one now is more

in demand with the American television cameras than Mr
Sassoon, who attributes his success to his stepfather, who
taught him how to cut hair and take elocution lessons to smooth
out his cockney accent.

But despite the film of *Shampoo*, (which portrayed the hairdresser as a super stud) and Mr Sassoon making the gossip
columns as 'millionaire crimper and health food freak inviting
400 close friends to the Hilton' – hairdressers will never be
accepted completely by the upper and upper middle classes
because of their pansified and plebeian image. Her hairdresser
may be the recipient of Caroline Stow-Crat's indiscreet
confidences, but he'll never be asked to dinner. Although
occasionally as a token working-class, he might get asked to her
wedding.

Manual work

> *While I was at University, I took a vacation job. To a nicely*
> *brought up girl from an academic family the horror of sitting at*
> *a conveyor belt eight hours a day packing chocolates was*
> *indescribable. I also remember the feeling of being a non-person*
> *to the manager and the secretaries of a small firm. I hope the*
> *custom of students doing manual work continues. For many of us*
> *it is the first time we have been in close contact as equals with the*
> *working classes.*
>
> Letter in *The Sunday Times*

The inclusion of the words 'working classes' is interesting. The
girl who wrote this letter must have met people from working-
class background at university, but then, perhaps by
definition, they had already become middle-class. Recently,
when a Sunday paper published a middle-class man's account
of how he swept the streets for six months as an experiment,
what came across was the monotony, the hard grind, and the
way people in the street behaved as though he didn't exist – was
a 'non person' in fact. Evidently the only compensation for
working in a factory is that it teaches you to lip read.

If the career is the supreme reality to the middle classes, the
worst thing about the working classes, according to Ernest
Bevin, was their poverty of ambition. They are far more

interested in good pay than 'job satisfaction'. In a recent survey, ninety-six per cent of clerks interviewed thought pay was less important than prospects, but only twenty per cent of the manual workers wanted to be promoted to foreman. Promotion would involve too much commitment to the management and much less overtime pay. If Mr Definitely-Disgusting is made a foreman, he finds himself in an ambiguous position. The management thinks of him as a junior executive, but he wants his fellow workers to think of him as one of the boys. He also finds he has to cajole and threaten to make the slacker on the assembly line pull his finger out. The only thing Mr D-D is really good at is assembling cars – and he doesn't do that any more. If he works too hard even on the factory floor, he'll show up his colleagues and they'll resent it. To rise is to feel less secure, paranoia is the disease of the upwardly mobile.

If Mr D-D wants to get on, therefore, it's far easier to become a shop steward and rise through the unions – then he can have a chauffeur-driven car, expense account, lunches, first class tickets, trips to Brighton, Blackpool and abroad, and the ear of the Prime Minister without losing the respect of the shop floor.

Monitor commissioned a recent advertising survey which goes as far as to say that the belief in greater social mobility for the working classes is principally held by the middle classes. The tradition of the working classes is a fatalistic acceptance of existing hierarchy and status. Mr D-D's hopes for the future are based on the price he and his mates can get for the work they do. This is emphasised by the belief that they will do better by collective bargaining under appointed union leaders, who often manipulate their demands, rigging ballots and forcing them to come out on strike. Striking is also a good way for union leaders, shop stewards, pickets and even Mr Definitely-Disgusting to get on Telly, and have Auntie Edna ringing up from Darlington after *News at Ten* screaming excitedly, 'We've just seen you.' Even Mrs Definitely-Disgusting was asked for her autograph the time she attacked a picket with her shopping bag during the lorry drivers' strike.

As work on the whole is hell, the working-class man likes to keep home and work quite separate. Mr Definitely-Disgusting comes home, having been bossed about all day, and wants his tea on the table. Nor does he see work as a place where he makes new friends, or joins social clubs. He couldn't go to one of these clubs in his overalls, all sweaty from work, and once he's out of the place, he doesn't want to have to go home, clean up, change and come back. Firms' social clubs and societies for this reason are almost exclusively middle-class.

When work is so exacting, monotonous and unrewarding, it is hardly surprising that workers seeing people having candle-lit dinners, frisking on sun-drenched beaches and driving blondes in fast cars every night on television, often fail to clock in in the morning. At British Leyland if Mr Definitely-Disgusting works for three months without taking a weekday off, his and Mrs. D-D's names are included in a draw for a fortnight in Majorca. For those who can go for two months without playing hooky there's a chance of five days in Belgian beer halls (after which you'll probably need a month to recover). If you don't go to work because you're ill, the working class refer to it as being 'on the sick', which sounds awfully slippery.

Within the working class itself there are also numerous hierarchies. We know of the Respectable and the Rough, and those in work despising those who are unemployed. There are also great divides between skilled, semi-skilled and unskilled. There is a lot of kudos in being skilled as my hairdresser pointed out: 'My Dad works at Vauxhall on the cars – skilled of course, then there's my father-in-law on nights at Fords, earns £200 a week, but he only does two hours a night, spends the rest of the time learning Spanish. He's skilled too.'

There is also status in having the power to paralyse. The biggest rewards go to the workers who, if they stop work, do the most harm to the country collectively. Thus, miners, power men, dockers, engineers and lorry drivers are the new élite who can bring the country to its knees. While the wretched postmen, firemen and ambulance men have no clout, and slink home without a decent rise. (The spiralist would call it a 'raise'.)

Mining and quarrying is regarded as much grander than building, because it's not casual work. Engineers regard themselves as the cream of the working class. Printers are evidently the most imaginative and intelligent. Miners in Britain know that their counterparts in Poland are paid twice as much as dons and doctors, and are biding their time.

Choosing a career

The great problem when the working-class school leaver looks for a career is the discrepancy between fantasy and actuality. According to a careers officer: 'Jasmin comes in with one C.S.E. in needlework and says she wants to be a brain surgeon. "How about nursing?" you say. No if she can't be a brain surgeon, she wants to be an architect. Some school leavers fancy science, but they think it's going to be all "Eureka. I've discovered a new gas and I'll be awarded the Nobel prize my first week." They also love anything with a 'Y': psychiatry, psychology, not having a clue what it involves. Of course all the E.S.N. automatically go into a factory.'

E.S.N. stands for educationally sub-normal, which Dive Definitely-Disgusting is not. With one C.S.E., he wants to be a helicopter pilot. He doesn't know how to fly, but they'll learn him.

Mrs Definitely-Disgusting who has accompanied Dive to the interview thinks he ought to learn a trade. Having scattered coke tins and crisp packets over Wandsworth Common all weekend she wants to know if they've got anything on The Environment, y'know pollution and all that. Dive thinks this involves rushing around in a Land-Rover rescuing oiled-up birds. Because he sees beaches, and Martini ads on telly, he would also like to be a courier. Anything where a golden-hearted employer will pay him to move about, and as he still identifies with Divid Bailey, as a great working-class hero, and, because six eighths of his holiday snaps comes out, he quite wants to be a photographer.

Looking for a job at sixteen, he'll probably be luckier than little Wayne Teale who's been persuaded by Jen and Bryan to stay on until he's eighteen, presuming there must be some lollipop at the end. A headmistress at a comprehensive school admitted that she uses class as a carrot, telling her girls if you stay on longer and take G.C.E. you'll get a job in a better firm, and make nicer girl-friends, and meet a better class of man. In fact, as the careers officer pointed out, it's easier to get a job at sixteen because the employer feels he doesn't have to pay you nearly as much as an eighteen-year-old.

Ten years ago Sharon Definitely-Disgusting's ambition would have been to become an air hostess, but, as it would take her away from her steady boy-friend for such long stretches, she'd prefer to be a ground hostess. Mrs Definitely-Disgusting likes her at home, anyway. She'd like Dive to get on; she doesn't have any real ambitions for Sharon. One working-class school leaver in a very depressed area of the North managed very creditably against a lot of competition to get herself a job as a hotel receptionist. Her parents refused to let her take the job, they thought it would make her 'too posh', and they didn't want her carrying on like they do in *Crossroads*.

Women

The greatest feature of occupational change in the last twenty-five years has been women of all classes going out to work. The telling statistic being that three fifths of all working women now take non-manual jobs, while three fifths of all working men do manual work. This is reflected in the vast shift to and swelling of the Census Class III (non-manual). With increased technology, most of the Class I and II jobs have gone to men, with women filling the increasing array of lower white-collar jobs. Consequently schools, for the first time, are taking seriously the fact that women will work before and after they're married.

One of the great job phenomena of the seventies is the way the upper classes have taken up cooking for money. All the debs take *cordon bleu* courses automatically now, instead of learning to type and undo the flowers. All their mothers cook like mad because they've got upper-class husbands with picky appetites to please, and have to organise grand house parties and dinner parties without servants. Therefore it is like falling off a log for them to cook for other people. The result is Caroline Stow-Crat organising directors' lunches and working wives' buffet parties, starting take-away food shops and running Mrs Nouveau-Richards' dinner parties.

Like the upper-class man who can't cope with the six-year training for a lawyer, the upper-class girl is incapable of long term sustained effort. If she works in an office, as has been already pointed out, she's always on the telephone, or sloping off on Friday, and not coming back till Tuesday, or, far far worse, not recognising any difference socially between Sharon Definitely-Disgusting in the typing pool, whom she describes as 'absolute heaven', and Thalia Upward who's doing significant research in the art department. As the Principal of a smart London secretarial college can be heard saying on the telephone: 'Saturday morning, oh that wouldn't suit my girls, they go to their country estates on Friday.'

My husband had one secretary who always used to ring up her mother when she was going home for the weekend, and arrange to have the train stopped, because the railway ran across their land.

The upper classes sometimes impose their tastes as interior decorators. 'I let Caro Stow-Crat have Carte Blank' says Mrs Nouveau-Richards.

'Mayfair Mercs.' who are the glamorous social climber invented by *Harper's* and are the female equivalent of spiralists, go into advertising, pop music, commercial radio, television, or else shop for Arabs. They also become stylists in advertising, which means they impose their frightful lower middle-class taste on all the sets in television commercials and press ads.

It seems insane, by the way, that all the lower middle and lower-class girls who come from Epping and Romford and the East End work in the City with upper and upper middle-class men, who wouldn't dream of marrying them; while all the upper- and upper middle-class girls who live in Knightsbridge, Fulham and Chelsea, can't face going any farther east than Mayfair on the tube, and therefore work with all the middle- and lower middle-class spiralists in advertising, whom *they* wouldn't dream of marrying either.

Upper- and working-class husbands don't like their wives going out to work. They want them waiting when they get home, always with a clean house, regular meals and the children under control. Only in the middle classes, is an outside occupation for a woman a sign of status, Samantha Upward hates saying she's 'just a housewife', although for her taking an interesting job is less of an economic necessity than it is for Mrs Definitely-Disgusting.

Mrs Nouveau-Richards has absolutely no desire to work. She saw her own mother working her fingers to the bone, and considers she's very lucky to be a 'lady' (she emphasises the word) of leisure.

Some upper-class wives tend only to play at jobs. They counter depression when the children leave home by doing charity work, sitting on committees, marriage guidance counselling, visiting the old, or spending one day a week in a smart boutique or a bookshop. 'I wouldn't possibly have time to do a job,' said one upper-class woman, 'If you have a private income you have far too many letters to write.'

In the office

The middle classes tend to take work home from the office and not take nearly so many days off. The working classes, feeling out of their depth socially in offices do best in backroom jobs – one remembers the spiralist who felt he had to switch over to admin in order to get on. The lower middles do best in sales and P.R. because they're so pushy. Gideon Upward is too laid back to sell, but he has polish and self-confidence which makes him good as an account executive, liaising with the client.

According to a fascinating book called *Managers and Their Wives* by J. M. and R. E. Pahl the working-class woman like Mrs Definitely-Disgusting would loathe the firm's dance. But Jen Teale would adore it, the atmosphere is lower middle anyway, and she likes to practise socialising in a formal atmosphere. Often she's been a typist before she was married and feels very much at home.

Samantha Upward would hate any of Gideon's office parties if she were asked. She would feel under-rated and neglected. She doesn't like being defined by *who* she is, rather than *what* she is. She can't bear being treated just as Gideon's wife.

Mrs Nouveau-Richards has a ball, and kisses all the directors on the mouth.

Jen Teale, because she is house-and-kitchen-proud enjoys entertaining Bryan's colleagues at home. She has read magazines and seen commercials emphasising the wifely role when the boss comes to dinner, and knows about cooking food that is delicious but not so obviously expensive that Bryan would not be thought to need a 'raise'.

Samantha Upward doesn't mind entertaining but she finds it more of a bore than an ordeal. She regards Gideon's boss as such a tedious little man.

Jen Teale, who would love Bryan to get on, gives him more practical help than Samantha gives Gideon. Because they don't often entertain she discusses work with Bryan in the evening, and being an ex-typist, helps him out typing reports when his sekketry is off with the curse.

The most terrible story is told of the very shy wife of a spiralist, who was bogged down by several little children at home, but who was invited to her husband's annual dinner dance. As he was doing well, she made a tremendous effort, buying a new dress, going to the hairdressers and arranging for her mother to baby-sit, and scouring the headlines for conversational fodder. The great day dawned and on arriving at the dance, she discovered she was sitting next to her husband's boss. Despite her trepidation, they got on terribly well, and it was only during the main course, when suddenly everything went quiet, that she realised she had cut up all his meat for him.

When Jen Teale worked in an office, she was a flurry of daintiness, fingerettes so she didn't have to lick her finger to turn a page over, plastic soap dishes, a shoe bag for her outdoor shoes, a mauve office cardigan to stop her good clothes getting dirty, a floral plastic sponge bag, and a blue plastic container for her Tampax, in case anyone should see anything. When she goes to the Ladies she rustles lavatory paper very noisily from the moment she shuts the door and sometimes coughs, too, so no one will hear anything. Afterwards she washes both hands with soap and water, unlike Samantha Upward who only bothers if there's someone there.

7 SEX AND MARRIAGE

My period has come upon me,' cried the Lady of Shallot.

As was pointed out at the beginning of the last chapter, the chief factors affecting social mobility are career and marriage. If Sharon Definitely-Disgusting blossoms into a beauty and lands Georgie Stow-Crat, her future will be completely different from that of her brother Dive, who marries a factory girl. If you marry beneath you, and have plenty of money, it is possible to yank your partner up to your own level. By the time King Cophetua had given the beggar maid a few elocution lessons and smothered her in diamonds and sables, she was probably indistinguishable, save for a few 'ta's and 'pardon's', from the other ladies of the court. But take a plunge both in class *and* financial status, and it's a different matter. If Queen Cophetua had fallen for a beggar, however, handsome, and then been cut off with 10p, and forced to live on his lack of income, they would have both vanished into obscurity.

Although kings have married beggar maids, and peers' daughters eloped with garage mechanics, the fact that gossip columnists get so excited when this happens, stresses both the news value, and consequently the rarity of such an event. Most of us commit endogamy – which is not a sophisticated form of bestiality, but merely marrying someone of the same class. In fact, a genealogist called A. R. Wagner has gone so far as to say a social class for him means 'an endogamous class, one, that is, whose members normally marry within it.' The main reason why the classes have tended to pick partners in the same stratum is to exclude the classes below. The upper classes, for example, married each other to keep their land to themselves.

The bourgeoisie did the same because they didn't want to share their capital with the working classes.

There has been much written about the social mobility triggered off by the sexual revolution of the sixties, with working-class lovers surging up from the East End; public schoolboys melting down their accents; and upper-class girls, in a glow of egalitarianism, taking on a string of down-market lovers: lorry drivers one year, Negroes the next, and beards the year after that. But as *Harper's* has pointed out, 'Her final choice remains strangely unaffected. Somewhere there is a chartered accountant with her name on it.' Or in Fiona Stow-Crat's case, it's back to Squire One.

Courting

The working classes get off the mark very early. Dive Definitely-Disgusting, having gone to school locally, meets the same members of the opposite sex all the year round. He goes about in mixed gangs at first, then one day on the way home from school, after knocking off Zacharias Upward's cap, offers to pay the bus fare of one of the girls, and has the mickey taken out of him by all his friends. From then on he and the girl go round entwined like a three-legged race. As neither has a telephone at home they spend hours on the doorstep necking, or gazing into each other's eyes like cats. If they ever do talk on the telephone, the conversation is punctuated by long, long pauses. Embarrassed by tenderness or compliments, they indulge in permanent badinage and backchat. This behaviour in extreme form was ritualised by the punk rockers; 'When you fancy a girl, you spit in each other's glasses, then the boy punk says, "Do you?", the girl answers, "Yes", and you go up to the toilets.' Jen Teale is very strict with Christine and hangs around at teenage parties, finally falling asleep at two o'clock in the morning under a pile of crisp packets, like a babe in the wood. Naturally Christine reacts against Jen, and she and her friends escape to London, live in hostels, go in pairs to wine bars, and pick up men with eye-meets. They are very keen on what they call 'Chinese Nosh' or a 'meal e-out', and use expressions like 'a curry' or 'a wine'. Having been told since childhood to behave like little ladies, they are the most overtly flirtatious of all the classes, fluttering their eyelashes, pulling faces and rolling their

'We're goin' steady!'

eyes like Topsy, which they call being 'unimated'. When she
goes into a party or restaurant Christine always looks round to
see what effect she is having on men. The upper classes never
bother – and they never fidget either. Zacharias Upward starts
courting much the latest. The middle classes haven't the self-
assurance of the upper classes, and, locked into a single-sex
school, Zacharias makes do with Thalia's friends who've been
asked to stay in the holidays. Howard Weybridge and his
friends are much better off. Too inhibited to pick each other up,
and considering it common anyway, they have evolved an
elaborate system of legitimate pick-up places: tennis clubs,
rugger, golf and hockey clubs, where sporting events take place
to heat the blood, followed by drinking to release the inhibitions
before anyone can get going. Jim Callaghan, who was
working-class, had to join the tennis club in order to court
Audrey, who, by his definition, was middle-class because her
parents had a car and a char and went on holiday.

Later the upper middle classes also escape to London, where
they share flats with other girls and boys of 'roughly the same
sort of background' (their euphemism for 'the same class').

They tend to meet the opposite sex through work, nurses going out with doctors, secretaries with bosses.

The upper classes have far more confidence. They all know each other anyway, and their parents, whom they call 'wrinklies' or jarryatrics' have full enough social lives not to bother themselves too much about their children's morals. They worry far more about drugs and car smashes after drinking than loss of virginity.

Georgie Stow-Crat meets girls at dances in the holidays, at the Fourth of June or Scotland in August, and at the Feather's Ball, once described by the *Observer* in very unsmart terms, as the 'do of the year for those of first class stock'.

Unlike Thalia Upward, Fiona Stow-Crat, if she sees a boy she likes will 'dance over and hope he notices me. If that doesn't work I find out someone who knows him, and get that person to introduce me. If he still isn't interested I give up.'

When they're older, the upper classes meet skiing, shooting and at various up-market occasions like Ascot and Henley. At parties they go in for lots of horseplay and shrieking. Linda in *Love in a Cold Climate* was more attractive to the opposite sex than the much more beautiful Polly, because she was a 'romper' – almost a sort of chap. The upper classes are inclined to lean out of windows and pour champagne and cigarettes on tramps and parked cars, or to charge around at dead of night changing road signs. The sexes also meet each other at drinks parties in the girls' flats in Knightsbridge and Belgravia. Even if the party isn't being given in her flat, the hostess send out 'At Home' cards, and the recipient automatically runs her thumb over the words 'At Home' to see if they're engraved. Mrs Nouveau-Richards, who has read somewhere that it's wrong to say 'My Home', has 'At House' cards printed.

The season

Up to the late fifties most upper-class girls 'came out'. One's mother who'd been presented herself, presented one to the Queen, and the Nouveau-Richards bribed some impoverished upper-class woman to do the same for Tracey-Diane. In 1958, however, the Queen abolished the whole presentation ceremony which meant that anyone could become a deb, the season was swamped by social climbers, and lost any kind of cachet.

Despite this setback, a few hundred girls still come out every year. The procedure is to write to Peter Townend, the social editor of *The Tatler* for a list of 'gairls' doing the season. Then follows a string of luncheons where the mothers get together see that party dates don't clash, and make sure that their daughters get asked to as many things as possible. Clued-up mothers have stickers printed with their own and their daughters' addresses on. The minute the first luncheon reaches the coffee stage, out come the diaries and everyone charges round seeing how many stickers they can get into other people's diaries.

Many of the upper classes sell farms or woods to pay for dances. It is also necessary to suck up to Peter Townend in order to get your daughter's picture in *The Tatler*. He can also produce young men out of a hat for dances whose background education, regiment or sheer cash flow make them eligible. Most of the young men live in the country or a precious stone's throw from Harrods.

One of the great dangers is that one's daughter may fall in love with one of them at the beginning of the season and wreck her chances with other men. 'Don't you dare go steady,' I heard one mum say recently, 'Just like the lower classes.'

One has the feeling that the mothers enjoy the season almost more than the daughters. Many of them, still youngish and pretty, suddenly have the chance to meet up with old gairl-friends and flirt with old flames.

And at the end of the season, I asked a deb's mum, did she feel all the expense had been worth it.

'Oh yes,' she replied, 'The gairls have all had such fun, and, at the worst, they'll have built up a network of jolly nice gairl-friends.'

'And even if they do go astray,' boomed her friend. 'One knows they'll go astray with the right sort of chap.' (Which is back to endogamy again.) When I went shooting in Northumberland I encountered a good example of this concern.

'Who's that ravishing girl who's been staying with Elizabeth?' asked one of the guns.

'Oh she's being stuffed by a man who says "cheers" and "pardon,"' said another, 'So her parents sent her up here to see if Elizabeth could find something more presentable.'

Rough diamonds are a girl's best friend

'When the mind is full of tit and bum,' a friend of mine once said, 'It tends to be a-critical.' Meaning that in the first flush of love, you don't mind what class a person is. The fact that he's not 'the right sort of chap' makes him even more attractive. When they are young, the insecure of both sexes tend to drop class. Older upper-class men love going to bed with working-class girls. It reminds them of Nanny. For the same reason, they adore big strapping Australian girls. One Australian journalist went to interview an earl about wealth tax, and only moved out six months later.

Equally, going out with a yobbo, gives the middle- and upper-class girl a feeling of superiority. She finds the working-class man more respectful but at the same time more dominating than his public school counterpart.

It should be pointed out here that the working and upper classes tend to be far more chauvinistic than the upper middle and middle classes. This is perhaps because they are more reactionary, but also because they tend to have everything done for them by their mothers or nannies; whereas the middle-class mother, struggling for the first generation without servants, is much more likely to have made her son run around fetching and carrying for her. The middle-class man will therefore be far more prepared to reverse roles. This is important because it is crucial to an understanding of the different class attitude both to sex, dating and women in general.

The first great love of my life was a miner's son who'd become a millionaire. I was working on a newspaper in Brentford. He passed by me in the street in a vast open dark green car, and screeched to a halt. I bolted into my office but when I sidled out two hours later, he was still waiting. He was the most handsome man I'd ever seen, and it was all very disgraceful and wildly exciting. He took me straight back to his house, whereupon he told me to go and make him a cup of tea. I was far more shocked than if he'd tried to seduce me. None of my stuffy middle-class boy-friends had ever bossed me round like that.

We went out for nearly three years. Whenever he went abroad on business, and, I suspect, pleasure, he never wrote. This broke my heart. I only discovered years later, that he was ashamed of being ill-educated. He was shocked if I said 'blast', and would never come to any of my parties, although I was dying to show him off, because he was frightened of not knowing how to behave. He went to see his mother every day.

He was bossy, yet socially tentative, prudish yet unfaithful, and mother-fixated – all working-class qualities – yet we had three marvellous years. He was incredibly generous, showering me with presents, which cost a fortune and which were returned (my middle-class background again) whenever we had our periodic bust-ups. And he was far more masculine, more reassuring and more fun than any of the uptight barristers, stockbrokers, and account executives I'd run about with before. If he had asked me to marry him, I should certainly have said 'Yes', but he had the good sense to realise we were far too different for it ever to work.

For when the class war and the sex war are joined, hostilities always break out in the end.

Alan Coren reports that when he was at Oxford, upper-class undergraduates screwed nurses and married upper-class girls, while working-class undergraduates married nurses and screwed upper-class girls, yelling 'One for Jarrow' at the moment of orgasm.

Richard Hoggart, that champion of the lower orders, alleges that one of the most valuable characteristics of working classes is the ability to take the mickey and say 'Come off it', which the middle classes usually translate as having a bloody great chip on one's shoulder. This trait frequently comes out in working-class intellectuals when they shack up with middle-class girls, one remembers John Osborne's Jimmy Porter constantly mocking his gentle, long-suffering wife.

Another example of working-class chippiness coupled with macho occurred recently with a beautiful girl friend of mine who was running two men at once, one of them an underwriter and the first man ever to wear full eye make-up to Lloyd's, and the other a working-class pop music promoter. One day the Lloyd's underwriter took her for a row in Hyde Park. They were just pulling into the shore, when the music promoter leapt out of the bushes where he'd been lurking and pushed the underwriter into the lake, where he stood spluttering and threatening to call the police.

'If he'd been working-class,' said the music promoter later,

'He'd have slugged me back. I didn't throw him in the water because I was jealous about you – but because he was upper-class.'

If Zacharias Upward goes out with Christine Teale, Gideon and Samantha will talk scathingly about 'Not quite P. L. U. [People like Us], darling' or 'rather Pardonia', and pray that Zacharias will grow out of it. Middle-class parents also become particularly lenient in the face of eligibility. If you go out with someone much grander than yourself, you tend to take on some of their mannerisms. Friends noticed that when Roddy Lewellyn was taking out Princess Margaret, he assumed the patrician poker face, used the pronoun 'one' instead of 'I', and started walking around with his hands behind his back like Prince Philip.

The date

When Dive Definitely-Disgusting takes a girl out on a date he's likely to be much cleaner than Zacharias Upward who often 'goes out straight from the office. Dive has a bath, and a good scrub before getting dressed for the evening. He'll reek of Brut and over-scented deodorant and wear an open-necked shirt to reveal a hairy muscular chest clanking with medallions. He'll be extraordinarily generous with drinks, but he won't give the girl dinner (having already had high tea so as not to drink on an empty stomach), because he's frightened of 'resteronts' as he calls them. (Harry and Gideon call them 'restrons'). Dive can't understand the menu if it's in French; he doesn't know how to order wine, or how to eat asparagus, and is terrified of making a fool of himself asking for steak tartare to be well done.

Being taken out to dinner is such a treat to Sharon Definitely-Disgusting, that she always works her way straight through the menu, and always has pudding. She won't comment on the food, or say 'Thank you' afterwards. One working-class girl I know went out with a lower-middle sales rep, who had an expense account acquaintance with 'resteronts'. 'He was so charming and well spoken' she said afterwards, 'And such a gentleman. He kept telling me what knife and fork to use, and correcting my conninenal accent.' George Stow-Crat, in fact, would never correct pronunciation or comment on table

'Waiter! There's an eyelash in my friend's soup.'

manners. If his companion wants an 'advocado pear', let her have one.

The manager of our local restaurant is a great observer of dating couples. 'You can always tell a girl who's escalated,' he says. 'She talks direct to the waiter, instead of letting the man order for her. Artichokes are a great leveller, I saw one girl trying to eat the whole thing.'

'People who belong', he went on, 'Always hold their coats in mid-air when they take them off. The *nouveau riche* never say "Good evening", are curt with waiters, snap their fingers, and then over-tip. They also put vinegar on their chips.'

Both Christine Teale and Sharon Definitely-Disgusting tend to prefer sweet drinks to dry: Sweet Cinzano, Martini, Baby Cham and Orange (a sort of Doe's fizz), Tia Maria, Crème de Menthe. If they drink gin, it's with orange.

Sharon also likes a man to be neatly dressed on a date. 'If he had a holey sweater, or holey jeans I wouldn't entertain him,' she says. 'And he must be clean. I couldn't stand all those rockers a few years back with dirty hair. I like a boy with a bit of life in him, but not rough.' She would also say 'I've got a snapshot of him indoors' (which is working-class for 'at home').

Christine Teale refers to a boy-friend over twenty-one as a 'boy', (e.g. 'I'm going out with a wonderful boy'.) Most people say 'boy-friend' or 'man'. The upper classes when they're trying to be democratic and trendy say 'guy' in inverted commas. One should never talk about an 'escort'. According to *U and Non-U Revisited* one should say 'male companion', which seems a bit pedantic. Most people merely say the person's Christian name, and leave you to guess who they're talking about. It is also vulgar to say, 'May I bring my girl?' as opposed to 'a girl' when you mean a girl-friend.

Unlike the working classes who don't bother about the morrow, Wayne Teale tends to be tight with money. To splash it around is both prodigal and cheap. He won't buy a girl dinner, so he'll put on a paisley scarf, which he calls a 'cravat' tucked into a sweater, and take her to a bar where he knows the landlord by his Christian name. This he calls 'social drinking'. If he's over thirty, he might wear a white orlon jersey which he'll call a 'rollneck' ('roll' to rhyme with 'doll') sweater, because a touch of white is so flattering close to the neck after a certain age, and the collar hides the wrinkles in his throat. He refers to a girl as an 'attractive young lady'. He would prefer her to wear a skirt rather than jeans, even though his trouser creases are sharp enough to ladder her tights. He's also read somewhere that it's common to say 'perfume', but 'scent' sounds too foxy, so he settles for 'fragrance'. Gideon would probably say 'That's a nice pong'.

Caution is the watchword of the lower middles. Wayne daren't be romantic, in case some unsuitable 'young lady' traps him into matrimony. He would call it getting 'invole-ved' with a long 'o'. His girl friends have corrugated left breasts from being pressed against the pens in his top pocket. He doesn't resort to insults and backchat like the working classes, but his conversation is arch, and rather hearty with an air of continual interrogation, rather like Bob Dale or the non-yokels in *The Archers*. He will use expressions like, 'Chop Chop, young lady,' or even worse address his girl friend as, 'Woman'. She will say in reply: 'Stir Your Stumps, Wayne Teal'. It is frightfully lower middle to address people by both their Christian name and surname. Any money Wayne makes will be spent on what he calls 'home-improvements' or on his car, which has a christian name, and is always referred to as 'she'.

Zacharias Upward likes entertaining girl friends in his flat where he can show off his gourmet cooking. This is cheaper than going to restaurants, saves on petrol, and is much nearer the bedroom. All his friends say Zach is very 'hos*pit*able' (the upper classes emphasise the first syllable). Howard Weybridge's idea of a really exciting date is to ask his girl-friend to freeze on the touchline while he grapples muddily with a lot of other fifteen-stoners on the rugger field. Later she will be expected to talk to rugger wives about deep freezes, while he frolics naked in a plunge bath with the rest of the team, and then make one warm gin and tonic last all evening while he downs pints and pints of beer. In summer she might get taken to cricket, which is sometimes warmer but goes on longer.

Georgie Stow-Crat will be very generous to his girl-friends, like Oscar Wilde who, when asked why he gave champagne to a barrow boy replied, 'What gentleman would starve his guests?' Georgie can't cook, and would starve in a well-equipped kitchen. So as he is too thick to make conversation for very long, he takes girls to dine in a night club or disco. Romance according to Tina Browne in *Over 21*, blooms in the twilight gloom of smart places like Wedgies and Annabels. As the upper classes tend to leave London at the weekend, Fridays and Saturdays are less good nights at Wedgies. To win Georgie, you'd probably have to engage Snipe's affections too.

Who marries whom

'Education'. I was always led to suppose that no educated person ever spoke of notepaper, and yet I hear poor Fanny asking Sadie for notepaper. What is this education? Fanny talks about mirrors and mantelpieces, handbags and perfume, she takes sugar in her coffee, has a tassel on her umbrella, and I have no doubt if she is ever fortunate enough to catch a husband, she will call his father and mother, Father and Mother. Will this wonderful education, she is getting make up to the unhappy brute — for all these endless pinpricks. Fancy hearing one's wife talk about notepaper — the irritation.'

Uncle Matthew in *The Pursuit of Love* by Nancy Mitford

*   *   *

As the upper classes all know each other, they get in a panic if their children get engaged to someone they haven't heard of.

Georgie Stow-Crat plays around with girls of other classes before and after his marriage, but he'll try and settle for one of his own kind. For what are a few nights of passion for a lifetime at the end of the wrong table. Lord Lichfield took out a string of models and actresses, but he ended up with Lady Leonora. More recently the Marquess of Druro married the Princess of Prussia. The Duke of Roxburghe married Lady Jane Grosvenor, while Prince Michael of Kent chose an Austrian baroness. As the aristocracy are forced to straphang through life like the rest of us, they are closing their ranks, and marrying the sort of gairl who will bring some cash or land with her, or as one aristocrat put it, 'can make a decent lunch for a shooting party,' preferably from the same class. 'The reason my marriage came unstuck,' said one friend, 'was because I was upper-class and he was only landed gentry.'

The moment Georgie Stow-Crat gets engaged he takes the girl to meet Nanny, which is far more of an ordeal than meeting Caroline. What the upper classes really dread is their child falling for someone middle-class.

'A thoroughly convential man in good society,' said Edward Lyttleton an ex-headmaster of Eton, 'Would rather that his son should resort with prostitutes than that he should marry a respectable girl of distinctly lower station than his own, indeed it is not going too far to say that he probably would rather his son should seduce such a girl, provided there were no scandal, than marry her.'

In order not to be continually irritated by class differences, the aristocracy often marry rich Americans or foreigners, whom they can instruct in upper-class English behaviour without being too insulting –

'In England Ortrud, we have a funny national custom of not saying "horse racing".'

If Georgie Stow-Crat did marry down, he would probably choose a very beautiful girl which is why the aristocracy is so good-looking. In general, good-looking people marry up – Tony Armstrong-Jones and Captain Mark Phillips being notable examples – and the insecure and ugly tend to marry down, Just as they dropped class, while dating, they tend to pick a partner who'll look up to them, and make them feel superior.

When people get married for the first time late in life – in their forties or fifties, parents are inclined to waive class prejudices out of sheer relief that their child is finally off their hands.

It is debatable whether the middle classes have any real desire to land an aristocrat any more. As has been pointed out already, the lord is no longer the favourite hero of romantic fiction (unless he's in costume of course) and has been replaced by the middle-class doctor or surgeon.

Heather Jenner told me her marriage bureau clients; 'don't give a hoot' what class people are any more. 'Why should they want to marry a lord and cope with a falling down overgrown house. On the whole blue collar men are far better at giving a woman a good time. One upper-class woman was so fed up with the sexual and financial ineptitude of the aristocracy she put "Working Class Only" on her form.'

On the other hand, another girl who ran a marriage bureau, discovering she had a baronet among her clients promptly whipped him off the books and married him herself. Then another friend of mine, born on a council estate can pinpoint the moment she fell in love with her future husband, who is a peer. 'He signed a cheque to pay for our dinner with his surname only.' Finally, one has only to read the small ads in *The Tatler*: 'Very attractive blue-blooded academic in his early thirties equally at ease on the hunting field or engaged in economic and political discussion' (sounds hell), to realise that class does have a pull, the Blue Bloody is still holding his own against the Blue Collar.

The upper middle-class man, preferring to get his career together before settling down, tends to marry late, between twenty-eight and thirty-two; his bride will be in her mid twenties. Often they live together first, particularly if one set of parents disapproves. Then gradually out of sheer force of habit, or desire for grandchildren, the parents come round.

Samantha Upward who's always taught Zacharias to be unsnobbish finds the thought of being a mother-in-law awfully trying. First there was Zulunka from the Fiji Islands, who was really wonderfully dark, but who spoilt it all by referring to all those nice Africans as 'no-good blacks.' And now there's Mikki (who's really called Enid) who appears to have no surname.

Mikki does something nebulous in the music business, is totally uncultured, but full of pretensions. In referring to herself and Samantha collectively as 'middle-class folk like ourselves' she is obviously totally unaware that Samantha's family is much better than hers is. Even more maddening, Gideon obviously thinks that Mikki is quite quite perfect, particularly as she doesn't wear a stitch in bed. Gideon insists on taking her a cup of tea first thing to admire her early morning teats.

The lower middle parents, being materialistic, aren't sure whether to oppose early marriage as unsound financially or welcome it as better than pre-marital promiscuity. One lower middle spiralist said the reason he finally decided to marry his wife was because she'd been brought up in a careful household, and therefore would be a good manager of his money. Believing in deferred satisfaction, Wayne tends to be engaged for several years, rather than live with a girl, so he can put a deposit down on a house. He will 'study for exams' in the evening, his fiancée will work in a bar, and bank the lot, so they have enough money to move in a perfectly 'decorated home'. His fiancée can't stand disorder – she must have everything nice. Whereas the upper middle girl who wanted to get married in a hurry would be perfectly happy to move into a rented box in Fulham, and run up an overdraft doing the place up, or expect Daddy to fork out for carpets and things later.

The Nouveau-Richards will be absolutely furious if Tracey-Diane doesn't marry up. In the same way the middle-class Princess Grace was livid, having hooked a prince herself, that her daughter settled for a middle-class industrial-ist.

Parents are very seldom cross about upward mobility. Even when engagements are broken off, parents make social capital, like the mother who went round telling her friends – 'It's such a bore having to pick all the coronets off the linen.'

Dive Definitely-Disgusting marries the earliest of all the classes. This is probably due to frustration. The working classes have got nowhere to make love – probably no car, no flat. If they go home Mrs. D-D and all the children are watching the telly and it's too cold outside except in summer. They also started dating earlier anyway, and if they do screw they often don't bother to 'take precautions', get pregnant and can't afford abortions.

'I didn't *have* to get married, I married for love,' a working-class minicab driver told me the other day, as if it were the exception to the rule.

Engaged at seventeen, Sharon Definitely-Disgusting gets 'eternized' at eighteen, which means she receives an eternity ring from her betrothed. At Christmas and birthdays, she will send him a four-foot square card padded with red satin, saying 'To my Darling Fiance' (without the accent).

The word 'fiancé,' perhaps because so many people live together now has become distinctly vulgar, particularly when it is pronounced 'fee-on-*cay*' with the weight on the last syllable. Debs get round it sometimes by saying 'my fiasco', or 'my intended' in inverted commas.

The wedding

The wedding is one occasion when the classes meet head on. People who marry up choose tiny churches, or have registry office weddings so they don't have to invite less grand relations. It doesn't matter having common friends, everyone thinks one's frightfully democratic, but common relations are quite a different matter. Wedding presents aren't displayed either because they might cause derisive mirth at the reception.

Embarrassing relations are less obvious at a stand-up reception with food you can eat with your fingers, so people's table manners don't show up – and with any luck working-class relations will push off early because they hate not being able to sit down.

There will invariably be a panic about protocol. One girl said her mother pored over *The Tatler* for months, studying every detail of the weddings, muttering firmly, 'We're going to get this right'. 'We even', she went on, 'put a sleeping pill in Grandad's cocoa, the night before, because he refused to wear morning dress.'

When John Betjeman married an upper-class girl he drove his mother-in-law insane at the pre-wedding party by wearing a made-up bow tie on elastic and flicking it all the way through dinner.

Conversely an example of aristocratic indifference to other people's opinions also occurred at a recent stag party held in a private room at a club. The men had just finished dinner, and the bridegroom's father, an old peer, suddenly beckoned to a waiter, and said: 'Pot'.

'We're not allowed to supply it, sir,' said the waiter nervously.

'Don't be bloody silly,' roared the Earl, 'I mean pisspot.' Whereupon a huge chamber pot was brought down from one of the bedrooms, and the Earl proceeded to use it, in full view of the other guests.

The upper classes get married in the country in their own churches. As they are accustomed to giving and going to balls and big parties, the wedding is not such an event as it would be in a middle-class family. Quite often the bride wears her mother's wedding dress. She usually doesn't have a long engagement or any of the hassle of finding a house, because her parents or her in-laws have already given them a 'place' with lots of 'pieces' in it. (One upper-class bride was so relaxed she spent her wedding morning washing her horse's tail.)

The wedding invitations are engraved in black, the service cards have the Christian names of the bride and bridegroom (pronounced 'bridegr'm' not 'bridegrume') printed at the bottom. Flowers in the church are usually something unostentatious like lilies of the valley,. with the bride's bouquet (pronounced *'book*-ay' not 'buke-ay') of white roses or spring flowers.

The men wear their own morning coats. There are usually hordes of little bridesmaids called Lucinda and Henrietta, a page with patent leather hair wearing a replica of a Blues and Royals uniform, and a labrador looking sheepish in a regimental bow. No one minds about the music. 'Here Comes the Bride' up, 'Mendelssohn' down. The bride agrees to honour and obey. It used to be unsmart to get married at the weekend, particularly in London as everyone had gone away. But now most of the upper classes and their show business friends have jobs, it is considered perfectly all right. Saturday police have to be deployed from the local football match to deal with the traffic. Several of the guests arrive by helicopter.

After the service the line-up to shake hands with the couple takes hours and hours. We queued interminably at a royal wedding a few years ago – it was rather like mountaineering. You crawled along for ten minutes, then turned into the next room to find another long queue, and then another up a stair-case and then another. People kept giving up, and doing U-turns to go out to dinner. One felt they ought to provide something to sustain one during the waiting: champagne at the foothills, or brandy at the South Col – or at least lay on buskers.

At another very grand wedding, having been nervously prac-tising my curtsy all the way, I found when we finally reached the bride and bridegroom that everyone was shaking hands with them.

'I thought we were supposed to bob,' I muttered to a friend once I was safely inside.

'I was damned if I was going to bob to that jumped up trollop,' said my mate. 'And after that everyone followed suit.'

The reception at an upper-class wedding is a very cheerful occasion, once again because everyone knows each other, and it doesn't matter that there's no introducing. None of the women look the least self-conscious in hats, the cake is decorated with white flowers, and often cut with the bridegroom's sword, the nearest it ever gets to active service. Really grand weddings include busloads of tenants from both families. Usually they sit around with red faces, shiny blue suits, and tumbrilcreamed hair. But at Earl Grosvenor's wedding recently, morning coats were hired for all the tenants so they wouldn't feel out of place, and they were all flown down by aeroplane.

The latest trend is to have a wedding followed by a small luncheon for the stuffier relations, followed by an afternoon rest for the stuffed bride, followed by a huge booze-up in the even-ing.

Georgie Stow-Crat hates his honeymoon because he misses Snipe. Upper-class girls often take Teddy on honeymoon.

When Georgie marries Tracey-Diane Nouveau-Richards, no expense is spared. Tracey-Diane's tiara is so heavy, her head droops like a snowdrop. The 'floral decorations' composed of 'Football Mum' Chrysanthemums, nurtured in Mr Nouveau-Richards's conservatory are described by the N–R's friends as 'tasteful'. Mrs N-R hires a hundred out-of-work actors to pose as relations, and two hundred more as tenants. They rather overdo the Somerset accents and rust-coloured country suits. The wedding takes place in Guildford Cathedral, with a recep-tion at the bridal home in Sunningdale. The marquee extends beyond the garden and covers the entire golf course. Guests keep falling down the holes. Three tons of Joy are squirted into the swimming pool on which float the words 'George and Tracey-Diane' written in salmon pink carnations.

Mrs Nouveau-Richards has had orchids and maidenhair corsages in little test tubes of preservative liquid made up for herself and Caroline Stowe-Crat, who surreptitiously tries to rip off the maidenhair during the service, and only succeeds in burning a hole in her new coat and skirt with the preservative. Signing the register takes longer than usual, as Mrs N-R's hat gets stuck in the door.

Harry Stow-Crat has a wonderful time. There's plenty of champagne – Tracey-Diane's endowment of worldly goods means he needn't worry about death duties any more. All Mrs Nouveau-Richard's hired relations turn out to be his show business cronies, which persuades him the N.R's do know some quite amusing people after all. And Snipe gets into all the photos with his back to the camera gazing at Harry.

The Upwards are simply furious they haven't been invited.

'I suppose they can't ask everyone,' says Samantha bravely.

Although Mrs Nouveau-Richards seems to have.

The upper middle wedding is far more depressing. Samantha and Thalia, wanting to be different and stress how 'cultured' and musical they are, choose hymns the congregation don't know. Lists are placed at Peter Jones or the General Trading Company, so everyone knows what they're getting. Waiters keep the napkin over the champagne to hide the lack of vintage. No one wears maidenhair behind their carnations apart from a few declassé cousins in lounge suits.

As the upper middle classes don't all know each other, but are too grand for a sit-down meal, their weddings tend to be very heavy going. The women's heels sink into the lawn so they can't circulate. The merriment is not aided by a long speech from the bride's parents' most upper-class friend. No one can clap properly at the end because they're holding empty glasses. Thalia's husband hates his honeymoon and thinks they're so called because they're so sticky.

Howard and Eileen Weybridge's wedding is held in the function room of the Olde White Hart (circa 1937) with French windows opening onto the patio. The women look very self-conscious in floppy hats, with too much hair showing in front.

The bride makes her own wedding dress, or buys it off the peg. According to one manufacturer, royalty influences far more wedding dresses than show business, and the less virginal a girl is, the more covered up she wants to look. Howard Weybridge and all his ushers are photographed outside the church in hired grey morning coats with maidenhair rampant behind every foiled carnation, and their top hats on the sides of their heads. The reception starts off with sweet and dry sherry followed by Asti Spumante ('bubbly', as they call it, is too expensive); everyone sits down to lunch of a nice smoked trout, chicken, and *bombe surprise*, after frightful rows over the seating arrangements. Likely to be local Councillors or secretaries of the Tennis Club, who adore the sound of their own voices, the speakers go on for ever, and every dismally unfunny telegram is read out.

The bride's mother finds the 'holl' occasion very 'meuving'. 'It's such a nice opportunity to meet and converse with relatives,' and Eileen's had 'some wonderful wedding gifts.' The father says 'looks after yerself,' as Eileen goes away in the Austin Princess and a navy costume with beige accessories. The honeymoon is spent in the bridal suite of a hotel in Devonshire.

The lower middles are the tiredest when they get married, because they've decorated and renovated their new property (Georgie Stowe-Crat would say 'done up their new house') themselves, all ready to move in.

Bryan Teale has his stag party two nights before the wedding because Auntie Jean has to be met off the train from Scotland on Friday and the Volks has to be put through the car wash before they go away. No one wears a morning coat, the men are in three-piece waisted suits. The best man goes off to buy shoes with built-up heels on the morning of the wedding so his trousers hang better. The 'bridal gown' is based on the latest royal soap opera with Mrs Fitzherbert sleeves. The photographer snaps away throughout the service in all the most solemn moments. People are shown to their seats by 'groomsmen' rather than 'ushers' and the results are put in a white album with spider tissue paper. The service cards are printed in silver gothic script and decorated with silver bells and the bride and groom's initials. The bridegroom has to remove his initialled signet ring to his right hand to make way for his wedding ring, and the happy couple, smothered in confetti and rice, leave the church in a white Rolls-Royce.

The reception is held at the Dainty Maiden Tea Rooms, and thirsty cyclists who've ridden over from Godalming are told to go to the Hand in the Bush Tea Rooms down the road, as the place has been taken over for a 'function'. Sherry is followed by rosé or sparkling hock. Everyone eats ham, chicken and salad. The wedding cake is topped by a papier mâché replica of the bride and groom both wearing lipstick, and decorated with silver shoes, horseshoes and plastic flowers.

The bride wearing a tangerine 'skirt suit', and the bride-groom in an even lighter coloured and more waisted suit go off to Majorca for a honeymoon where the new Mrs Teale loses her virginity on the third day.

The working-class wedding is the most jolly. Mrs Definitely-Disgusting has even forgiven Stan for putting Sharon in the club – at least he's white. The hall is hired at the Goat and Boots, the bar is open all day, everyone sits down or dances – the working classes never stand because of their corns. Dad soon gets down to the piano, and starts playing 'golden oldies' like 'You Made Me Love You'. Auntie Eileen leads the singing. Even Mrs Definitely-Disgusting is persuaded to do a knees up. Sharon wears an empire line dress to hide the bulge, and feels sick all the time. The honeymoon is spent in Jersey. Having never been away from home before Stan and Sharon are very homesick.

Oh Come Oh Come non-Manuel

It is difficult to generalise about sex and class. Hunter Davies, a working-class writer so successful that he has certainly become middle-class in his life style, in a *Sunday Times* piece expressed his bewilderment at his thirteen-year-old daughter going out with boys, and demanding parties with drink. 'Brought up on a council estate in the sixties,' he wrote, 'I married the school swot, it took me three weeks even to hold her hand. My dad knew what it was like to be me when I was courting, but things have changed so much in the last ten years, that I haven't a clue what it's like to be Caitlin. She's a different age, a *different class*, a different society.'

With the advent of the permissive society, one hopes that the young of all classes are getting better at sex, and more aware of 'the great discovery of the age', as Hugh MacDiarmid called it. 'That women like it too.'

But there are still vast pockets of male chauvinism among the upper and lower classes, particularly in the north. It is possible that young Georgie Stow-Crat and Dive Definitely-Disgusting are fairly competent operators having picked up a few tips from the cinema and Anna Raeburn, but their fathers are probably still floundering around in the dark ages.

Harry Stow-Crat's attitude to sex, for example, is the same as that of our late lamented English setter, who was spoilt, goofy, terrifyingly tenacious and possessed of a totally unbridled sex drive. If he got on the trail of a bitch, he would charge across three main roads, race twenty miles until he caught up with her, and then mount her from the wrong end. His libido was only equalled by his sexual ineptitude – rather like one peer who discovered after three years when no heir appeared that he'd been using the wrong entrance.

Another married aristocrat I know was so wild to pull a girl he'd had lunch with, that he secreted them both into the Great Western Hotel by a side door without paying, locked himself into a bedroom, and was just settling down to work, when the management rumbled him. Only a lot of fast talking and a fistful of fivers stopped him being arrested, and the most frightful scandal ensuing.

If Harry fancies a girl, particularly a lower-class one, he will pester her until he gets her, and then it's 'wham bam, thank you ma'am'. He's far too used to poor Caroline shutting her eyes and thinking of England to believe a woman should have any pleasure.

The telly-stocrat and the pop singer have the same exalted approach. 'It's so easy,' sighed one rock star, 'You have all these groupies, there's no time to romance [lower middle for to 'court'] on the road, so you just say "get your gear off".' A sort of 'droit du Singer'.

My favourite mini-cab driver has a theory that tall people are good in bed because only they can reach the sex books that librarians insist on putting on the top shelves. But this doesn't explain why aristocrats, who are generally tall, tend to be so hopeless – maybe they never go into public libraries, or don't read anything except *The Sporting Life* and Dick Francis, like

Harry Stow-Crat. Harry's sole aim is vaginal penetration – he can't even count up to foreplay. When a girl kisses him, she can feel his narrow stoat's head under his straight mousy hair totally devoid of any Beethoven bumps. As he thinks after-shave and deodorant are vulgar and doesn't have any of the middle-class hangups about being nice to be near he might even be rather dirty.

Aristocrats often break their toes on stone hot water bottles climbing into other people's beds at house parties. One wonders what the procedure is, does the hostess sleep with the man in the right hand bedroom for the first half of the night, and the man in the left hand bedroom for the second half. Presumably anything goes, as long as you're back in your own room at dawn so as not to upset the servants. Most of the upper classes share their beds with their dogs for warmth. When a noble lover leaps into bed, and thinks he has encountered something interesting and furry, he may easily get bitten.

As they have all the freedom and restlessness of inherited wealth, there is a wild decadent fringe of the aristocracy, whose sexual appetites are so jaded that they're into every perversion under the eldest son. Having enjoyed beatings at Eton, both Harry and Georgie Stow-Crat adore being whipped. You can recognise an old school bottom – striped with red, white and blue weals – anywhere.

Most life peers, who have been far too busy making it to the top to get any practice, are absolutely hopeless in bed.

Once you have found her never let her come

The upper middles used to be even worse than the aristocracy. They were too inhibited even to have Harry's *joie de vivre*: their upper middle lips were far too stiff for them to be any good at oral sex. Colonel and Mrs Upward's generation must have had terrible sex lives because of overhead lights in the bedroom. Once they'd switched the lights off by the door, the room was plunged in darkness. So it was a miracle if they ever found their way into bed with one another. In fact it's remarkable they succeeded in producing Samantha and Gideon at all.

Moving down the generations, Gideon is very enthusiastic, but a bit mainline – *Playboys* in the lavatory and a finger under his next-door neighbour's roll-on at New Years' Eve parties. He knows all about the middle class sophistication and de-furred satisfaction and longs for Samantha to shave her bush off. She did once but it was awfully itchy, and as the whole family have baths together, it might have put Zacharias off his O-levels. But she's frightfully understanding about Gideon's *Playboys* and allows him to do anything he likes to her in bed, shutting her eyes and thinking of Great Britain and the Common Market. She does her yoga every morning to keep herself young and attractive.

The best lover of all is the upper middle-class intellectual. Having been made to run round by his mother when he was young, he's into role reversal and a woman having as much pleasure as a man. His already vivid imagination has been encouraged by voracious reading. He's just as randy as the aristocrat, but he tempers it with finesse and humility. Lucky the girl that lays the golden egghead.

A male stud who has done extensive field work agrees that middle-class intellectual women are also best in bed. *The Guardian* reader, he specifies is the easiest lay of them all, because she feels she ought to be liberated and knows all about rejection and blows to the male ego. She always refers to coming as 'a climax' says 'penis' and 'vagina', and talks about her friends having 'lovely breasts'.

The lower middles tend to be too cautious. It's all 'nudge nudge' prurience and not much joy. Jen Teale is also terribly difficult to get at because she wears such an armour plating of full length petticoats (which she calls 'slips') corselettes, five pairs of 'punties', tights with trousers (which she calls 'punts'), and 'punty girdles'. Bryan, on the other hand, sometimes forgets to take off his driving gloves. Dainty and fastidious, Jen would never make love during the curse (which she calls a 'period') and she is 'revollted' by anything slightly off-centre. Afterwards she says, 'That was very pleasant, Bryan.'

Mandy Rice-Davies, interviewed in a sex book, is a good example of lower middle refinement: 'Looking sexy is a low class turn on, I've had affaires with Lord Astor and Douglas Fairbanks. [Here she displays parvenu boasting and lack of discretion.] But none of them involved anything remotely kinky.'

Working-class sex

The working classes have a reputation for potency and being good in bed. A myth probably started by middle-class novelists and by graphologists who claim anyone with loopy writing must be highly sexed. Randy they certainly seem to be. According to an Odhams Survey, the working-class couple makes love more frequently than any other class, but the woman enjoys it less.

'We don't fight,' said one builder's wife. 'Only over money and sex, especially sex, he always wants it. He'd do it now if he came in and you weren't here.'

Geoffrey Gorer maintains that the skilled worker (Class III), would appear to have more sexual energy than the other classes. But he says that there does not seem to be any factual basis for believing the working classes in general are more sexually potent. He quotes an upholsterer who only had sex three or four times a month, and a welder who only had it once a month (perhaps he got stuck).

Mrs Definitely-Disgusting calls sex 'having relations' or 'in-ercourse'. If there were any sexual problems, she would be far too embarrassed to discuss it. Mr Definitely-Disgusting is not into foreplay, he uses that finger to read the racing results.

A divorce lawyer also told me that the working classes hardly ever see each other naked, probably because they often sleep in one room with the children, and if Mr Definitely-Disgusting takes his clothes off, Mrs Definitely-Disgusting might see 'Rosy, Mum and Nancy and Doreen' tattooed all over his body and get jealous. And as he also imagines all women have retroussé tits, sopping wet hair, and full make-up like Page 3 of the *Sun*, Mrs Definitely-Disgusting undressed might be a bit of a disappointment.

Marrying up

No one understands the nuances of class better than Chekhov. At the beginning of *Three Sisters* Andrey's fiancée, Natasha, is seen as a lower middle-class social outcast. Everyone laughs at

'Oh my Gawd!'

her, and the three sisters tell her her clothes are all wrong. Then she marries their brother, and gradually she gains ascendancy. She starts bossing the sisters, henpecking her husband, and being beastly to the old servants ('I don't like having useless people about'). Soon she is cutting down trees on the estate, and moving the sisters into smaller bedrooms, by the end they are meekly taking criticism from her about their clothes.

People who marry up are far more insistent than most on having their new status recognised. I'm sure the Beggar Maid, despite her lovesome mien, made a perfect nuisance of herself queening it all over everyone. Women who marry up also become frightfully strict about their children's manners, because they're terrified that any lapse in behaviour will be attributed to a mother who doesn't know what's what. In the same way, stupid women who marry clever men are pushy about their children's education. Middle-class women who marry into the upper classes say 'se-uper' a lot, and become very good cooks to cope with picky aristocratic appetites.

When men marry up, they usually move away from their home town, buy horses and farms, and take up patrician pastimes like hunting and particularly shooting. They also become totally bilingual, putting on very grand voices when they're out hunting, and lapsing into their mother tongue when they're talking to garage mechanics.

If you marry someone who constantly tells you you're pretty, you begin to think you are. In the same way if you marry someone who thinks you're frightfully grand, you begin to believe him. As a result lots of middle-class women married to working-class men get very smug and think they're far more upper-class than they really are. Men who marry up, often put their wives on pedestals, and then run around with other women. Parvenus within marriage in fact, are invariably unfaithful. It's a back-handed blow for the class war – John Osborne's Jimmy Porter is a classic example. So was President Kennedy. Upper-class women brought up to expect infidelity can handle this, that's why they build up that network of jolly nice gairl friends to fall back on, and anyway they're so busy sitting on committees, organising charity balls, and wondering what to wear at Ascot they don't miss sex much.

The middle classes like Eileen Weybridge and Samantha Upward can't cope at all.

'Oh Charles,' said one middle-class wife, 'I can't bear to think of your penis in Mrs Peacock.'

Which brings us to. . . .

Adultery

The way to helly is paved with bed intentions

Harry Stow-Crat has never been faithful to Caroline, like the earl who made a good start to his marriage, by asking all his old girl friends to sleep with him as a wedding present. Traditionally, as was pointed out in the first chapter, marriages were arranged to improve one's cash situation, to increase one's land, and one got one's fun elsewhere. Not all aristocrats are rich of course, but it is much easier to play around if you don't have a job, own several places, have a helicopter to whisk your mistress round the country, yachts to sail about the Mediterranean, and plenty of cash to take her to smart restaurants and hotels. Upper-class males also tend to lead separate lives from their wives in any case.

'Where's Daphne?' I remember asking one peer. 'Oh she's stalking in Scotland' came the reply (the prey wasn't specified).

If ennobled, aristocrats also have the perfect alibi in the House of Lords. One's wife never knows if one's in the House or not. In fact a friend recently discovered a peer screwing a girl on the woolsack, but no one sneaked on them: there is honour among strawberry leaves.

Location can also curb the libido. One girl friend of mine said her lover, who was an Hon., wouldn't even hold her hand if they were walking across the Knightsbridge side of the Park, but would neck ferociously on benches on the non-smart Bayswater side (because he was unlikely to see any of his wife's friends up there). And in the undergrowth of Wimbledon Common he would fornicate freely ('because there's not the slightest possibility of ever bumping into anyone I know in the suburbs'). An aristocrat once came up to London to take me out to lunch, and booked a table at a restaurant in Holland Park, which he also regarded as Suburbia and quite safe. Alas we couldn't get a taxi afterwards, and to his extreme consternation, had to walk all the way to Knightsbridge before he could find one.

Upper-class wives can occasionally be just as unbridled sexually. One even has two telephone numbers, one for business, and an ex-directory hot line for lovers. She was livid with one editor (who'd been an ex) who rang her about a feature by mistake on the lovers' telephone.

The upper middle classes used to concentrate on their careers to keep sin at bay. But all changed with the advent of the country cottage. With Samantha in the country, and Gideon at his little flat in the Barbican, the fun is unconfined although Gideon's frolics are slightly inhibited when Thalia decides to leave Wycombe Abbey early and take a secretarial course in London and live with Daddy.

The seven-year itch often finds some basis for truth among the middle classes. Samantha marries at twenty-four has Zacharias at twenty-six, and Thalia at twenty-eight. Three years later when she's been married exactly seven years, Zacharias starts full-time school, and Thalia goes to play group. Eureka, she has the house free for the first time in years, coupled with the feeling of nagging inadequacy that the children are no longer a full-time job justifying her being just a housewife. Hey Presto, in moves the lover.

The upper middle classes, not having living-in servants, often have a sexual renaissance when the children go to boarding school and they have the house to themselves. On the debit side, one friend said it was very difficult to keep lovers at arm's length, when one no longer had the excuse after a liquid lunch that one must rush away and pick up the children from school at four o'clock.

All adultery grinds to a halt during the school hols, which is the main reason – not tiredness – why mothers get so bad-tempered.

The lower middles tend to be too cautious to commit adultery, it might upset the extra bright children. Occasionally they go to wife-swapping parties and pool all the children with what they call a 'sitter'. Bryan Teale, when not working out the commission he's made that morning, makes love in a car on the edge of the common in the lunch hour, which is why he furnishes his car with cushions and coat hangers so his cheap suit won't crease.

Working-class adultery, however, is much harder to achieve. No telephone to arrange appointments, possibly no car to draw up in lay-bys. Because of shift work and overtime, the lover never knows if the husband will be there or not ... when the coast is clear the wife puts a packet of OMO in the front window (which stands for 'Old Man Out'). Mrs Definitely-Disgusting says she doesn't hold with it.

The upper and upper middle classes talk about 'having an affair' with someone. The media and the trendy middle class call it 'having a relationship'.

In-laws and parents

Many working-class couples – unable to afford a place of their own are forced to live with one set of parents after they are married, often with the wife's mother bringing up the children. This is why the mother-in-law problem is more acute among the lower echelons, and is the basis for so many music hall jokes. In the past when the mortality rate was very high, and husbands were likely to desert or be put off work, the wife's only protection was herself, so she clung to her own family, particularly her mother. As has been pointed out, many working-class men visit their mothers every day, and, if their wives are working, go home for lunch. Although the old matriarchies are breaking down now that some couples can afford cars, and move to jobs away from home, working-class mothers still tend to be far more possessive than middle-class ones. At Christmas and birthdays, they have truces with their sons' wives and they send each other large spangled 'Dearest Mother-in-Law' or 'Daughter-in-Law' cards.

Among the middle classes, the social gradations are so complex, you often get both sets of parents thinking their offspring has married down.

'Oh Zacharias has got a nice little wife,' a mother will say, 'We're getting used to her saying "garridge" and "port-rait".' ('Little', as in references to 'Little shopgirls', is always a euphemism for 'common').

If however, the 'nice little wife' looks after her husband well, and produces a son fairly quickly, she will soon be forgiven her low caste. Heirs are a daughter-in-law's crowning glory. In many ways, too, a slightly common daughter-in-law is preferable, as long as she's respectful, because it makes the mother-in-law feel superior. One girl friend said she didn't speak to her husband for three days after a weekend with her in-laws. In the middle of dinner, her mother-in-law asked her to pass the cruet, and her son half-jokingly said: 'Oh Angie thinks the word "cruet" is common.'

The middle classes, disliking friction, try to keep a superficial peace with their in-laws, even if they disapprove. The upper classes don't bother. A middle-class friend of mine was once very pointedly told by her extremely grand old mother-in-law:

'Divorce is considered perfectly respectable now.'

On the middle-class front, one often gets antagonism between two sets of in-laws, if the wife is working. Samantha's parents say 'You must be getting *so* tired, and Gideon really ought to be able to support you, darling.' Colonel and Mrs Upward, nettled by such disapproval retaliate with 'poor Gideon being hampered in his career by having to help with the housework, and cook dinner when he gets home in the evening.'

Parents whose children marry up and move away, often complain that young people today are selfish and ungrateful. 'He's become like that Greta Thingamy,' grumbles Mrs Definitely-Disgusting, 'he wants to be alone.'

One girl who married a man in the R.A.F. said it was

a nightmare every time her working-class parents came to stay.

'Dad sneers every time Don brings out a bottle of wine at meals, and says 'We *are* pushing the boat out, aren't we?' Then he expects Don to take him for a drink at the Officers' Mess. If only they'd behave like the jolly kind of people they normally are.'

'My daughter goes to sherry parties now,' said another working-class mother sadly, 'and has a little car of her own. She asks me to go and stay but I don't go, I might show her up.' Stay in your own world you're OK, move up and you're out of step.

As Tracey Nouveau-Richards says: 'If Dad wasn't my Dad, I'd laugh at him myself.'

One lower middle girl I know describes a horribly embarrassing occasion, when she got engaged to a peer and his father came for a drink to meet her parents.

Her mother's first words were: 'We're all of a flutter, we don't know whether to call you "Your Grace" or "Dad".'

Divorce

As you go down the social scale, the more rigid and unforgiving you find the attitude towards infidelity. . . . The upper middle-class couple, according to Geoffrey Gorer, believe in talking over the situation if they discover one of them is having an affair. The lower middles would try and reconcile their differences, and get over what they consider a passing fancy. The skilled worker might advocate separation but not divorce. But Social Classes IV and V would be all for punitive action: clobber the Missus and clobber the bloke, and after that the only answer is divorce.

Of all the social classes, in fact, Class V clocks up the second most divorces. This is probably because they marry so young, often having to get married, and because they find it impossible to discuss their problems when things go wrong. The husband can't cope with the pressure of so many children, and as he often takes casual labouring jobs in other parts of the country, the temptation to desert and shack up with another woman is too strong. He can also get free legal aid, and doesn't have to pay for a divorce, and finally, because the parental bond is so strong, it is quite easy for both husband and wife to go home and live with their own parents, whereas the middle-class wife, having achieved a measure of independence, would find this far more difficult.

What else wrecks a marriage? The middle classes mind most about selfishness, conflicting personalities and sexual incompatibility, while the working-class wife objects to drinking, gambling and untidiness, and the husband going out on his own with his mates.

Despite all the country cottages, Social Class I (engineers and oculists) has the fewest divorces, probably because they can't afford two mortgages and two sets of school fees, because no one's going to give them legal aid, and because they think divorce would be bad for their careers.

According to Ivan Reid's *Social Class Differences in Britain*, lower middles get divorced more frequently than skilled workers. Maybe this is because the lower middles, working together in offices, have more opportunity to meet the opposite sex on a long-term basis, while the skilled worker is stuck on the factory floor assembling tools. Maybe, too, the skilled worker has enough potency to keep both girl friends and his wife happy, and has no particular desire for divorce.

The aristocracy, statistically negligible though they may be, tot up even more divorces than Class V. Since the turn of the century, thirty-three per cent of all marquesses and earls have been married twice, twenty-four per cent of viscounts and twenty per cent of barons. That's why *Debrett*'s is such a fat book, listing all the marriages.

'The reason for this,' explained one life peer, 'Is that few blue-blooded aristocrats have inhibitions about what their neighbours think.' Presumably if you live at the ends of long drives, the neighbours don't get a chance to see much.

One of the saddest victims of the class war is the wife of the ambitious spiralist. While *he's* been living it up in foreign hotels, eating expense account lunches, and playing golf with the boss, she's been stuck at home with the children. He has a whole new life-style, and he wants a new wife to complement it, someone more glamorous, and more socially adept. Husbands justify abandoning the first wife by saying: 'Anita didn't travel with me', or 'I married a local girl [euphemism for 'common'] first time round'.

People who've been married several times tend only to mention the grandest ex they've been married to. Woodrow Wyatt has had several wives, but in *Who's Who* only lists the one who was an earl's daughter.

8 HOMOSEXUALITY

*'The middle age of buggers is not to be
contemplated without horror.'*

Virginia Woolf.

Heterosexuals, as we have seen, tend to marry and go out with
people of their own class. But as Harry Stow-Crat might drop
class if he had something on the side, because there would be
less likelihood of his own set finding out, homosexual relation-
ships (because until recently they were against the law in
England), tend to be between people of different classes, simply
for safety reasons. Harry Stow-Crat pursuing rough trade in
Brixton would not be likely to bump into any of Caroline's
friends, any more than Dive Definitely-Disgusting bouncing
around in the four-poster of some stately home would be likely
to meet any of his mates.

There are fewer homosexuals (about one in ten) around than
heterosexuals. Therefore it's more difficult for them to find
someone of their own class. Nor would you find a class of people
more insecure socially than most homosexuals, and, as we've
already pointed out, the insecure tend to drop class. The
upper-class man having an affair with Dive Definitely-
Disgusting is given a nice feeling of social superiority.

Perhaps most important of all, there is the psychological
motive: if you're going to descend into the pit of sodom you
might as well degrade yourself further by dropping class. Hence
the often tragic addiction of upper- and upper middle-class
queens to the criminal classes, laying themselves open to goodness knows what blackmail, beatings-up, and being left
trussed-up naked like a chicken for the char to discover in the
morning.

'Well Doctor – it's like this – I feel queer.'

Sometimes there are happier outcomes. A famous painter surprised a burglar rifling his house, and invited the burglar to stay: he did – for the next twenty years. Another friend has a running affair, going with a wonderfully handsome married burglar. He was particularly enchanted the last time the burglar came out of prison, 'because he lied to his wife about the release date, and spent his first night out with me.'

There's also no doubt there is something very attractive about a butch, muscular working-class boy. 'I'm simply not turned on by people who don't have accents,' said one aristocrat. While a middle-class man said his father 'warned me never to look below for a friend – how wrong he was.'

'If I want to attract a toff,' said one East-Ender, 'I always thicken my accent, and talk about "fevvers": they think it's marvellous.'

On the other hand the queen, whatever his class, tries to be more upper-class, ironing out his accent like mad, and putting on what my East End friend calls a 'posh telephone voice'. Because the middle classes tend to articulate – and emphasise their words more, the homosexual voice is often very difficult to distinguish from Jen Teale Refained. This is why the working

classes roar with laughter at people like Larry Grayson and
Frankie Howerd, and Dick Emery when he does drag acts,
because they think they are putting on lower middle airs.

The higher classes are attracted to the working classes not
only because they like the butch image, but also because, like
women, they are drawn to people who give them a hard time.
E. M. Forster, after years of falling in love with unreliables, said
he was convinced that the working classes are incapable of
passionate love; 'All they have is lust and goodwill.' Ironically
Forster later found happiness with a married policeman, who
after he died said with typical lower middle caution he'd never
realised Forster was homosexual.

But earlier Forster had advised the writer J. M. Ackerley,
who suffered from a string of unreliable boxers, burglars,
guardsmen and deserters to bear in mind that the lower-class
lover could be quite deeply attached to you, but suddenly find
the journey up the social scale too much.

Certainly if Dive Definitely-Disgusting gets taken up by the
upper-class fag mafia he can lead an amazingly grand and
glamorous life. I knew a plumber who spends his weekends
moving from one stately home to another, the sort of life Mrs
Nouveau-Richards would give her capped teeth for.

According to Geoffrey Gorer, the higher the social class, or
rather the more educated people are, the more likely they are to
be tolerant of homosexuality. As he was basing his findings on
the census classifications, by the highest classes he would mean
Gideon and Samantha Upward rather than Harry Stow-Crat.
Certainly Jen Teale and the lower middles who don't enjoy sex,
and disapprove passionately of promiscuity would be the most
intolerant, not being able to comprehend how anyone could do
anything so 'revollting' for pleasure. The upper working classes
are also very intolerant. One thinks of the poor electrician who
wrote to *Coal News* saying he was homosexual and pleading for
acceptance, who was promptly pilloried and sent to Coventry by
his workmates. There is even less tolerance in the Midlands and
North East. In Newcastle working-class homosexuals are so
terrified of being rumbled, they always take girl-friends with
them to the gay pubs.

London, of course, is much easier going. When I went to a
CHE (Campaign for Homosexual Equality) meeting in
Streatham, I gathered that one lorry driver came up to meet-

ings from Wales regularly, because 'you can't come out in Cardiff.' And the boy who worked in the London betting shop, said that when he told his mates at work that he was queer, they were very understanding about it. 'What they simply couldn't understand, and I think this is a working-class attitude, was how I could sleep with a man and not get paid for it.' Whereas in the old days, it was the great fear that one's daughter would become a prostitute now it's the young lads, who are referred to as 'rent boys', who run away from home, go up to what is known as the Meat Rack in Piccadilly and hawk their bodies to any likely buyer for £15 a throw.

One interesting point, however, is that the working classes seem to get less flak than other classes when they tell their parents they're homosexual. 'My parents found out when I was about eighteen,' said my East-End friend, 'this boy kept writing to me. We don't get many letters in our house, and I told Mum I was going to spend Easter with him. She said "Is there anything you want to tell me?" I said, "No." Well, I had a lousy Easter worrying about her, and the moment I got home I said: "I have got something to tell you, I'm homosexual." Her reaction was: "Oh Thank God, I thought it was drugs." I went to a shrink and he wasn't any help, so now everyone's accepted it. A lot of my gay mates are frightened of shrinks, the moment you tell them you're gay, they leap on you. There's a change in my dad too, before he was always very undemonstrative, but now we get on very well, and he often puts a hand on my arm and says "Are you all right, son?" My mum and dad don't mind what friends say, because they haven't got many friends, they're too much into the family.'

One gets the impression that because the mother–son link is so strong in the working classes, a lot of them are subconsciously not displeased if their sons turn out queer; if this is the case there won't be any daughter-in-law problems and there won't be the macho rivalry between father and son, when the son gets married to some lovely girl and starts jackbooting around the house. Since the working classes have large families, there'll also be other children to provide Mum with grandchildren, and there isn't this middle- and upper-class obsession with carrying on the line. Nor, like Jen Teale, do they care quite so much what the neighbours think, in fact they enjoy their sons bringing home all these nice young men.

Further up the social scale, middle-class parents put appalling pressure on only sons who turn out to be 'queer' and don't produce heirs or grandchildren, to be boasted about at bridge parties.

The upper-class attitude to homosexuality, is the same as it used to be towards heterosexuality. Marry well and produce an heir at all costs, and then do what you like.

Some of the happiest marriages, in fact, are when homosexuals marry upper-class ladies, a kind of 'with my buddy, I thee worship'. The sex side works, because the upper-class woman doesn't expect much, and the man just shuts his eyes and thinks of Benjamin Britten. Being a raging snob, the homosexual adores all the grand side of it, organising smart parties and inviting all his prettiest men friends. While the wife, used to the male chauvinism of the aristocracy is entranced by a husband who can help her decorate her house, run her social life, advise her on clothes, cook delicious meals, and provide hordes of endless personable young men to chat away amusingly for hours to all the girl friends.

Samantha Upward being very 'aware' would be particularly nice to homosexual men, trapping them at parties, because she wants to show them that she feels no animosity towards men she knows can never find her sexually attractive.

Howard Weybridge 'comes out' on the golf course at forty-five, and suddenly emerges at dinner parties in white suits with brushed forward hair. His son, similarly inclined, would work in a prep school.

Bryan Teale would have an absolutely miserable time at the office party avoiding all the secretaries and longing to dance with one of the packers. If he's single, he also has problems when his boss give him two tickets for a function. He can't take a man and if he takes a girl, she's bound to get ideas and expect him to kiss her goodnight. If the office gets too much for him he might easily become a male nurse or a purser, or work in the men's department in a department store.

Homosexuals, because they are insecure and sometimes effeminate and feel they have therefore to try harder, are often *raging* snobs. They worry terribly about accents, vocabulary, and laying the table properly. They always write letters after dinner parties, and send you change of address cards saying 'Crispin and Terence are moving to...' Because they have such good taste, their houses are often better-class than they are.

I think because it's euphemistic, Harry Stow-Crat would not use the word 'gay' nor would he say 'homo', or 'lezzie.' Harry Stow-Crat's mother would say 'roaring pansy'. Harry would probably say 'homosexual' with a long 'o', Samantha to show off her knowledge of Greek would shorten the 'o'. Gideon would say 'queer'. Jen Teal would say 'one of those Nancy boys'. Mr Definitely-Disgusting, luxuriating in alliteration, would talk about 'effing fairies', like. An old fashioned expression used to be 'is he T.B.H.' (which Samantha Upward muddles up with G.B.H.) meaning 'To Be Had'? Also in the old days, one used to say 'is he *so*?'

9 HOUSES

Though the pipes that supply the bathroom burst
And the lavatory makes you fear the worst
It was used by Charles the First
Quite informally,
And later by George the Fourth,
On a journey north.   Noël Coward

It is not possible to gauge what class a person is just from the house he lives in. Some of the upper classes have execrable taste and don't give a fig about their surroundings, while some working-class people – perhaps a homosexual – may have an instinctive sense of what is beautiful. How people do up their houses is also considerably affected by fashion. A few years ago, flying ducks were only acceptable if they were outside and moving, now they've become fashionable *kitsch*, and the young and trendy, raising two fingers to convention, are putting them on their walls again.

Electric logs have long been considered a Jen Teale indicator. My husband once worked for a man, whose son an old Etonian (whom I will call Ambrose) asked us to dinner. The other guests were a very smart couple, whom Ambrose was determined to impress. We arrived first to find him switching off some electric logs in the drawing room. He was worried that the smart couple might think them common. 'My mother, being Spanish, has terrible lapses of taste,' he said apologetically.

So the three of us sat frozen to death until the smart couple arrived an hour later. Instantly some devil overtook my husband, he crossed the room and switched on the logs.

'Have you seen Ambrose's mother's splendid fire?' he asked the smart couple.

There was a ghastly pause. Ambrose's face whitened like that of someone close to death. The merry flickering of the electric logs was nothing to the blaze of rage in his eyes. The evening was a disaster. My husband was fired within three months. And yet I know two peers of the most ancient lineage have electric log fires. One even has bright blue water in his lavatory.

Nevertheless the house that you live in, like the education you receive, and the accent you speak with, is one of the determining factors that indicate the class you belong to. One girl was terribly keen on a tall, thin very aristocratic-looking friend of mine until she discovered he lived in a bungalow in Sheen with his mother.

In Putney, where I live, the people who live in the big Victorian houses on the Common slightly, albeit unconsciously, look down on the large but semi-detached houses in the next road leading down to the Common, whose owners in turn look down on those living in similar houses in a street with slightly heavier traffic; the occupants of these look down on the people in the Neo-Georgian houses on the edge on the Common, whose occupants in turn despise the people in the terrace houses behind them, who won't have anything to do with the council estate beside the river.

In *Voices from the Middle Class* by Jane Deverson and Katherine Lindsay a journalist is quoted as saying:

'A house is a complex thing, it represents a social position. We found living where we were (a smartish London suburb) without meaning to we had acquired several friends who see themselves as the same sort of people as we were because they live in the same sort of house. Painting and decorating is a middle-class thing,' he went on. 'You say you've been decorating and you get an immediate response.'

Harry Stow-Crat wouldn't dream of painting his own 'hice' (as he pronounces it) or putting up shelves and would regard any such activity as distinctly 'working-class'. But, as it happens, Mr Definitely-Disgusting wouldn't bother to do up his house either because he considers it the council's responsibility. The moment he buys his own house, however, he crosses one of the great class divides from Council Tenant to Owner Occupier and starts to become bourgeois. He'll immediately drop the word 'mortgage' in the public bar, and begin building a new porch or slapping different coloured paint on the front of his house, to distinguish it from the houses on either side, and to show he's not Council any more.

The expression 'they live in a bought house', would be a term of approbation from the working classes, but a term of contempt from the upper classes, who have usually lived in their own 'hice' for generations, inheriting it, as they inherit all their furniture and silver. (One of the upper-class definitions of the middle classes is the 'sort of people who buy their own silver' – particularly when they call it 'cutlery'.)

Another crucial point to remember is that the Stow-Crats of today were the Nouveau-Richards of a few hundred years ago. 'How often have I wondered,' wrote Lord David Cecil 'at the difference between the stately beauty of a great house, so exalting and tranquillizing and the fierce, restless unscrupulous character of the men who were so often responsible for its original building. Perhaps a gentler more contented spirit would not have felt the urge and vitality to create such buildings.'

Blenheim Palace, for example, described at the time as 'England's greatest house for England's greatest man', was built to celebrate the new Duke of Marlborough's victories. Then there was the very rich Yorkshire baronet, Sir John Smithson who at the beginning of the eighteenth century married Elizabeth, the sole heiress to the rich and ancient Percy family. So great was the extent of their joint estate, that Sir John was able to persuade George III to grant him the Dukedom of Northumberland. Anxious to establish his new status, the first Duke set about transforming Alnwick, the neglected castle of the Percies. Capability Brown (who'd been such a success at Warwick Castle) was called in to rebuild the towers and add seven turrets, and a complete new garrison of stone warriors was stationed on the battlements. At the same time Robert Adam arrived to re-gothicise the interior. Everything was done to make the castle as luxurious and self-consciously picturesque as possible. And no doubt the old aristocracy, who regarded any peer created after the middle ages as an upstart, thought the whole thing at the time both phoney and vulgar.

So it was that generations of new noblemen harnessed the

best talents of their time, just as today David Mlarnaric and David Hicks move around forming the tastes of the uncertain and the newly rich.

What is regarded as the height of *nouveau riche* vulgarity today, the huge oval bed humming with dials, perhaps, or the onyx and marble double bath with 22-carat gold-plated mixer taps – will probably be considered exquisitely beautiful when it is unearthed from the rubble in the year 2500. Certainly the furniture and building trades would grind to a halt if it weren't for people erecting monuments to new splendour or ripping out the taste of previous owners because they considered it too grandiose or too vulgar.

Harry Stow-Crat does not refer to his house as a 'stately home' but as an 'istoric hice'.

Although they may have originally been built as what Ivy Compton Burnett called 'huge monuments to showing off', few buildings quicken the pulses more than the great English country house. Vita Sackville-West points out that the best historic houses grew in a leisurely way over generations, sprouting a wing here a tower here, like the oaks and elms, that surrounded them. It is the feeling that each succeeding owner acquired furniture and pictures as the taste and fashion of his generation dictated – and imposed his own taste – that makes up the glorious hotch-potch of the great house.

Lord Weymouth, who has contributed his own splendidly colourful murals to the walls of Longleat, says that everyone in his family 'has been raised from birth to be an acolyte in the temple'. This sums up the attitude of the aristocrat, good husbandry, rather than good husbands, or 'Old Masters and young mistresses, as Peter de Vries called it. 'I don't mind black sheep in the family,' said Lord Carrington recently. 'What I can't stand is people who don't put something back into the house.'

Most upper-class houses therefore have a certain shabbiness about them. (There ought to be a shop called 'Shabby-tat' where Mrs Nouveau-Richards could buy aged-up furniture and materials.) The festoons and rosettes on the ceiling show the traces of the years, the pink and white striped silk cushions are falling to pieces, the faded red damask sofa covered in yesterday's dog hairs. On the walls are squares of much lighter red flocked paper (like the circle on the spiralist's lapel) where a

Rubens or a Romney has been flogged off to pay taxes. When you go to bed you draw the pale blue watered silk curtains with care. The aristocracy believe in buying the best – silks especially woven in the colour they want – and then making them last. They'll probably only re-decorate their rooms every fifty years. Upper-class colours therefore tend to be faded into softness by antiquity – like a Beatrix Potter picture. The faded rose-reds and golds of the Tailor of Gloucester's coat are particularly popular, and ice blue is very in, too, at the moment. Green is rarely popular because there's so much of it outside in the park. In the upper-class London houses (perhaps because their owners miss the green of the country) you'll get a chilly Eaton Square eau de nihilism.

The floors are polished, and three quarters covered with very good, very old, patterned carpet. Caroline Stow-Crat wouldn't dream of buying a modern patterned carpet, but Casa Pupo rugs are somehow considered all right. Until recently she's resisted plain fitted carpets, as being an example of the middle classes boasting that they've got enough carpet to cover the entire floor. But convenience is a great leveller, and if you haven't got a servant to polish the floor, you may sink to a fitted carpet. In the same way duvets are being surreptitiously smuggled into four posters, particularly for the children, and the silver centrepiece in the dining room, which used to be made up of forty individual bits, and take two men three days to clean, has now been lacquered over.

Caroline also resists any man-made fibres, and certainly anything plastic, which Harry's mother still calls 'plarstic'. The upper classes wear leather on their feet, and the elbows of their coats, but not on their sofas or their backs. Their rooms tend to be very leggy, like the bottom half of the paddock, because all the furniture has long spindly legs. Huge libraries of memoirs and sermons, probably acquired by the yard back in the eighteenth century are kept behind grilles like Snipe. The bedrooms have slots on the door for the guest's name, and interlocking doors, so people can bedhop easily without the servants finding out. The ceilings are particularly beautiful, so Caroline Stow-Crat can admire them when she's in the inevitable missionary position. On the whole the upper classes prefer things to be either beautiful or functional. They wouldn't hide the television in a repro cabinet, or the paper handkerchiefs in

'One has one's own piped music.'

the spare room in a dainty flowered box with a slit in it.

The rooms are lit by crystal chandeliers or candelabra or by lamps with no tassels. Tassels on anything, umbrellas, lights or chairs are considered slightly flash. The bath and basin are always white, the lavatory is white with a chain that pulls and a wooden seat which is often agonisingly cracked. All upper-class loos smell of asparagus pee in June. The kitchens are traditionally hellish because that was where the servants lived.

As the outdoor life has always been more important to the English gentleman than indoors, the field more alluring than the hearth, their houses tend to be terribly cold, and smell of blasts of icy air. (One member of the landed gentry always asked you to bring old telephone directories when you went to stay, to feed an insatiable boiler). On the walls they have huge paintings of battles, hunting scenes and their ancestors, gazing down and reminding them of their heritage. They also have portraits painted of their dogs, their horses and their children. As the latter go off to boarding school so early, it's important to be reminded what they look like.

The upper-class man always has a dressing room. Even though Harry sleeps in the same room as Caroline, he would refer to it as 'Caroline's bedroom' if he were talking to an equal, 'my wife's bedroom' if he were talking to a higher echelon servant like the woman who organises people seeing over his house, and 'Lady Caroline's bedroom' to a maid.

One very grand old lady said 'When Willy and I went to stay with some people in Norfolk, they didn't give Willy a dressing room but they provided a screen in the bedroom so we managed very well.' This was after they'd been married forty years – shades of the Definitely-Disgustings.

One of the ways the upper classes exclude the classes below is by pronouncing the names of their houses differently from the way they are spelt – Woburn, Holker, Althorp, (pronounced 'Woob'n', 'Hooker', 'Alltr'p'), being typical examples. And because they have had their houses for hundreds of years, they also tend to take the beautiful things in them for granted, and tend not to comment on such things in other people's houses.

'Fellow praised my chairs, damn cheek,' said a duke, after a visit from a new neighbour.

Equally, it is not done to show someone over your new house, unless they ask specifically, or they pay at the gate. There was an awkward moment when an actress we know, who was justifiably proud of her very expensively decorated house asked an upper-class friend if he'd like to see over it.

'Whatever for?' came the curt reply.

In very grand houses, they have an estate carpenter permanently on the premises doing repairs. One friend got locked in the lavatory when she was staying in Yorkshire, and the host fed her bloody Maries through the keyhole with a straw, while they waited for the carpenters to come and free her.

Paying guests

The poor man in his castle
Sells tickets at the gate.
While all the rich plebians
Have fun on his estate.

Leonard Cooper

'Between the duties expected of one during one's lifetime, and the duties expected from one after one's death, land has ceased to be either a profit or a pleasure. It gives one position, but prevents one from keeping it up, that's all that can be said about land,' said Lady Bracknell, admirably summing up the plight of the aristocrat.

In the old days, Harry Stow-Crat's ancestor would have looked out of his top window and owned all he surveyed, now he probably only manages it. Most of the upper classes are feeling the pinch, and the days when they could field a chauffeur's second eleven against a footmen's third eleven are over. Only the hugely rich, like the Westminsters, are still not allowing the public to see over their houses. Some peers like Lord Montague and the Duke of Bedford, who obviously have a strong streak of showmanship in their make-up, seem to rather enjoy it. Others hate it, like an earlier Lord Bath who was found cowering in a cupboard by one of the visitors, or Vita Sackville-West who hid in the roses. Some peers try to keep up standards and shock visitors to the house by putting up signs saying *lavatories* rather than *toilets*, but most of them descend to the level of public taste by flogging the most appalling souvenirs: key rings, caps, tee shirts, replicas of the house in a snow storm, bottled Welsh or Scottish garden fragrance, in order to keep going.

When we went to spend the weekend at Longleat, we drove up the endless drive and my children's eyes grew rounder and rounder as they took in first the green mist of flat bottomed spring trees, then the herds of cows and sheep and then the lions, leopards, rhinoceros, monkeys and a giraffe. Finally, as the great golden tawny house with its battlements, turrets, and flags came into sight, my son turned to my daughter...

'He's got an awful lot of pets,' he said in awe.

Buying-up and doing-up

The upper middle classes, not subscribing to the law of primogeniture, and tending to move where their jobs take them, seldom live in the same house for several generations. They tend to start off in a flat in Fulham, or some big town when they get married, then move to a terraced three-bedroom house with the first child, then to a five-bedroom house when the second child arrives, because they need room for an *au pair*, or possibly for a lodger to help with the mortgage. Samantha Upward prefers a student, so she can combine altruism, free baby-sitting and help with Zacharias's maths prep, which will soon – despite workshops – be quite beyond her. To live in a house with more rooms than you have family is regarded by the working classes as a middle-class characteristic.

The major change in the upper middle-class house in the last twenty-five years, has been the kitchen, which used to be an airforce blue barracks where a sucked-up-to maid sourly banged saucepans. In the seventies, this change was speeded up when financial necessity coupled with the absurd stigma attached to unpaid domestic servitude, forced all but those wives with very young children out to work. The status-conscious upper middle classes therefore promptly re-vamped their houses. If Samantha Upward has to sink to housework or cooking she must do it in congenial surroundings. Kitchens therefore became more and more like drawing-rooms, with sofas, low lighting, welsh dressers covered in ornaments and books, pictures on the walls, and a low pine table for the children to play improving games.

As it was essential for the children to play on the ground floor near their parents, the dining-room was also turned into a 'playroom', and in order that Samantha needn't miss a word of the intelligent dinner-party conversation, as she was flambé-ing chicken breasts, or whipping the zabaglione, the kitchen was turned into a dining-room as well. The drawing-room by this time was feeling a bit neglected, and was consequently filled up with plants, and natural earthy colours until it resembled Kew Gardens. The garden in its turn filled up with furniture, reclining chairs with gaudy seedpacket upholstery, stone lions, white wrought iron chairs and tables, hammocks. What was once the 'terrace' became the 'patio', or as Mrs Nouveau-Richards would say the 'pate-io'.

A peer, recently flipping through a *Habitat* catalogue, remarked how extraordinary it was that the lower middle classes today furnished their houses with the sort of stuff you'd once only have seen in the servants' quarters. As stripped pine and William Morris are taken up by the lower middles, the upper middles have latched onto rattan, and art deco sofas and chairs, French and English antiques (when they could afford them), good Chinese furniture, and Laura Ashley itsy-bitsy cottage prints – (sort of William Morris Minor). Recently a friend heard a builder showing a plumber over the house at which he was working.

'They've got Philip Morris curtains in the lounge,' he said.

A word might be said here about the words 'drawing-room' and 'sitting-room'. Both seem to be perfectly upper-class except the 'droin' room' would be slightly more formal, and the 'sitting-room' more easy and relaxed. You'd never have a 'droin' room' in a cottage for example. 'Living-room', as a ghastly modern compromise, is extremely vulgar. So are 'lounge' (except in a hotel), 'front room' and 'parlour'.

In Samantha Upward's house, you would find a few antiques, and some good china and silver. She thinks 'repro' furniture is very common, and whereas she might hang reproductions in the lavatory or the children's room, they wouldn't be allowed in the drawing-room. Nor would a Victorian painting from her parents' house, of a four-year-old girl in a boat with a grizzled fisherman entitled 'His Mate', get farther than the landing. All her curtains would be on brass rails. Her carpets would be plain

'Zacharias is very creative at the moment.'

but fitted, and relieved by a few rugs, and her counterpane would be distributed evenly over the whole bed.

Samantha is gradually installing 'continental quilts', as she insists on calling them, in every bedroom. She thinks the word 'dewvay' is so vulgar. The most difficult Beethoven sonata lies open on the piano. Zacharias's 'cello is allowed to stay in the drawing-room among the *Spectators* and *New Statesmans*. Samantha would spend a lot of time removing book jackets to make the books look more read. Dried flowers, or honesty in a pewter mug would gather dust on the window ledge.

In the lavatory downstairs, as a sort of 'bogography', Gideon modestly records his achievements, with photographs of himself in hockey, rugger and cricket teams of his house at Rugby; of a freshmen's match. His dressing room would be the repository for all the atrocities little Zacharias and Thalia had given him and Samantha for Christmas over the years; china poodles, cats wearing bow ties playing the banjo, glazed china flowers, boxes encrusted with shells. He also has to put up with all rich Uncle Alan's paintings on the walls (these are whipped down to the drawing-room when Uncle Alan comes to stay), and a photograph of Samantha taken twenty years ago, and framed by herself at evening classes, when she had a beehive. Samantha waits till the daily woman goes home before loosening up the serried ranks of cushions on the sofa.

Upper middle-class houses smell of beeswax, drink and sometimes cats. As their owners are always knocking things over when drunk and not being able to afford new ones, they have a lot of Christopher Wray lamps with bites out of them.

On Saturday mornings all through outer central London – Fulham, Clapham, Islington and parts of Hackney, the streets are alive with the sounds of 'gentrification', as coats of paint are slapped on the fronts of Victorian terraced houses, rooms are knocked through, and the net curtains of previous occupants are shoved in the rag bag. The upper middle classes would far rather spend a bit of money knocking a Victorian or Edwardian workman's cottage back in to shape than move into a modern house where everything worked, so they quite happily rip plywood and hardboard off doors to reveal the original mouldings, strip banisters, and replace aluminium windows with wooden frames as close to the original as possible. Soon follow the French number plate, the brass letter box, and the trellis for the honeysuckle from the garden centre and a bay-tree that quickly gets nicked. Blue tubs, bought cheap from the brewery round the corner, are soon filled up with bulbs or pink geraniums (Samantha thinks red ones are rather common). And on Saturday morning, Vivaldi pours out of the Hi Fi into the street, and balding architects can be seen sitting in the window drawing lines at their desks and drinking coffee out of Sainsbury's mugs.

Having also cottoned onto the fact that they can get £25,000 tax relief for an extension, and with the price of houses being so prohibitive, my dear, and the traffic being so frightful we never get down to the cottage till midnight, the upper middle classes are beginning to sell up their 'shacks' in the Isle of Wight or Gloucestershire, and build onto their houses instead. Gideon Upward and Zacharias are working so much at home now that they each need a study. And as Samantha so often wants to watch opera, and Gideon the late night sport, it avoids so many rows if they have two televisions in different rooms. And now that Thalia's getting a bust it's not quite right for her to entertain boys in her bedroom, which calls for a second sitting-room where they can all play pop music as loudly as possible. As a result £300 worth of clematis and hydrangeas are crushed under foot, as an extension is slapped onto the patio.

One of the tricks of the middle classes is to buy their old houses then form a pressure group to have their street declared a Conservation Area so as to stop the compulsory purchasers touching it or building flats nearby. But they then get absolutely livid when the council rather understandably drags its heels over planning permission for an extra music room or a new bathroom.

Don't say 'Pardon' say 'Surrey'

Merridale is one of those corners of Surrey where the inhabitants rage a relentless battle against the stigma of suburbia. Trees, cajoled and fertilised into being in every front garden, half obscure the poky 'character dwellings' which crouch behind them. The rusticity of the environment is enhanced by the wooden owls that keep guard over the names of the houses, and by crumbling dwarfs indefatigably poised

over gold fish ponds. The inhabitants of Merridale Lane do not paint
their dwarfs, suspecting it to be a suburban vice, nor for the same
reason, do they varnish the owls, but wait patiently for the years to
endow these treasures with an appearance of weathered antiquity, until
one day even the beams in the garage may boast of beetle and
woodworm.

John Le Carré *Call for the Dead*

'Oh look,' said a friend as we drove through a rich part of
Surrey. 'All those houses have been Weybridged.' This is a
practice of the socially aspiring who've made a bit of money and
want to shake off the stigma of suburbia by living in Sunningdale, Virginia Water, or any rich dormitory town.

First you buy a modern house, which you refer to as a 'lovely
property', then you 'age it up' to look like a Great West Road
pub. Rustic brick with half timbering and leaded windows are
very popular, with a lantern or carriage lamp outside the front
door, and a name like 'Kenilworth' or 'De Cameron' carved on
a rustic board. The burglar alarm would be discreetly covered
by creepers. An alternative is white pebbledash with a green
pantile roof and matching green shutters with cut-out hearts,
and the name in wrought iron treble clef writing on the front of
the house. Wrought iron, in fact, is everywhere.

A few years ago, a Weybridged house would have had a
chiming doorbell, but, suspecting this is a bit suburban, the
owner has responded to an ad in *Homes and Gardens*:

'No more electric bionic ping pongs. . . . every lover of style
can now capture the elegance and tranquillity of less hurried
days with a real brass doorbell, complete with mechanism and
most attractive pull arm to enhance your doorway.'

The hall, as Anthony Powell once said, looks like the inside of
a cigar box with a parquet floor, panelled walls, and a very thin
strip of carpet running up the polished stairs. At the top is a
round window with a stained glass inset. The Weybridged
house smells of self-congratulation and Pears soap.

In the living-room (again, they've heard 'lounge' is suburban
but can't quite bring themselves to say 'drawing-room'), you
find wall-to-wall glossies, and coffee table books. On the walls
are imitation candle lights, with fake drips and little red hats,
bumpy white gold mirrors, and pictures by real artists from
Harrods and Selfridges. The carpet is tufted two-tone, the

curtains pinch-pleated, the 'settee' and 'easy chairs' are covered in terra cotta velvet Dralon. Repro furniture is inevitable to give a nice 'Ollde Worlde' look: 'period doors', a Queen Anne 'bureau', and Regency Chippendale cabinets to hide the TV. (the upper middles call it 'the box', the upper class 'the television') and the 'stereo'. Every piece of furniture has mahogany or teak veneer. The Weybridged house suffers from veneerial disease. A Magi-Log fire flames in the repro Adam fireplace – 'the ultimate in realism' with incombustible oak logs knobbly with knotholes and twigs. The alternative might be a 'feature fireplace' in stone. The *Radio Times* is wrapped in a sacking cover with a thatched cottage embroidered on the front. If you came for drinks, you would be offered goblets.

In the dining-room, lacquered silver candlesticks sit on the Elizabethan repro table even at lunchtime, and an Ecko hostess trolley keeps the rack of lamb, creamed potatoes and garden peas piping hot. There would be an overhead light, or more lights with fake hats and little waxdrips and six chairs with oxblood and silver regency stripes.

Howard has a 'den' where he's supposed to work at weekends, but in fact does nothing but read *Penthouse* behind Saturday's *Financial Times* and long to be asked to a wife-swapping party. Poor Howard feels he is not 'ollde' enough for the house, and if he plays with himself a lot, it might age him too.

The kitchen is usually very pretty, and quite indistinguishable from the upper middle, or even modernised upper-class kitchen. Next door a 'utility' room is filled with expensive machinery – the word 'dishwasher' as opposed to 'washing-up machine' is very Weybridge, so is 'freezer' instead of 'deep freeze', and 'tumble' instead of 'spin dryer'.

In the 'master bedroom', tufted carpeted steps lead up to a dais on which a huge brass four-poster swathed in white Norfolk lace sits like a wedding cake. The lampshade matches the duvet cover and the wallpaper.

Next month Mrs Weybridge will receive her eighth German porcelain coffee cup and saucer from the 'Collector of the Month Club' special offer, and be able to hold her first coffee morning.

Better nouveau than late-Victorian

The Weybridged house is very 'ollde' and tasteful, as opposed to the Nouveau-Richards mansion which is very plush, ostentatious, and modern – another great monument to showing-off.

Reacting against the in-and-out-of-their-houses familiarity of the working class, Mr Nouveau-Richards has high walls built round his house, and it is burglar-alarmed to the teeth. Ten-foot-high electric gates protect him from the street. As he arrives in the Rolls he presses a button and the gates open. The drive is lined with toadstools which light up at night. The garage for five cars opens by remote control, and so you don't get wet a lift takes you up to the hall.

Every room in Mrs Nouveau-Richards's house has a rake for the shag pile. The daily woman's visit is a sort of rake's progress, nor does she much like having to climb into the onyx and sepia marble double bath to clean it, and having to polish up the 22-carat gold mixer taps with headworks of solid onyx. She nearly got her hand chopped off when she was shaking her duster out of one of the electric windows the other day. When she answers the telephone she has to say: 'Mrs Nouveau-Richards's residence.'

In Mrs Nouveau-Richards's lounge acrylic pile tiger skins with diamanté collars lie on the ebony shag pile. Mrs Nouveau-Richards reclines on the leather chesterfield, in front of the heated coffee table, while Mr Nouveau-Richards revolves in his captain's club chair in deep buttoned hide. On the walls is black and silver flocked wallpaper. When the maid in uniform hacks her way through the 'house plants' to bring in 'afternoon tea', she is sent back because the sugar bowl doesn't match the tea cups. A ship's bell summons people to dinner, and the naval motif is continued by a bar in the corner with a straw ceiling covered in lobsters. After a few drinks they crawl by themselves. In the bar, every drink known to man hangs upside down with right way up labels. Mr Nouveau-Richards doesn't drink very much, because he knows it makes his face red and his accent slip. Off the lounge are the swimming pool, constantly kept by the pool attendant at eighty degrees, the solarium and the gym. The stables are built under the lawn, so the horses can look out of their boxes into the pool like Neptune's mares. In Mr Nouveau-Richards's library, where he has bought all the books

by the yard, he has eighteenth-century repro library steps.
When he presses a button the entire works of Walter Scott slide
back to reveal yet another bar. Even the goldfish tank is
double-glazed.

Mr Nouveau-Richards is very proud of his dimmer switches,
in a mellow mood he'll give guests a *son et lumière* display. In
every room, musak pours out of speakers, even in the loos,
which have musical lavatory paper, fur carpets and chandeliers. The lavatory has a wooden seat. Mr Nouveau-Richards
responded to an ad in *House and Garden:*

'After years of mass-produced plastic, feel the warmth of
solid mahogany. Each seat is individually sanded and french
polished. Hinges and fittings are made of brass, and we offer as
an option at no extra cost a brass plaque recessed into the lid for
your personal inscription.'

Mr Nouveau-Richards has 'Piss Off' wittily inscribed on his.

In the 'guest bedroom', as Mrs Nouveau-Richards calls it,
everything is upholstered in peach satin, with a peach fur
carpet. The master bedroom, however, has a vast suède oval
bed, so humming with dials for quadrophonic stereo, radio,
dimmer switches, telephones, razors and vibrator (which Mrs
Nouveau-Richards uses for massaging her neck), you don't
know whether to lie on the thing or hi-jack it.

Nouveau-riche houses are always blissfully comfortable to stay
in. 'Chandeliers in the loo, and a bidet on every bed,' said my
mother after one visit.

A word about nets

The world is divided into 'Haves' and 'Have-Nets'.

The upper classes never had net curtains because, if you lived
at the end of a long drive, there was no likelihood of being
overlooked and, never being worried about other people's
opinions, you didn't give a damn if anyone saw what was going
on anyway.

The upper middles, aping the upper classes, don't have net
curtains either. They traditionally had servants to keep their
houses tidy so it didn't matter anyone seeing in, and, as they
only had sex at night (unlike the shift worker coming home for
lunch), they drew their curtains if they wanted privacy.

Samantha Upward wouldn't dream of having net curtains, she wants the whole street to look in at the gay primary colours of the posters and the extra bright drawings in Zacharias's playroom.

The middle classes sometimes have net upstairs. If Eileen Weybridge is changing out of her tennis shorts in the middle of the day, she doesn't want the workman mending the road looking in. If they have nets downstairs, they might explain it by saying they've got an American mother.

The rough friendly element of the working class, who float in and out of each others' houses never bothered with net at all, and have an expression for someone putting on airs: 'Net curtains in the window, nothing on the table.'

It is where the more thin-lipped respectable element of the working classes blend into the lower middles that net reigns supreme. You can see out and chunter over everyone else's behaviour, and twitch the nets to indicate extreme disapproval, but they can't see you. Suburban privet hedges and Weybridged latticed windows provide the same function.

Jen Teale, however, wanting to priss everthing up and shake off the stigma of upper working class – which is a bit too close for comfort, hangs pink jardinière festoon cross-over drapes, which leaves three-quarters of the window clear. This allows space for 'floral decorations' on the window ledge, makes the windows look 'so feminine', and enables the neighbours to see how 'spotless' (a favourite lower middle word) her house is. Other examples of the lower middles trying to go one better are ruched nets, putting a row of package tour curios on the window ledge outside one's nets, or hanging one's curtains so the pattern shows to the outside world. Mrs Definitely Disgusting tried yellow nets once, but they made the whole family look as though they'd got jaundice.

Behind the mauve front door

Jen Teale, liking to have everything dainty, wages a constant battle against dust and untidiness. Bryan Teale sits in the lounge with his feet permanently eighteen inches off the ground in case Jen wants 'to vacuum' underneath. In the bedroom a Dra-lon button-back headboard joins two single divans with drawers underneath for extra storage, into which Jen might one day tidy Bryan away for ever. Gradually all their furniture: wardrobes, sideboards, cupboards, is replaced by fitted 'units' which slot snugly between ceiling and floor rather like Lego, and leave no inch for dust to settle.

As soon as the Teales move into a house, the upper middle process is reversed, all the doors are flattened so the mouldings don't pick up dust anymore, the brass fittings replaced by aluminium, which doesn't need polishing, and all the windows and old 'French doors' (as Jen Teale calls French windows) replaced by double-glazed aluminium picture windows. Being hot on insulation, because they loathe wasting money, the Teales even have sliding double glazed doors round the porch. Bryan does all this with his Black-and-Decker.

The mauve front door has a rising sun in the bottom left hand corner of the glass. The doorbell chimes. The house smells of Lavender Pledge and Freshaire. In the lounge the fire has a huge gnome's canopy to concentrate the heat and keep smuts at bay. Beside it stands the inevitable Statue-of-Liberty combination of poker, brush and shovel in a thistle motif. On the walls, Bryan and his Black-and-Decker have put up storage grids, like vast cat's climbing frames, with compartments for the Hi-fi, records, scrabble, the odd spotlit bit of Wedgewood, or 'vawse' of plastic flowers (real flowers drop petals, and paper ones gather dust). A few years ago the Teales wouldn't have had any books – too much dusting – but as culture seeps downwards, there might be a few book club choices tastefully arranged at an angle to fill up a compartment.

The lounge suite has easy-fit nylon William Morris stretch covers which have interchangeable arms that can be switched from unit to unit, or rotate on the same chair to give that straight-from-the-showroom look, which is the antithesis of the shabby splendour of the upper classes. Jen also rather likes the continental habit of offering lounge furniture as a group comprising three-seater settee, two-seater settee, and one armchair called 'Caliph'. (Down-market furniture invariably has up-market names like 'Eton' and 'Cavendish'.) There is also a Parker Knoll recliner in case an 'elderly relative comes to visit'.

As well as her books Jen also has her Medici prints, and her Tretchikoff (under a picture light, to show there's no dust on the frames), and in the dining room there's a David Shepherd elephant gazing belligerently at Bryan's vintage car etchings. There is no bar, because the Teales are tight with drink, Bryan keeps any bottles in another room with measures on. Just as a guest is putting his glass down, a mat with a hunting scene is thrust underneath to stop it making rings on one of a nest of tables called 'Henley'.

The kitchen is like a laboratory. No ornaments alleviate the bleakness. As the lower middles disapprove of money spent on luxuries (and can't afford them so readily), Jen probably wouldn't have a washing-up machine. She doubts it would get things really clean. She calls washing-up 'doing the dishes'. She washes, Bryan 'wipes' with a 'tea towel' rather than a 'drying-up cloth'. (Caroline Stow-Crat would call it a 'clawth'.) Jen also does a lot of 'handwashing' and, as she's very conscious of understains, she 'boils' a lot. Friends say her whites are spotless. She also calls hoovering, 'vacuuming'.

In the bedroom a doll in frills, to show Jen's just a little girl at heart, lies on the millpond smooth candlewick bedspread which is edged in a fat sausage under and then over the pillows. (Caroline Stow-Crat has a worn teddy bear.) 'Robe units' with motifs and very shiny lacquered brass handles slot into the walls. Jen tidies her make-up away in a vanity case. The only ornament on her white formica-topped vanity unit is a circular plastic magnifying mirror. When she makes-up and brushes her hair, she protects her clothes from 'dandruff' with a plastic pink cape. The matching bathroom suite, in sky blue or avocado, with a basin shaped like a champagne glass, has a matching toilet cover, toilet surround, and bathmat in washable sky blue nylon fur. A Spanish 'dolly' with Carmen skirts discreetly conceals the toilet tissue (pronounced 'tiss-u' not 'tishu' as Samantha Upward would pronounce it). Jen, being obsessed with unpleasant odours, has Airwick, pot pourri and a pomander on top of the cistern, and a deodorant block hanging like a sloth inside. In the toilet there is bright blue water. Bryan and Jen prefer showers to baths, they waste less water, are easier to clean up after. Jen calls a bathcap a 'shower cap'.

Although she keeps her house like a new pin, Jen always does housework in tights and a skirt rather than trousers. Her whole attitude is summed up by her feather duster, which keeps dirt at a distance.

The chrome squad

There was an advertisement recently in a magazine called *Home Buying* offering 'Modern houses in Wood Green, the ideal site for those who want a convenient rung on the home ownership ladder'. Among the other attractions was 'garage with space for work bench'.

This was aimed at the spiralist who is continually buying houses, doing them up, selling them at a profit, and moving on to a better part, which means a safer suburb, with a nicer class of child, more amusing parents at the P.T.A. and no danger of coloureds (although a black diplomat's O.K.). Usually the process is to start with a flat, then move to a terraced house, then on to a large 'period semi', where you let off the top flat to pay the mortgage. Then as soon as the house is done up, you buy a cheap flat for the sitting tenant, put it on the market, and look for an even bigger house. The process is basically the same as that of the upper middle-class couple, except that the spiralist moves as soon as he's got the house together, while the upper middles wait until they've run out of room.

Spiralists like anonymous furniture: chrome, glass, and unit sofas and chairs, because they can be shifted around to fit into any size house. Just as they often adopt a phoney American accent to hide the Cockney or the Yorkshire, so spiralists embrace American terminology: 'trash cans', 'garbage', 'closets', 'chaise lounges' and 'car ports'. Even in the short time they stay in a place the spiralists are deeply competitive.

They are likely to buy a three-piece suite in a sale, then put it in a Harrod's depository, so it can be delivered three weeks later in a Harrod's van.

They are the estate agent's nightmare, because they never stop hassling and expecting more for a house because of another brick on the night storage heater. Evidently the upper middles treat the agent like a pro, because they're used to one chap doing one job.

Home suite home

When Mr Definitely-Disgusting thinks of buying a house other than his own council house, he fills in a coupon and goes off and sees a show house on an estate called some grandiose name like

'Well it's the Council's job, innit?'

Northumbria, and puts his name down for it if he likes it. Attractions include 'teak laminated kitchenette, stainless steel sink, coloured bathroom suite with matching vein tiles, veneered doors in the living room, kitchen dinette and shower room'.

Ads in the 'homebuying' press show neighbours looking welcoming and helpful in widebottomed trousers, so as not to intimidate Mr Definitely-Disgusting who is used to his friendly familiar street. In a comic strip guide to 'homebuying', the solicitor has spectacles and brushed back hair, and wears a suit and a tie, while the buyer has wide trousers again, an open-neck shirt, and hair brushed over his ears. His wife has shoulder-length hair, swept back from her forehead by a kirby grip, and a skirt on the knees. This is presumably the ideal working-class prototype.

The Definitely-Disgustings hurry now and buy everything from Williams's sale, even the once-famous actor with tired eyes doing the telly commercial. Up to their necks in H.P., they get carried away by the ads and buy three-piece suites in deep pile uncut moquette and wildly expensive domestic appliances, which go back when they can't keep up the payments. The house-to-house upstaging is as subtle as the spiralists'.

'You can't hang your washing out any more, because everyone'll know you haven't got a tumble dryer', said one wife.

Mrs Definitely-Disgusting on the other hand buys a fridge for the first time and stands at the front door saying: 'I'm worried the kiddies will catch their fingers in the door', just to show she's got one.

(My favourite advertisement of all time appeared in an Indian magazine showing a woman and child gazing admiringly up at a huge fridge with the caption: 'Just right for our living room'.)

Mrs Definitely-Disgusting's front room, if she's feeling flush, will be dominated by a black cocktail cabinet with interior lighting, containing every drink known to man like the Nouveau-Richards's, and a glazed tile fireplace with a gas fire (although the council are beginning to put in what is known as a 'fuel alternative'). Most of the ornaments look as though they have been won at a fair, or bought for his mother by Zacharias Upward: china alsatians, glazed shire horses, china ladies in poke bonnets and crinolines. Here also are the curios from a hundred package tours, green donkeys with hats on and panniers, matadors under cellophane, a mass-produced plastic bull with a piece of the next bull's back attached to its cock, fifteen glass fishing floats and ashtrays barnacled with olives (brought for Mrs Definitely-Disgusting by various Samantha Upwards on their return from holidays), and souvenirs from trips to historic houses. There might be a few very small reproductions, Constable's Haywain, Van Gogh's Sunflowers, or the Queen by Annigoni.

The colours are garish – with everything, wallpaper, sofas and chairs, in different patterns. The carpet, a symphony of yellow, nigger brown and orange exploding in circles, wouldn't cover the linoleum. On the huge colour television there might be some candelabra, or a carriage clock with the works well exposed by a pyrex dome. Mrs Definitely-Disgusting's plastic flowers differ from Jen Teale's in that they make no attempt to copy the originals, mauve snapdragons and blue roses, pink primroses and da-glo tulips would mass gaudily together in a sharply cut glass vase (Mr Definitely-Disgusting would probably rhyme it with 'praise'). In Mrs Definitely-Disgusting's mother's house the décor would be mostly brown, from design and chip fat fumes.

The less respectable element of the working classes would have no ornaments or pictures, having smashed the lot during drunken brawls. The room would be furnished with a huge colour television and biked beans tins.

Working-class houses and flats tend to smell of cabbages and leaky gas and, Jen Teale, wrinkling her retroussé nose, would claim, dirt. (A major casus belli, one of the great rows in the class war, is the fact that Samantha Upward, Eileen Weybridge, Jen Teale and Mrs Definitely-Disgusting all accuse each other of being sluts.)

The Bronco is hung up with string in the outside lavatory which explains why so many of the working classes suffer from constipation. Only two per cent of the professional classes are overcrowded compared with over fifty per cent of the working class.

10 GEOGRAPHY

Oh to be in Great Britain now that April's here.

Where you live is just as important as what you live in. I myself keep very quiet about being born in Hornchurch, always justifying it by saying we were only there temporarily because my father was working at Fords. At the time my parents' friends used to laugh it off by saying: 'Bill and Elaine live in the slums. Ho ho ho.'

With relief after two years, we moved back to Ilkley in Yorkshire which was where my father was born. Even here people looked longingly across to the Myddleton side of the valley, which was much smarter than the town side, because it was greener and got the sun all day. But at least Ilkley was smarter than Otley, because the inhabitants were richer, and because it was farther away from the industrial towns of Bradford and Leeds. And Harrogate was much smarter than Ilkley or Bradford or Leeds, because it was more rural and nearer the East Riding – which was much smarter than the industrial West Riding, but not as smart as the North Riding. And so it went on.

All over the North, as in the South, there are snob patches, immortalised by John Braine as 'T'Top'. Hoylake is 'T'Top' for Liverpool. Cheshire is 'T'Top' for Manchester. Ilkley is 'T'Top' for Bradford and Leeds. 'You can't get anyone local to char for you', said a friend who lives there now. 'When people move to Ilkley they think they've arrived.'

Certainly when we lived in Ilkley, which was devoid of anyone one would have thought of as upper-class, the upper middles (or people who considered they spoke the King's

English) stuck together. There were plenty of people we knew well who came to our parties but only a handful of them were invited to meet friends who came up from the South, particularly London, because the southerners were so easily bored, and so much pickier about Yorkshire accents. One Ilkley woman was described as having 'snobbed her way out of friends', because she never invited any of the locals to meet any of her friends from London. The North think, quite misguidedly, that they're much less snobbish and more open than the South, despising the emollient phrases of the southerner, which they think smack of insincerity.

Fulham, in South West London, is interesting from a class point of view. In the early sixties it was principally working-class and considered very unsmart. We lived in Redcliffe Square, (which called itself Kensington in those days), and I remember saying in shocked tones to my solicitor, 'But you can't live in Fulham'. Fifteen years later Fulham is swarming with upper-class and upper middle young marrieds in their first house, probably before moving out to the country. And in estate agents' ads, Redcliffe Square is not described as 'Kensington' any more but as 'Fulham'.

As the Arabs take over Mayfair (they must have access to strip and gambling clubs) and Saudi Kensington; and Paddington and Maida Vale are colonized by West Indians, and more and more residential property in central London is taken over for offices, the upper classes and trendies are tending to move farther and farther out. In the old days, they liked to keep their 'S.W.s' low: one, three, five and seven being best, like the Beethoven Symphonies, but now one finds them in Battersea, Clapham, Camberwell, Kentish Town and particularly Islington and West Hackney, because the two latter are so convenient for the City.

As birds of a feather traditionally flocked together, the B.B.C. sound radio people, who worked at Langham Place, the *New Statesman* readers, and the left-wing trendies tended to go north to Hampstead, Highgate, and St. John's Wood. While the Tellystocracy polarised around Barnes, Putney, Chiswick and even Hammersmith, because it was near the television centre. The richer ones even bought houses along the Common in Wimbledon, regarded by the upper classes as somewhere you only visited during the tennis fortnight. Certainly the older generation of the aristocracy still think of North of the Park (Hyde Park) and South of the River as beyond the pale, regarding anyone who lives there as a taxi-exile. (You can't pick up a taxi in the area and you can't get a taxi to take you out there because they won't get a fare back.)

If you pick up upper-class address books, they are still full of the old Flaxman, Fremantle, Belgravia, Knightsbridge, and Mayfair numbers. And the upper classes still tend to congregate in Belgravia in places like Cadogan and Eaton Square (although even these are getting a bit 'araby'), where they set up an elaborate system of one-way streets that make it impossible for the hoi polloi to enter them. They often also own huge chunks of London.

'Is this our street?' asked a very grand old woman, as we drove through Kensington.

But, despite their flats or houses in London, the upper class live mainly in the country, while the upper middle classes live in London and have cottages in the country. I know one Mrs Nouveau-Richards who has the only country cottage in the A–Z. Despite pleading poverty, the middle classes still have a million second houses.

Harry and Caroline Stow-Crat would never be in London at the weekend – which they would call 'Friday to Monday', although Georgie and the younger generation call it 'weekend' and tend to stay up more often.

'You'd never have got this sort of person in Harrods on Saturday in the old days,' a friend overheard one Harrods shop assistant saying to another recently.

Harry Stow-Crat is usually out of England skiing in February, and in Scotland shooting in August. Scotland is always smart, and packed with upper-class English, but the Highlands are smarter than the Lowlands. Northumberland and the border country is considered pretty grand too. Although you will find upper-class people in all counties, there tend to be more in Yorkshire than in Lancashire. The Midlands are shunned, except for Rutland, Herefordshire and Lincolnshire. Norfolk and Suffolk are much smarter than Cambridgeshire, which is not as grand as Berkshire and Oxfordshire. Of the 'home (that word again) counties', only Sussex and Kent are tolerable.

Just as the upper middles in Ilkley stuck together, the grander aristocracy might just deign to know the people who own the next-door estate, but on the whole they prefer to go into another county to dine with people they regard as their own level – this presumably is where the expression 'county', to describe the upper classes, came from. Hence you get those interminable forty-mile drives just to go out to dinner. The richer upper class buy planes, thinking nothing of flying a hundred miles to dine: 'It's only ten minutes in the helly.'

If they were going to stay with the Tavistocks at Woburn Abbey, or the Sitwells at Weston Hall, they would tend to say, 'I'm going to Woburn' or 'Weston', and expect the other person to know where they meant. They always spell out the whole county, i.e. 'Warwickshire' not 'Warwicks', and 'Devonshire', not 'Devon' on envelopes, writing paper, and in conversation.

It is very lower middle to talk about 'Great Britain' rather than 'England' and to describe oneself as 'British' rather than 'English', 'Scottish' or 'Welsh'.

In London the richer of the middle classes have tended to polarise round greens and commons, and on hills like Hampstead, Harrow-on-the-Hill, Richmond, Kingston, Putney. The exception is the Thames. Water in a city plays a dual role, it repels the rich where there are docks and industry, but attracts them where there are not.

The papers a year or two ago quoted a taxi-driver grumbling about the erosion of cockney London by the middle classes, who, as we have seen, are pouring into places like Barnsbury (Islington), Fulham, De Beauvoir Town (Hackney), even Whitechapel, the Old Kent Road, and the Isle of Dogs, wanting a house with a bit of garden for the children, within bicycling distance of the library. Soon the new settlers start action groups to have their own areas barricaded off against the traffic, so it spills into peripheral working-class areas, football is stopped in the streets, prices rocket, and the pubs are full of people called Nigel drinking gin and tonic. The old shops are rapidly replaced by antique shops and expensive delicatessens catering for career couples ('Ossie's Taramasolata is so delicious it would be crazy to make it myself') and the garish-looking dress shops crammed with skirts and sweaters in da-glo pink and royal blue, vanish in favour of ethnic boutiques catering for size fourteen upwards.

One of the great urban middle-class movements of the late

'Oh Bryan – it must be the great community feeling they told us about.'

seventies has been the development of community associations. When we were in New York in 1971, a publisher's wife was talking about a block fête, she and her friends had organised, and what fun it had been. Didn't we think fêtes were fun, she had asked my husband.

No we didn't, my husband answered, appalled, they were absolute anathema, one of the best reasons for living in London was to escape from that sort of thing.

'But we met so many nice new middle-class people', the publisher's wife had said.

Where America leads, England usually follows, and now eight years later, community and conservation societies flourish and every bit of urban grass has its own horse show, street party, or block community fête to raise money for park benches and shrubs round the churchyard – all organised by the middle classes banding together to protect their own property.

'I may have a large beautiful garden crammed with climbing frames,' says Samantha, 'But I don't want a hair of the common outside touched by kiddies' adventure playgrounds, and hockey pitches. And don't you dare build houses in the churchyard, to pay off your parish debts, or the price of my house will plummet.'

You can often tell the difference in London between a principally lower middle-class street, and an upper middle-class one, as the authors of *Voices from the Middle Class* pointed out. The first has narrow terraced houses, with no room for a front garden. People are cleaning their cars and windows, and painting their houses. Mongrels roam around the streets chasing cats away, an occasional cake tin, painted to look like a burglar alarm, hangs on the walls, and there will be several 'For Sale' signs, as the spiralist, having done his house up, is ready to move on.

His aim is the upper middle-class street, probably only blocks away, which has big houses set back from the road hidden by a hedge or wall with full-grown trees in the front garden, burglar alarms and cats asleep on the window sills. There is very little do-it-yourself, no-one is seen cleaning their cars, or their windows. You might even find a couple of horse boxes parked. This is the sort of quiet road, in fact where instructors teach learners to drive. There are very few 'For Sale' signs here, because people usually stay until their children leave home, whereupon they retire and move into a smaller house.

The lower middles tend to colonise in suburbs like Worcester Park, Cheam, Morden and Hendon.

Home county

To the spiralist, as we have seen, St. George's Hill, Weybridge, East Horsley, Cobham and Sunningdale are social meccas. Here he will meet more people in *Who's Who* than in any other county and rub shoulders on the train with more commuters from Social Classes I and II of the Census (stockbrokers, architects, Harley Street specialists, and rich businessmen) than anywhere else. These are the people the spiralist regards as upper-class – he doesn't realise that the real upper classes – except for people like the Earl of Onslow whose family have lived near Guildford for centuries – wouldn't be seen dead in Surrey.

There was a television programme on the inhabitants of Cheam, Surrey, recently where they interviewed a lot of spiralists with brushed-forward hair who all talked about the importance of 'competing' and 'living in an upper-class he-ome'. There was great community feeling in Cheam they said, the 'holl' thing had exploded at the Jubilee Party in 1977' and they all got on because they had the same sort of sense of humour, and enjoyed the same sort of hobbies: going 'horse racing and playing for Esher Rugby Club'. (The wives organized coffee evenings if their husbands had a night down at the Club.)

According to a brilliant book by John Connell called *The End of Tradition*, which explores rural life in central Surrey, there are only two classes left there. The middle-class 'foreigners', i.e. rich town dwellers who've moved in and bought up the old cottages, doing them up at vast expense, and the villagers who used to live in the same cottages but who now live on council estates.

Or as Geffrey Bernard put it a few years ago in the *New Statesman*: 'The place is divided into two halves. At one end, it's lavender, medium sherry, the *Daily Telegraph* and what a won-

'Now do tell me – does one go *up* or *down* to Weybridge?'

derful job the Conservatives are doing, and at the other end it's baked beans, bicycle clips and what a lousy job Sir Alf Ramsey's doing.'

What is happening in Surrey is that gradually the 'foreigners' are imposing their own middle-class life-style at the expense of the council tenants. The middle classes form their own preservation societies, rather like the community associations in London, and reject any improvement as 'smacking of suburbia', John Connell points out a scarcity of bowling greens and football pitches, while there are plenty of tennis courts and rugger, cricket and hockey pitches. Proposals for launderettes, children's playgrounds and more shops are quashed in case they spoil the beauty and quiet of the countryside. For the same reason the street lighting and bus shelters asked for by the council tenants are rejected. The middle classes, of course, are all right Jack, they've got cars to take them shopping at Bentalls, and out to their 'rack of lamb' dinner parties. What does it matter if they run a few council tenants over on the way, they're only spoiling the rural look of the countryside?

The tragedy is that the council house tenant has no mobility, the man who owns his house and who doesn't fit into the bridge and golf club set, can always move away, but the council tenant is stuck where he's put and with whom he's put.

Meanwhile the chasm between the house owner and council tenant grows bigger. 'The trouble with Surrey', grumbled one of the foreigners who couldn't find a char, or get someone to re-thatch his roof, 'is that there are no real yokels left'. Rather like the earnest woman, who said the trouble with the Third World was there was no middle class.

In other parts of England, of course, the class division is much more hierarchical, the upper classes in rural areas getting on much better with the working classes, than the middle-class professional man whom they both despise and regard as an upstart.

All the way down any hierarchy, in fact, you are likely to find each class trying to segregate itself from the class below. In Wolverhampton, council tenants had to make a three-quarters-of-a-mile detour, rather than walk two hundred yards through an owner-occupied estate. 'I don't want them coming through here,' said one house owner, 'Playing their radios, dropping ice cream papers, pulling up tulips, and our little willows. Someone even stole our pet rabbit.'

Another example was in Dawlish, where the council planned a two-storey housing estate, but was subjected to such an outcry from nearby house owners, that they turned them into bungalows. 'I mean,' protested one woman, 'They would have been able to look into our large picture windows, and seen us at our meals and in our private life.'

Finally, at the bottom of the scale, when some Romney Marsh gypsies were re-housed in a council estate, all the council tenants got up a petition and had them thrown out.

'These people are really not our class. We don't think New Church is the right place for them.'

11 GARDENS

Climax onto the patio, Maud.

The Englishman traditionally loves his garden almost more than his family. It needs cherishing and tending, but doesn't answer back. It is hardly surprising, therefore, that class distinction should be almost more rampant outside the house than in. Once again garden centres – like furniture shops – do a roaring trade because of snobbery – people ripping out the plants and paving stones of previous owners – that were 'too ghastly, my dear'. I remember being mystified once when a friend came to stay. we were having tea outside, enjoying the sunshine and the quiet (for once the aeroplanes were silent), when suddenly she fixed me with a beady eye, and said, 'You know, it's frightfully common to have Peace in one's garden.'

It was a few minutes before I realised she was referring to the beautiful pink and yellow rose next to the magnolia which flowers so gallantly and continually all the summer, which she thought vulgar, perhaps because it is so universally popular.

In the same way, Caroline Stow-Crat wouldn't touch gladioli, begonias, chrysanthemums, most dahlias, or fuschias (except in the conservatory). Also on the index would be gaudy bedding plants like petunias, French marigolds, calceolarias, cinnerarias, calendulas, salvia, californian poppies, zinnias, astors, and yellow daisies, although michaelmas daisies and white daisies are O.K. Colour would also be important, the white and green tobacco plants, are much more upper-class than the red or mauve ones; dark red wallflowers better than yellow or mauve. Trails of pale blue lobelia are all right, but Oxford blue is very common, particularly when combined in military rows with white allysum and scarlet geraniums.

Caroline wouldn't be very keen on any flower of a different colour to that which nature intended; blue roses, brown irises, pink forget-me-nots or daffodils. Daffodils, and most bulbs, she feels should be planted in long grass not in flower beds. She hates tulips. If she had rhododendrons she would not have individual ones, but a thousand in clumps lining the drive. A friend once asked a West Country peer how he achieved his magnificent multi-coloured display.

'Oh I move them around,' said the peer. 'When I want to change the colour schemes I just get sixty men up from the factory.'

'Yellow and green should never be seen', so Caroline would soon rip out anything variegated – laurels, or, even worse, privet and mother-in-law's-tongue in the house.

Some trees are also more upper-class than others; one thinks of the great flat-bottomed oaks, beeches, limes and chestnuts, that look, as Taine said, as though they'd been tended for hundreds of years like the children of rich parents.

If you discount the ancient cedars of Lebanon planted by Capability Brown, indigenous trees are considered much smarter than foreign ones, which is why the white cherry scores points over the pink ones, and why the Stow-Crats tend to despise the silver birches, pines and conifers of Surrey. Weeping willow trees are all right growing 'naturally' by a lake or stream, but a willow would be considered the height of vulgarity in the middle of a lawn, particularly if it were planted in a circle of earth. While the suburbs in Spring with their candy floss mass of blossom, pink and white cherry, dark pink crab-apple, almond, laburnum, and lilac are quite beyond the pale.

The names of buildings in the garden are also pronounced differently. Harry Stow-Crat says 'garidge', Samantha Upward wanting to show off her French pronunciation says '*gar*arzh'; the Weybridge set say 'gar-*arge*' in order to upstage the lower middles who say 'garidge' like Harry Stow-Crat. Mrs Nouveau-Richards has a 'carport'. Harry has a 'gaz-ee-bo' in his garden; Samantha calls it a 'summerhouse', while Mrs Nouveau-Richards reclines in her 'gayze-bow'. Harry pronounces 'loggia' like 'lodger', but the Weybridge set call it 'lowdjea' in case there is any confusion about paying guests when someone says Howard is relaxing on the loggia. A friend claims his very grand great-grandmother used to refer to ants as 'aunts', saying 'there's an aunt-heap in the garden' – which sounds like a great fleshy pyramid of maiden ladies.

The point about the upper-class garden is that it should look as 'natural' as possible, great sweeps of mown grass leading down to the lake, huge trees with new little saplings always being planted and nurtured, trout streams, parks full of deer, and cows, swishing their tails knee deep in the buttercups. Away from the house, there might be a series of flower gardens, divided by walls, or hedges of box or yew; a conservatory full of nectarines, peaches and the oldest vine in Europe, a herb garden and a huge vegetable garden. Around the house, plants will grow in genuine Versailles pots, which are made of wood and square but narrower at the bottom and topped with balls. (All balls are very upper-class says Harry Stow-Crat.)

But everything would be mellowed and weatherbeaten, the walls and roof of the house 'stained by time and many coloured lichens, and overgrown with creeper to a richly variegated grey-ish red'. The drive would be made of stone chippings or gravel – not black tarmac or concrete like the M.1.

The Stow-Crats are very keen on vistas (Mr Nouveau-Richards thinks they're something to do with chicken curries). Through a gap in a wood you might see a temple of Flora, or a folly or a bend in the river.

The secret of their gardens is sweet disorder. Weeds in moderation don't matter, because the plants are so closely massed they don't show the earth beneath. A dearth of earth is very upper-class.

Percy Lubbock, writing about the 'easy abundance' of a particular upper-class garden, realises that it's not the plants themselves but the way they are planted, that matters. 'Lobelia stripes, for example and those marigold patches, which might have looked harsh and hard, (one knows how smartly odious marigolds can look in an over-tidy garden) all rejoiced together, rambling and crowding in liberal exuberance. The gardener might wreak his worst will, but the free soul of the garden escaped him and bloomed tumultuously.'

A garden like that, however, requires not just money and genius ('Planted 400 bulbs in the orchard this afternoon,' wrote Vita Sackville-West to Harold Nicolson) but also gardeners you can bully.

In the old days, gardeners used to wash all the vegetables,

and take the thorns off the roses before they were sent up to the house. A handbook published in the eighteenth century, advised them to look clean and neat. 'Your employer will not wish to look on a dirty ragged uncouth grinning or conceited bi-ped, in his garden.' They were also instructed to 'Put the manure on the flower beds, early in the morning, so the putrescent vapours may not prove offensive to the owner of the garden and his friends.'

But as 'corsts' get higher and gardeners get scarcer, it is more and more difficult to keep up a large and beautiful garden. In the country, gardens tend to get smaller and smaller, and orchards bigger and bigger. Donkeys are becoming increasingly popular for keeping the lawn down. And I heard that mixture of concern and self-interest which always colours the master-servant relationship, neatly summed up by a woman I met at a party the other day who said: 'Our darling old gardener died last week – isn't it *maddening*!'

In Harry Stow-Crat's London garden you find a few bulbs in window boxes, followed by pink geraniums and ivy followed by irises and Albertine, a pale pink rose which stops flowering in June. After that the upper classes are always out of London so it doesn't matter what their gardens look like.

In the country, the upper middles tend to have beautiful gardens with shrubberies and herbaceous borders more related to the house and not set aside in separate gardens, as they are in Harry Stow-Crat's place, although the vegetable garden will be separate. Plants and flowers grow round the house and on the terrace you might see imitation plaster Versailles pots by Julian Jenkinson, an old Etonian who copied them very successfully from the authentic wooden pots at Lord Harcourt's place. The lawn will be well tended, but there will be more brown patches on the lawn because upper middle-class dogs are less likely to pee in the house than upper-class dogs. As manure is seldom available all the time, there will also be greater interest in compost. The roses and dahlias will be very fine and the colours slightly brighter than in the upper-class garden. As we go down the social scale, gardens tend to become neater and gaudier.

Samantha Upward is very proud of her green fingers, particularly as she lives in London. She reads Wordsworth to her potted plants, rushes out with a shovel every time the police horses go by, and, by feeding Zacharias' daffodil with John

Innes and Liquinure, she won him first prize in his form's flower growing competition. But, alas, the herb garden she planted so she could have all the ingredients in Elizabeth David's recipes has been turned into a cat's lavatory by visiting toms.

Samantha knows that plastic flower pots and plastic hanging baskets are frightfully common, but such is the greenness of her fingers, that she couldn't possibly afford pottery flower pots for all her plants. She's also far too soft-hearted to rip out that variegated horror donated by a neighbour that time she had shingles, or that rose that looked the palest pink in the catalogue, but turned out bright crimson and horribly clashing with the da-glo orange rose beside it. She knows, too, that dear, funny John Betjeman said that every time he looked at a rhododendron, he thought of a stockbroker, so she moved her two mauve ones under the catalpa, but, alas, they're doing terribly well. At least she hasn't descended to crocuses in a wheelbarrow, or a plastic Venus de Milo like the one on the patio next door which melted at their last barbecue party.

Her garden would be really quite lovely if only she could stop the gardener who comes two hours a week edging the lawn so the flower beds are never full up, and planting tulip bulbs in serried ranks like the ones outside Buckingham Palace. But if she checks him, she's terrified he'll take offence and not turn up next week.

Gideon and Samantha sit in their garden on a Sunday morning, swilling back the chilled white, saying 'This is the life!' and watching the half leg of lamb rotating jerkily on the barbecue, wafting, intimations of garlic, rosemary and envy into the nearby council estates.

The suburbs

Ewbank'd inside and Atco'd out, the English suburban residence and the garden which is an integral part of it stand trim and lovingly cared for in the mild sunshine. Everything is in its place . . . The leaves of the virginia creeper which climbs the rough-cast wall just beside the window of the best bedrooms hardly stir.' J. M. Richards, *The Castles on the Ground*

Nothing has really changed in the suburbs. When we lived in a working-class part of Fulham, no-one minded that we never

bothered with our garden. A few neighbours grew vegetables
and fought a losing battle with visiting tom cats, but the rest of
us let the weeds flourish and chucked our beer cans and spare
rib bones over each other's fences when we ran out of dustbin
space. Only when we moved to Putney, a Madam Butterfly
land of cherry trees and flowering shrubs, and inherited a
beautifully-kept garden which we promptly let go to rack and
ruin, did we discover that gardening here was taken very
seriously indeed. Soon the whole street were clicking their
tongues over our hayfield of a lawn, and making cracks about
calling in the forestry commission to deal with the weeds.
Finally, a kindly neighbour could bear it no longer, and found a
gardener to come in three hours a week to sort us out.

More recently, the local conservation association, which
howls with protest if even a harebell is touched or a sapling
uprooted on the common, produced stern proposals, which
were circularised round the district for the tidying up of the
garden of the only house along the common that happened to be
owned by the council. This, they felt, was letting down the tone
of the road by its number of weeds. At any minute one
expected the dandelion detector van to start policing the streets
bleeping noisily outside the offending garden. My husband

suggested it would be far cheaper to declare the garden in question an Area of Outstanding Natural Beauty: then the weeds and wild flowers could riot unimpeded.

Though Putney is more upper middle than suburban, the notion of not letting down the street is shared by the suburbs farther out. Few people here are dedicated gardeners in the winter. Unlike the upper classes they stay inside in bad weather. But come the first temperate weekend, suburban man peers out of his window at his colourless plot, and thunders off to the garden centre to load up the car with bags of John Innes, bedding plants, do-it-yourself cucumber kits, and a plaster fig-leafless cherub to upstage the plastic dolphin regurgitating blue water on the patio next door.

The suburban gardener is deeply competitive: he doesn't want anyone else to let down the street, so that his own glory may be greater when his garden is the best. Rivalry is particularly fierce over roses. Hybrid teas and floribundas and dahlias mass in clashing colours above totally weedless flower beds. You can't get a lie-in at weekends either; it's like the pits at Silverstone with the roar of all the mowers revving up, interspersed with the occasional excruciating teeth-grating rattle as they drive over the crazy pavement. Some people acquire a second mower for difficult patches as a status symbol.

The patio is a focal point of the garden, a mosaic of Italian tiles, covered with plastic urns containing striped petunias, deck chairs with foot rests, and sun umbrellas mostly bought with Green Shield stamps.

The Weybridged house has a circular gravel drive bordered by 'rhodos'; 'in' and 'out' entrances with no gates; an up-and-over garage door; a swimming pool which, despite its barrage balloon cover, is filled in winter with dead leaves and sparrows; and a dog yard for the terriers to dry off in. Having gone one step up from the suburban garden with its high laurel hedges, Weybridged gardens are often open plan with no dividing fences at all, although there might be a hedge of conifers to shelter the roses from the wind, or interlaced larch fencing round the vegetable garden. Here Howard and Eileen Weybridge sit in their summer houses admiring the well-tended lawns with their crazy pavement stepping stones; the conifers and golden willow in their little circles of earth; the beautifully kept shrubberies full of pampas grass and bamboo;

and the thrushes pecking at the 'rack-of-lamb' bone which hangs from the dovecote (pronounced 'dovecoat': Harry Stow-Crat says 'dovec't'). A heavily ferned stream flows under a wooden willow pattern bridge and into a waterfall through the heaths in the rock garden. Heather, except on the moors, is considered very vulgar by Harry Stow-Crat. Even its Latin name, 'Erica', sounds frightful.

On Monday, aping the upper classes, Eileen Weybridge feels it her duty to pick up the litter dropped by trippers in the nearby beechwoods before she goes out to bridge or a conservative coffee morning.

Believing that upper-class women spend their leisure hours doing the flowers, the Weybridged middle classes are heavily into flower arrangements by numbers, ramming salmon pink 'glads' into green foam blocks so they stand up in the plastic dole-phin vase, and pick up the apricot décor in the lounge.

Yellow 'chrysanths' and button dahlias have always been a talking point, too, when arranged in the white basket held by a naked cupid on the dining-room table, when Howard's business associates come to dinner. While the orchids Howard has raised in the '*con*serve-a-tory' (the Stow-Crats say 'c'n*serv*'tri') look so well in driftwood in the vestibule. The expression 'fresh flowers', to distinguish them from dried or plastic flowers is also very Weybridge.

Although Jen Teale lives in a house with a number, she has re-named it 'Jenbry' which combines both her and Bryan's names, which she puts in inverted commas on her notepaper. This drives the postman crackers. Her wrought iron gate also incorporates the name. On either side Bryan has built a bright yellow wall, shaped like a doily. A plastic flowerpot container, holding a plastic flowerpot filled with purple and shocking pink petunias hangs by the mauve front door. Jen remembers to remove the dead heads night and morning. There are no creepers up the house. Jen doesn't want earwigs in the bath. Most of the back and front gardens have been crazy paved by Bryan because it looks so much neater, but there are a few crescent shaped flower beds. They might have been dug out with a pastry cutter. Here in neat rows in the spring stand military lines of blue grape hyacinths, yellow 'daffs' and scarlet tulips. In the summer these are replaced by white allysium, french marigolds, Oxford blue lobelia and scarlet geraniums, or, by

'For God's sake pull the plug out!'

way of a change, calceolarias and salvias. Jen loves bedding plants because once they've finished flowering they can be thrown away. There is not a weed in sight. The garden is oblong, regular and compact like a park garden.

When Bryan is not in his toolshed, he tends his 'chrysanths' and his 'toms' in the greenhouse. It's better than being hoovered under. Occasionally, on summer afternoons, Jen and the family sit out on tubular steel picnic chairs, that can fold away neatly afterwards. There was a nasty moment once when 'an elderly relative come to visit' got stuck in the couch hammock with aluminium frames. Harry Stow-Crat ties hammocks to trees.

As a first generation gardener, Mr Nouveau-Richards pulls out all the stops. Apart from illuminating his tarmac drive and technicolour lawn with toadstools, he has all his flowerbeds floodlit, and coolie-hat lamps are stationed like street lights round the garden.

Weeding, watering and edging is all done by electricity, which also keeps the earth warm under the cloches. In the propagating frames, all-night fluorescent lighting forces tulips into bloom in November, and vast strawberries to ripen in time for Christmas. Plastic grass lines the outdoor swimming pool (which is constantly kept at 80° like the indoor one).

Mr Nouveau-Richards reclines on the underfloor heated 'pate-io' and plays with a computerised mowing machine, a new toy newly imported from Texas.

He has just mixed a mint julep from his portable drinks trolley which glides over tiles and shagpile and was described in the catalogue as 'the ultimate way to enjoy a cocktail on the patio, an aperitif by the pool, or those after-dinner drinks in the lounge.'

Mr Definitely-Disgusting hasn't got a garden, but he grows tomatoes and geraniums on his balcony, and he also has an allotment which means a lot to him. It is illegal to sell 'produce' or 'provender', both very Jen Teale words, from one's allotment, but at least he can grow vegetables and flowers for all the family. Here stand neat furrows of potatoes, curtains of runner beans, rows of lettuces and 'caulies' and at the end a blaze of annuals and bedding plants in primary colours to rival Samantha Upward's playroom. When he pulls up a lettuce he calls it 'picking a salad'.

12 FOOD

Let them eat gâteau.

'When a woman asks for back, I call her "madam"', said a grocer. 'When she asks for streaky I call her "dear". You can always tell the gentry,' he went on, 'by their knowledge of cheese. They don't have trouble saying the foreign brands.'

The food you eat often indicates what class you are, the way you eat it, namely your table manners, does so almost as much.

The upper classes, for example, don't have any middle-class inhibitions about waiting until everyone else is served, they start eating the moment food is put in front of them. This stems from the days when they all dined at long baronial tables, and if you waited for fifty other people to be served, your wild boar would be stone cold. Nor would Harry Stow-Crat comment on the food at a dinner party, because there's no point in congratulating your hostess on something that's been cooked by someone else. Equally if he knocked his wine over, he wouldn't apologise, because, traditionally, there would be a fleet of servants to clean it up.

The ritual of table napkins is interesting too. The working-class man tucked a handkerchief under his chin to protect his shirt and waistcoat (he would never eat in a coat). The lower middles daintily thinking 'napkin' sounded too much like babies' nappies, and wanting to show off their knowledge of French called it 'serviette'. The middle classes, wanting to go one up, talked about 'napkins', but being frugal also wanted them to last a few days so they introduced napkin rings, whereas the upper classes who had plenty of people to do the laundry (Harry Stow-Crat's mother calls it 'larndry') had clean napkins at every meal, and regarded napkin rings as the height of vulgarity. One peer, when presented with a pair in a velvet box, after making a speech, had to ask the mayor hastily what they were for. Even today Caroline Stow-Crat would rather use paper napkins than napkin rings. Mrs Nouveau-Richards having read in some etiquette book that the word 'serviette' is common, calls them 's-napkins'. In the same way, she only just remembers in time that dinner in the middle of the day is called 'lunch' and talks about 'd'lunch', which sounds faintly West Indian. Harry Stow-Crat's mother still calls it 'luncheon'.

Both Harry and Gideon Upward would lunch from one o'clock onwards, have tea around four, and dinner at eight to eight-thirty in the evening. The Teales would breakfast very early because they don't like to be rushed. So would the Definitely-Disgustings because Mr Definitely-Disgusting has to get to work early. Both Bryan and Mr Definitely-Disgusting probably have a cheese roll or a bar of chocolate at nine-thirty, followed by 'dinner' at twelve and 'tea' the moment they get home from work about six to six-thirty.

The worst thing about the working classes, complains Caroline Stow-Crat is they never know when to leave. If she asks them round for a quick pre-dinner drink, they've always had their tea first, and are all set to carry on drinking until midnight. Samantha Upward gets round the problem by asking Mrs Nouveau-Richards at seven, then lies that she's frightfully sorry she and Gideon have got to go out to dinner at eight-thirty. Unfortunately, Mrs Nouveau-Richards spoils everything by asking if she can see round the kitchen, and discovers three large baked potatoes, and a casserole cooking in the oven. Samantha stands on one leg, and says: 'The *au pair* has the most enormous appetite.'

Then there's a whole different ball game about what to call the courses. Caroline Stow-Crat would never use expressions like 'starter' except in quotes, or 'the soup' or 'an appetiser'. She would talk about the 'meat' or 'main course', or 'cold cuts' but never the 'entrée' or 'the roast'. (The middle classes say 'joint'.) Nor would she refer to chicken or grouse as 'the bird' or 'poultry' although Harry might use the word 'poultry' as a farming term. Howard Weybridge says 'polltry' or 'casseroll' with a short 'o'. Everything from lemon water ice to jam roly-poly pudding, Caroline would call 'pudding'. She would never say 'sweet' or 'dessert'. Cheese would be served after pudding, never before. Then, to muddle everyone, this might be followed by 'dessert', which is fruit, even bananas, being eaten with fruit knives and forks.

A few months ago, I went to the annual general meeting of the 'Istoric' Houses Association, a gathering bristling with members of the aristocracy and the henchmen who organise the people who see over their houses. Having been gossiping in the bar, I arrived late for lunch, and found a fat lady henchman sitting by herself, the rest of the table having gone off to help themselves to pudding.

'Who else is sitting here,' I asked, 'anyone exciting?'

'Well ay don't think they were ducal folk,' she said, 'Because they were holdin' their knives like pencils.'

Indeed she was right.

One of the great class divides, along with living in a 'bought house' and saying 'pardon', is the way you hold your knife. The lower echelons hold them like pencils, the upper and middles to a man putting their first finger (the one Mr Definitely-Disgusting uses to read with) on the knife where the handle joins the blade. Harry would also turn his fork over to eat his peas, if he felt like it, and pick a bone. Behaviour that would horrify Jen Teale.

Michael Nelson, in *Nobs and Snobs* tells a story to illustrate what a gentleman his grandfather was. When sitting next to his hostess, he saw a slug on his lettuce. Rather than embarrass her, he shut his eyes, and ate it. 'And your grandfather', the story ends 'managed not to be sick until after dinner.'

Whilst it is a touching story, I think this was the act of a gentleman, but not necessarily an aristocrat – the two are not synonymous. In my experience Harry Stow-Crat wouldn't swallow a slug, nor eat anything he didn't like. Nor would he ever resort to the lengths of a Jen Teale who once dropped in on my brother and his wife, and was asked to stay for lunch. To eke out the sausages and mash, my sister-in-law fried three kidneys, which this Jen Teale was too polite to say she couldn't eat. In silent glee, my brother watched her whip a kidney off her plate, when she thought no-one was looking, and hold it in her hand all through lunch. Afterwards, she sidled inch by inch towards the fire, and choosing a moment when my sister-in-law was pouring out coffee, flicked the kidney discreetly with a brisk backhand into the flames, whereupon it let out a prolonged and noisy hiss.

If someone else was paying for lunch in a restaurant, and the food wasn't up to scratch, Mr Nouveau-Richards would complain noisily to the waiter. Harry Stow-Crat would keep his trap shut. If, on the other hand, he was paying, he would never be too embarrassed to complain, like Gerald Lascelles lunching at the Ritz, who sent a trout back because it was too small. Or the crusty old baronet, who peered into the communion cup, at early service, and because it was only a quarter full, bellowed, 'That's not enough.'

If you stayed with the Stow-Crats you would go into dinner at eight on the dot, because it's inconsiderate to keep the servants waiting, and you wouldn't sit around the table swilling brandy until midnight, because the servants want to clear away. But the men would stay behind with the port for a while, and grumble about estate duty, while the women would go into the drawing-room and probably grumble about constipation.

Things are changing, however. These days you find far more upper-class people telling the hostess her food was lovely, because she's probably cooked it herself – and if you've spent two days slaving over a dinner party you want a bit of praise. In London fewer and fewer men wear black ties, although the upper classes and upper middles still tend to in the country, with many of the women still sticking to their horse blanket long skirts and frilly shirts.

With the inroads of women's lib, upper middle women are less and less often shunted off to drink coffee by themselves after dinner, the merry-tocracy in particular believing in a port in every girl, and as the husband often cooks the dinner to cries of approval which his wife would never get, he's the one who needs to go upstairs and tone down his flushed face.

The other great change in the upper middle-class life-style is the swing back to traditional English food. In the fifties and sixties, on those three-week holidays to various costas, the wives picked up tips for five course dinners. If you put garlic and green peppers in everything it showed you'd travelled. Samantha Upward even used the same plate for all courses, so you could still taste the squid vinaigrette, and the beef proven-çale when you were eating your *Poire Belle Helène*.

As a reaction to all this the trend now is for simple English cooking designed to bring out the flavour of good food instead of concealing it in a cordon blur of cream and wine sauce with grated cheese and breadcrumbs on top. At dinner parties, Samantha now serves fish pie, pink beef, and, particularly, English lamb (she and Gideon have had best end of neck four times during the last five times they've been out the spiralists call it 'rack of lamb'). And for puddings it's treacle tart, jam roly-poly and bread and butter pudding, which at a time of national unrest reminds Samantha of Nanny, childhood and security.

Meanwhile other trends move downwards, the patrician habit of not commenting on the food for example is reaching the suburban spiralist belt. 'Dinner gets more elaborate,' said a wife on a Neo-Georgian estate, 'but people pretend not to notice, it's all passed over to prove we're used to brandy in everything, and avocado pears.'

And although the Surrey commuters are still wafting out garlic like dragon's breath – a sort of last gaspachio – the return to traditional food is just reaching the Weybridge set. Determined not to let the Chancellor ruin their 'wholl' new fun lifestyle, 'they are into communal dinner parties with one wife cooking each course, and all keeping a stern watch on anyone getting too elaborate and putting in too much cream.

The foreign food bug in fact has just filtered down to Jen Teale, Colman's Cook 'n Sauce is the best thing that has ever happened to her. She has also started tarting up the Oxo stew with package Hungarian Goulash, and finds that Chicken Marengo mix gingered up with garlic salt, makes a nice change from an 'assorted platter of cold meats', and all these mixes do save bothering with messy ingredients. Packet *Boeuf Bourgignon* was a smash hit, too, the time Bryan's boss came to dinner. Bryan's boss's wife also admired Jen's table. Pink paper napkins in the glasses, a matching pink doily in the basket under the slices of 'crusty bread', pink flowers in the centre of the table, and pink needle-dick candles casting a lovely light. Jen, who believes things that look good, taste good, has decorated everything with radish flowerets and cucumber hearts. And her new tupperware Jel'n Serve bowl set the orange mousse in a rose shape and Jen garnished it so prettily with piped cream and mandarin segments. The one bottle of table wine looked so attractive in its basket too, (in the old days Bryan used to

'It would never 'ave bloody well 'appened, Ricardo, if you'd 'eld yer
knife proper.'

decant it – so people wouldn't see the V.P. label) and Jen made
sure no-one got tiddly by serving little glass bowls of crisps and
nuts with the Bristol Cream before dinner.

Jen's knives have stainless steel handles and resemble fish
knives, the forks look like tridents and have long thin handles to
keep you farther away from the messy food – on the same
principle as her feather duster. Jen never 'cooks', she always
calls it 'preparing a meal'. After she'd been to a 'resteront',
she'd expect the waiter to say 'enjoyed your meal?'. The word
'meal' is a convenient cop-out when you don't know whether to
call it 'lunch', 'dinner', or 'tea'. Bryan's Rotarian father says
'repast'.

The Nouveau-Richards still overdo their dinner parties –
smoked salmon and caviar soufflé to start with; sole flamed in
brandy with a pernod cream sauce; *boeuf en croûte*; and a moated
sugar castle for pudding, followed by After Ape mints. 'Cha-o-
bo-elled wine' flows throughout. Afterwards all the guests are
sick.

The Definitely-Disgustings don't give dinner parties. Everything is geared towards Sunday dinner. In the old days you

were paid on Saturday night, rushed off to the pawn shop, got out your Sunday suit, and then hurried down to the late-night market to buy food for 'dinner' the following day. The warmth and friendliness of the pub often proved too seductive for the wage earner, and his wife would try to drag him out before he blued all his earnings. If there wasn't enough money to pay for dinner, Charlie Chaplin remembers himself and his brother being told to sit down to empty tables and clash their knives and forks together so the neighbours wouldn't realise they were going short.

Today the tradition is continued. Mr Definitely-Disgusting starts Sunday with a good breakfast, fried egg, bacon, beef sausages (because they're cheaper than pork) and fried bread. At twelve he goes to the pub, and is dragged home at two-thirty for the 'roast and two veg', followed by apple pie and custard, or, as a treat in the summer, tinned peaches and cream. Having slept off the excesses while the family watch football on telly, he would then have whelks and two slices of 'ovis for tea, this being the only roughage he has had during the whole week.

Growing, shopping and cooking

Like Mr Definitely-Disgusting, Harry Stow-Crat has always liked plain unmessed about food – the Costa Brava Elizabeth David revolution having hardly touched him. Harking back to the old days, when mediaeval barons had to take care of themselves, the upper-class estate has always been self-sufficient. The upper classes tend to be unimaginative in their tastes. Lord Lucan used to go to his gambling club every day and have cutlets in winter, and cutlets en gelée in summer. I have a friend whose father always has Stilton and rice pudding for lunch.

As has been pointed out, lack of servants has only recently prompted the upper classes to take an interest in cooking. Lord Montague may get up early and roast a woodcock or snipe for his guests' breakfast on Sunday, but more characteristic is a story told by Nancy Mitford about the evening her maid went out and left her some macaroni cheese to put in the oven for three quarters of an hour. After the allotted time, she took it out, and was surprised to find it stone cold. It had not occurred to her to turn on the oven.

In Harry Stow-Crat's house an eternal battle rages between
the cook who keeps pulling tiny young carrots, and potatoes
from the earth because they're more tender, and the gardener
who wants them to grow to flower show size.

Conversely in street markets you can't sell tiny potatoes,
tomatoes and sprouts to Mrs Definitely-Disgusting because
they look poverty stricken. Many working-class eating habits
are based on eking things out further. Sandwiches are left with
the crusts on, lettuce is served with Heinz salad cream, so you
only need use as much as you want, rather than wasting the
whole thing by drenching it in French dressing. Mrs
Definitely-Disgusting's cabbages always seem overcooked,
because she uses everything and by the time the stalk and tough
outer leaves are tender, the inner leaves are overdone. As
recently as 1973, only thirty-seven per cent of the working
classes in Britain had refrigerators, which explains why they ate
so much out of tins, and why so many things: beetroot, onions,
herrings, cockles and whelks are stored in vinegar to make them
last.

Because Mr Definitely-Disgusting likes frozen and marrow
fat peas, Jen Teale would refer even to peas that came out of a
field in Norfolk as 'garden peas'. She would ask for 'green
beans', to distinguish them from 'biked beans', while Samantha
Upward would say 'French' or 'runner beans'. Equally Jen
Teale would talk about 'creamed potatoes' because it was one
up on the working-class 'mash', not realising that the upper
middles and uppers talk about 'mashed potatoes' too. She also
calls baked potatoes 'jacket potatoes', which she'd cut in half
horizontally, spread out like two halves of an easter egg on a
separate plate, and fill with sour cream. Another lower middle
expression, attempting to put down the Definitely-Disgustings
is 'fresh fruit' or 'fresh cream' to distinguish it from tinned fruit
or cream. The classes above would just say 'fruit' or 'cream'.

Fish holds numerous pitfalls for the socially unwary. Shortly
after John Betjeman's poem 'Phone for the fish knives,
Norman', received wide circulation when Nany Mitford's
Noblesse Oblige was first published in the fifties, the antique
shops were flooded with unwanted fish knives, and the upper
middle and even some of the upper classes sat solemnly at
breakfast trying to bone kippers with forks.

Mr Definitely-Disgusting thinks fresh salmon is utterly tasteless, and prefers salmon out of a tin. A similar reputed preference once made Harold Wilson the subject of widespread scorn. Mr Definitely-Disgusting likes pilchard salad too, and cockles, rollmops and eels either jellied or in a pie with mash, which he eats with a viscous green sauce. But the working-class northerner, however, wouldn't touch mackerel, regarding it as the scavenger of the seas, 'If my Missus gave me mackerel for tea,' said one fishmonger, 'I'd go to a marriage guidance council.'

A fashion that has moved downwards is the 'quiche', which was once called 'bacon-and-egg pie', until it got tarted up with peppers, onions, mushrooms and corrugated pastry, and was produced every time Caroline Stow-Crat had to provide something for a charity luncheon or Samantha had a buffet party. The merry-tocracy also found it much cheaper than china to hurl at each other at the end of drunken evenings: 'And then I shut her wild eyes with quiches four.'

The Weybridge set produced it for rugger and cricket teas, and the trend has finally filtered down to Mrs Definitely-Disgusting who calls it a 'qwitch'.

I think the popularity of quiche may be explained by the fact the people no longer feel easy about using the word 'tart'. 'Treacle tart', and 'apple tart' sound all right, but expressions like 'savoury tartlets', or 'My son says I make a good tart,' usually get a snigger. 'Queer' and 'Gay' have gone the same way. Only Mrs Definitely-Disgusting could still get away with saying: 'I turned queer in the night. It must have been them prawns.'

As one moves through the day, the class indicators come thick and fast. The higher classes have coffee for breakfast, the lower have tea, which they drink very strong and usually sweet. Jen Teale says she doesn't favour either a 'cooked breakfast' or a 'continental breakfast', and instead has 'just a drink in the morning', meaning tea. (When Gideon Upward or Harry Stow-Crat use the word 'drink' they mean alcohol.) Jen sometimes has 'segments' instead of 'cereal', which means tinned grapefruit pigs. Caroline Stow-Crat has Oxford marmalade on her toast, so does Samantha. She doesn't like it very much but she read somewhere that Golden Shred was common. Mr Definitely-Disgusting has 'two a drip, a chuck a bubble, and a cup of bug,' which translated means two slices of bread and dripping, a plate of bubble and squeak, and a cup of tea (which rhymes with flea, hence 'bug'). Jen thinks the word 'chuck' has a nasty derivation so she says 'portion'. Samantha says 'helping'.

On to luncheon where gentlemen, according to Harry Stow-Crat, never have soup – presumably because the upper classes were always out slaughtering wildlife, and soup would be difficult to eat if you were crawling through a bracken, or sitting on a horse. He pronounces venison 'ven'son', and truffles 'true-ffls'. Jen Teale, knowing the importance of eating a proper lunch, has frozen cod in cheese sauce boiled in a cellophane bag, which is indistinguishable from the dishcloths, and tea towels she is always simmering on the hob. 'On the weekend' she and Bryan sometimes have 'an assorted platter of cold meats followed by the cheese board.' As a first generation 'resteront' goer, Bryan has picked up some of the ghastly terminology – 'bill o'fare', 'sweet n' sour', and 'turkey and all the trimmings' (which means a teaspoon of cardboard packet stuffing and one burnt chipolata).

On to tea, which for the unwary is also full of pitfalls, it is very unsmart to call it 'afternoon tea' to distinguish it from 'high tea'. Now that people of all classes in a hurry use tea bags, everyone puts the milk in second, so this is no longer an upper-class indicator. The upper classes drink china tea out of china teacups, 'but it's awfully difficult drinking out of hand painted cups', said one spiralist's wife, 'so we have mugs when we're alone, and por-cell-aine when we have guests'. (Caroline Stow-Crat calls it 'porsl'n'.)

Jen Teale's tea is a symphony of doilies under pastries and gâteaux, cake forks, scones (with a long 'o'). She provides paper napkins and a knife even if you're only eating sandwiches – which she pronounces 'sand-witch' like 'spin-itch', Caroline Stow-Crat says 'sanwidge', and 'spin-idge', the Weybridge set say 'sani'. Mrs Definitely-Disgusting says 'butty' or 'booty' if she lives in the north.

Jen would be shocked by Mrs Definitely-Disgusting's milk bottle and bloater paste on the table, by the way she holds the bread in the palm of her left hand and spreads it with the right, and dips her biscuits in her tea, because of her sore teeth (spiralists call it 'dunking'). Caroline Stow-Crat has Earl Grey or China tea the colour of washing-up water (just the colour Mr

Definitely-Disgusting likes his coffee). White sliced bread is particularly lower middle because of its lack of roughage.

A fellow journalist however tells a wicked story of the time he interviewed a famous romantic novelist who was also a passionate health food freak. During the interview at her house, he was subjected to a long lecture on the merits of wholemeal home-made bread, but just as he was leaving, a little Sunblest van came jauntily up the drive.

'Surely,' said the journalist in mock horror, 'You're not buying sliced bread.'

'Oh that, darling,' said the lady novelist airily, 'Is for the servants.'

13 DRINK

Say 'Cheers' to me only with thy peep holes.

I was talking to a man in the pub the other day, who'd done very well for himself, and we got on to the subject of class: 'I was born working-class,' he said. 'But I must be middle-class now because I'm drinking wine.'

This recalls the working-class father who sneered that his son-in-law was pushing the boat out, every time he produced a bottle of wine for lunch. But if drinking wine has come to be a middle-class indicator, it wasn't always so.

Angus Wilson at Oxford just before the war says that only the richest of his middle class friends was used to drinking wine regularly at home, and goes on: 'I think this lack of regular wine drinking was much more common in middle class homes in the inter war years, not only than now but than it had been in late Victorian times.'

Certainly my own mother, being a vicar's daughter remembers the horrors of having a completely dry wedding in the twenties, and right up to the end of the fifties, I remember my parents hardly ever drank wine at home. They had dry martinis before dinner sometimes, and if they were having a dinner party, occasionally a bottle of claret between eight guests. Then there would be whisky and soda at the end of the evening to tell people it was time to go home. There was a set who drank a lot in Ilkley, whom I regarded as rather exciting, but whom my mother considered were fast and very jumped-up.

The wine-drinking habit seems to have caught on in England in the late fifties and early sixties when 'bistros' started replacing coffee bars, and the middle classes went to Spain, Italy and

'We've just had a terrible, terrible row and finished off those two rather good bottles of Latour you gave us.'

France, and discovered, along with all those tips for their dinner parties, the pleasures of drinking the local wine. Soon the husbands were enjoying Sauterne with watery sprouts at their cricket dinners, and showing off in restaurants – 'Let it breathe, Luigi.'

Rapidly wine-drinking spread, particularly in the seventies when the middle classes, believing they were being slowly squeezed out of existence, started drinking themselves insensible. During the austerity years of the middle seventies, the merry-tocracy gave up their foreign holidays, but not their booze.

The middle classes also have totally dislocated values about other people drinking. Every time a T.U.C. leader entertains a few foreign union leaders in a smart restaurant there is a frightful sanctimonious uproar in the popular Tory press over the price of every item on the bill. No wonder Wedgie Benn and Jim Callaghan are tea-total.

The Stow-Crat family have had cellars filled with wine for generations, so Harry's always drunk it but not to excess. Because it's there he doesn't feel the need to swill it all round the clock. Before dinner, he would probably offer guests a glass of sherry, or chilled white wine – he might say, 'Have a glass of wine' (meaning champagne) – nothing to rot up the palate, unless he were an alcoholic, whereupon he would keep topping up everyone's drinks, to the frenzy of his wife who is longing to dine. Harry doesn't taste wine in restaurants to see if it's all right, just swings his nose back and forth in the glass to make sure it is not corked. He tends to drink at home rather than in pubs, but if he went into a pub, he wouldn't feel it necessary to buy a round of drinks to curry favour with the locals. He doesn't need their approval. He probably owns the place anyway. Mr Nouveau-Richards finds himself picking up the bill far more often, both in 'resteronts' and bars. Tightness with drink isn't entirely to do with class, although the working classes are very generous, and so are the merry-tocracy because they want an excuse to fill their own glasses.

The lower middles who enjoy dressing up in hired dinner jackets and 'taking wane' with each other at Rotarian ladies nights, are given to euphemisms like 'partaking of liquid refreshment', 'imbibing potations', and 'just a wee dram'. Howard Weybridge is very up on bar terminology, he has 'snorters,' 'snifters', 'ones for the road', 'hooch', 'noggins' and 'a few jars'.

The Weybridge set are also very keen on barbecue parties. Samantha tried them and gave up, it just meant midge bites, charred pork chops in the flower beds, everyone losing their glasses in the dark when they were half full, and wanting new full ones, so Samantha had to spend the evening frenziedly washing up, and her face got so covered in smuts from the barbecue, she looked like a token black.

Among the working classes, the great divide between the rough and respectable is summed up in two words: 'the drink'. One of the reasons for the heavy drinking of the poor in the nineteenth century was that drink took away the misery and the appetite, and gin and beer were much cheaper than food. It was Nathaniel Hawthorne's opinion that the poor in England could only maintain their animal heat by means of alcohol, without which the harsh climate would destroy them. Today, when gin is so prohibitively expensive, Mr Definitely-Disgusting drinks beer because television advertisements, extolling the male cameraderie and virility that will stem from it, tell him to.

14 APPEARANCES

When in Crimplene my Julie goes.

Clothes

In the past fifteen years we've been through a complete sartorial revolution. There was the self-expressionism of the late sixties, when everyone did their own thing, followed by unisex and jeans for all classes and all sexes, followed by the punk revolt of the late seventies. And now, as Christopher Sykes has pointed out, after the age of turmoil, an age of conservative consolidation has set in. As a result, it is almost impossible to tell what class the young are from their appearance.

On the one hand you have the tear-away from Eton wearing polyester trousers and shirts with key motifs to irritate the establishment, on the other the working-class undergraduate, determined to identify himself with the establishment, who smothers himself in college regalia. The hacking jacket has just about filtered down the class system to Sharon Definitely-Disgusting, while Fiona Stow-Crat turns up at a party with bright purple hair wearing a leopard skin rayon jump suit and gold stiletto-heeled boots. And although the upper classes usually settle down sartorially with marriage, I met an extremely grand, much divorced old woman recently wearing orange satin drainpipes, and a white T-shirt with 'I AM A VIRGIN' printed across the bust. Meanwhile the majority of parvenu Tory ladies living in Weybridge, terrified of betraying their origins by putting a foot wrong, dress exactly like the Queen.

Recently I went to a lunch party, where some Americans had been invited to meet a duke's daughter. The daughter of the house who was middle-class, called Rosemary, and equally apprehensive about meeting a member of the aristocracy, wore a tweed coat and skirt, flat shoes, a pale blue cashmere jersey, and pearls. The duke's daughter roared up from a drinks party on a motor bike wearing a leather skirt, fish-net stockings, a tight black sweater, and punk eye make-up. The Americans who arrived just after her made a justifiable mistake.

There is a rather touching story told me by one of the Queen's dressmakers. The Queen was visiting his shop, when she admired a very beautiful evening dress, glittering with crystal and rhinestone. When both the dressmaker and her lady-in-waiting urged her to buy it, she shook her head wistfully saying, wasn't it a pity, but really she hadn't got anywhere smart enough to wear it. What she probably meant was that it was too tarty and glamorously ostentatious.

Traditionally the aristocracy survived because they were the wiliest of the tribe, and knew when to lie low. Let the Nouveau-Riche swagger around in their finery, showing off their wealth, and getting their heads chopped off by royalty, or later by revolutionaries. Harry Stow-Crat's ancestors were prepared to dress up in their peer-robes when the King commanded it, otherwise they camouflaged themselves and blended in with their surroundings. Thus today Harry is only copying his forbears, when he wears a dark suit in the grey of London, and green, dung-coloured, or brown clothes in the country. There was an additional reason for this. Harry's ancestors lived on what they shot, hunted and fished. It was easier to land your prey whether it was a girl in London, or a salmon in the Tay if you were indistinguishable from your background.

If there is one single class indicator therefore where clothes are concerned – it is colour. The upper classes tend not to wear crude garish, clashing colours. Not for them the da-glo oranges or reds, the jarring lime greens and citrus yellows, the royal blues, mauves and cyclamen pinks. A friend of mine was once witheringly written orf as 'the sort of girl who wears shocking pink in the country'. Mrs Nouveau-Richards can pore over *Tatler* and 'Jennifers Diary', and find out exactly when and in what styles different clothes should be worn, but while the photographs go on being printed in black and white, she'll never get the colours quite right.

Traditionally, too, because the upper classes believe in supporting their own industries, they regard anything that's lived: wool, leather, silk, cotton, as all right, but anything man-made, crimplene, polyester, or plastic as decidedly vulgar.

At a meeting of the Historic Houses Association, Edward Montague the departing president and Clive Jenkins the trade unionist, wore identical clothes – dark blue suits, slightly lighter blue plain shirts, and dark blue ties with red spots. But, because Clive Jenkins' materials were all man-made fibres, they looked somehow much shinier, and less substantial.

The upper classes, as Michael Fish has said, also believe it is morally wrong to buy more clothes than you have to. So as clothes have to last they have to be conservative and of decent stuff. It is a point of pride for Harry at forty to be able to get into the same trousers and coat he wore at Eton.

In fact the higher up the social scale you go, the taller and more finely boned people tend to be, because of diet, work patterns and extra vitamins over the years. Harry has no bum, Caroline no bum or bust, both are tall and thin, so their clothes, which have the advantage of being very well cut, tend to look good on them, and set them apart. Leanness, as Mrs Gaskell pointed out, is a great aid to gentility. Even if Georgie horrifies his father by buying an orf-the-peg suit, he'll probably get away with it because of an etiolated figure and self-confidence. Aristocrats, even if they live in London, and have little opportunity to take exercise, seldom allow themselves to put on weight.

Harry Stow-Crat is therefore very conservative in his dress. But from the way he describes what he's wearing, 'black tie' for a dinner party, 'white tie' for an official occasion, or a 'morning coat' for a wedding, you'd think he was going about half-naked. One asristocrat I know got caught out very badly in this way. He was going to spend a weekend at a very grand house in the country, and asked his batman to pack his dinner jacket. It was only when he was dressing for dinner, he discovered his batman had taken him at his word, and only put in the coat. In the end he was reduced to borrowing a pair of trousers from his host, which were midnight blue, half his size, and about three times too large in the waist. No one made any comment at dinner or afterwards. Harry Stow-Crat's own dinner jacket is almost green with age and wear and tear. He would never call it a 'dinner suit', or have one in midnight blue, particularly in terylene with braiding. Georgie however might easily wear a different coloured velvet tie, but not a waterfall of duck-egg blue frills like Jison Richards.

Harry, as has already been pointed out, would wear a dark suit in London, but he wouldn't call it a 'lounge suit', or a 'three piece suit', or a 'business suit'. At the back he would have a slit (Bryan Teale calls them 'vents'). The buttons on the sleeve would undo, and there would be a real buttonhole for a carnation in the collar, which he could do up in bad weather on a button hidden under the collar on the other side. He would still wear fly buttons, rather than zips to protect his member for carrying on the line, but Georgie would probably have a zip, just as he might easily wear a leather belt to hold up his trousers. Harry would wear braces, which he would take off before removing his coat. His shirts would be striped, checked or plain coloured, and never have pictures, patterns or initials on them – initials on anything are considered very vulgar. Harry would never wear a striped tie with a dark suit, but he might wear a Guards tie with a tweed coat in the country. Georgie probably wouldn't bother to wear a tie at all, but it is interesting that when the tieless fashion was at its height in the late seventies, girls started one-upping each other by wearing the smart old school, club and regimental ties their fathers and brothers had jettisoned.

Harry would wear one 'han'k'rchif' (not 'hand-ker-cheef') in his trouser pocket, and another in his breast pocket – not up his sleeve. But it would not match his tie, and it would be casually arranged just to show a tip of a corner and bit of fold. It would not be folded across in a white rectangle, as though, as someone bitchily said, 'You'd forgotten to post your pools envelope' (although Prince Philip wears it this way), nor in a neat right angle, nor in a made-up mountain range on a piece of cardboard, like Bryan Teale. Mr Definitely-Disgusting wears a handkerchief on his head at the seaside.

Pottering about at home, Harry would probably wear old corduroy (pronounced 'cord'roy') or whipcord trousers, and a tweed jacket, which he would refer to as a 'tweed coat', or, as he called it at Eton a 'change coat'. He would never use the expression 'sports jacket'. He would never wear a blazer, in fact he tells Georgie he would have been thrown out of the Guards for using such a word. He might occasionally wear a polo neck sweater, but never in pastel colours or white and always in wool. He would call it a 'polo neck jersey', because the upper classes think the words 'jumper', 'sweater', 'pullover', 'slipover', 'woollie', 'cardigan', and particularly 'cardi' extremely vulgar. He would never wear a mackintosh in London nor call it a 'raincoat', or even worse a 'showerproof'. He would never carry an umbrella in the country (only vicars are allowed this privilege) except at point-to-points or the races, or anywhere where a woman might be dressed up and need cover – on the moors they can drown. The umbrella would be black and without a tassel. He would wear gum boots in green or black, but never call them 'wellington boots', or, even worse, 'wellies'. If he wore an overcoat he would refer to it as a 'coat', or a 'covert coat' (pronounced 'cover' – to fox the unwary).

If Georgie wore just a shirt and trousers, he would take off his tie, undo the top button and roll his sleeves up to below the elbow. Mr Definitely-Disgusting would do the same except that he'd roll the sleeve up above the elbow. Bryan Teale would leave his tie on and his shirt sleeves buttoned up. (What does it matter if his cuffs get dirty? Jen can drip dry them in a trice tonight.)

If Harry wore a signet ring, which is unlikely, as he doesn't need these kind of status props, it would have a crest, and be on the little finger on his left hand. Georgie might wear a wedding ring merely to irritate the upper middles who all wear signet rings with crests, on their little fingers, and think it's awful to have rings, with initials particularly, on any other fingers.

Harry would probably still decant his cigarettes into a cigarette case, although Georgie wouldn't bother. Not long ago one officer in the Guards got frightfully bawled out for offering the Duke of Gloucester cigarettes in a packet. 'You're not in the garage now', said his Commanding Officer in a furious aside. Mr Definitely-Disgusting smokes his Woodbines between finger and thumb to eke them out, and curled in the palm of the hand to hide them from the foreman. Howard Weybridge and Colonel Upward smoke pipes, Mr Nouveau-Richards smokes very expensive cigars and leaves the label on, like a signet ring. Georgie Stow-Crat would certainly smoke in the street if he felt like it. His mother would not. Harry Stow-Crat keeps his money in a 'notecase' not a 'wallet'.

Gideon Upward, trying to be trendy but slightly out of date, would still be squeezing himself into jeans. He might wear a blazer but not with a badge, more likely a corduroy or a velvet coat, or last year's denim, which Samantha bought him: it has four buttons and a high neck and makes him feel slightly silly. Since Zacharius and Thalia went to boarding school he can't afford to buy suits any more so he wears his old ones. All his Christmas presents are chosen by Samantha, usually sweaters from Marks and Spencer, in colours which suit Samantha and which Samantha wears during the week, so they have two bumps in front when Gideon puts them on at the week-end. He has reluctantly started to wear part nylon socks, because Samantha shrinks his wool ones to Action Man size in a few weeks. He knows that shirt collars ought always to be worn inside a coat and a sweater, and he never wears a hat although when he goes shooting occasionally, his grander friends force him into a cap, saying: 'You'll be frightfully cold, Gideon'.

Howard Weybridge dresses straighter than straight, not unlike Colonel Upward. Howard wears regimental ties, golf club ties, the Hurlingham Club tie, and an old school tie if he's got one. Occasionally he wears a paisley scarf, which he refers to as a 'cravat' with a brass scarf ring. At the pub he wears a very clean blazer with an Esher Rugby Club badge, and slightly too new cavalry twill trousers, although the nearest he's got to the cavalry is an hour-long horseback ride through the pine trees in Oxshott woods. He has never gone in for wide trousers, but his suede ankle boots are slightly too ginger. When he goes to Twickenham he wears a sheepskin coat, often with brown fur, and an assortment of hats, Russian fur, flat caps, and deerstalkers. 'A hat designed for shooting Scottish deer/ Though Haywards be the only Heath he's near.' wrote Paul Jennings. He wears huge riding macs, and his spectacles have no bottom rims to them. In bed he wears a red wool nightshirt from Bentalls, grandiosely called a 'sleep coat'.

Mr Nouveau-Richards wears too much jewellery, huge gold cuff-links and a huge gold watch. He likes wearing bow ties so he can show glittering collar studs on his shirts, but if he wears a tie, he puts on a huge gold tie pin. In his early working-class

'I am your demon lover in my new red sleep coat.'

days, like Mr Definitely-Disgusting, he wore a tie clip, and
sleeve garters. He wears a camelhair coat with a belt, and in the
evening changes into a burgundy velvet smoking jacket, with
his initials in frogging.

Jison Richards, as a member of the telly-stocracy, wears
three-piece suits in white with a black shirt and no tie, or very
light blue suits, with the jackets so waisted and with such long
slits at the back they look like miniskirts. He used always to
wear very fat, flamboyant ties borrowed from Wardrobe at the
B.B.C. but the knot is getting slimmer. He often leaves his
make-up on after a programme when he goes to the pub to
remind people he's a telly star.

The spiralist who is climbing very fast, but hasn't got the
same kind of money as Jison Richards, studies the fashion
magazines slavishly and co-ordinates carefully. He might select
a neat check jacket to go with plain beige slacks, add a 'wesket'
to match the slacks, and the whole ensemble can double up as a
business suit during the week. He's also very keen on herring
bone suits, which, worn with a sporty cravat, will double up as a
sports suit for leisure wear. He likes British accessories, a jaunty
check cap matching the check insets of his high button jacket or

a donegal tweed hat with the brim turned down, worn with a matching coat and 'holld-all'. He's also heavily into luggage. Last year's gold plastic bag on a coathanger has been replaced this year by a 'travel robe', in tartan which has a handle enabling him to carry all his co-ordinates vertical. Nattiness reigns.

Bryan Teale is dressed from top to toe in drip-dry clothes. One day Bryan thinks Jen may well put him through the washing machine under the setting for 'whites lightly soiled'. Bryan wears burgundy crimplene slacks which never fit because Jen brought them by Mail order in the *Daily Mail*, rust cable stitch cardigans, and cavalry twill-style trousers in brown/black/lovat/fawn in 100 per cent washable polyester. He wears his rotary badge on his lapel. Instead of pants he wears tartan jockey shorts. He also wears striped ties which the shop categorizes as a 'Club tie', but which have an old-school-tie look, 'that's very nice'. Bryan also has a whole robe unit in the bedroom for his car wear: woolly hats, zip-up car coats, fake sheepskin coats for cold days, overalls to save his good clothes when he's lying under the car, and driving gloves with holes in the back.

Gideon Upward changes out of a suit into old clothes, when he gets home or at the weekends. Mr Definitely-Disgusting changes out of old clothes into one of Gideon's old suits, which is a bit shiny but still has plenty of wear in it, that Mrs Definitely-Disgusting bought at a jumble sale. She likes a good fight at the jumble on the weekend. Indoors Mr Definitely-Disgusting always removes his coat, and sits in a waistcoat, and collarless shirt, any shoes he wears inside the house will be called 'slippers'. His bedroom slippers he calls 'carpet slippers'. If he wears a shirt with a collar with a coat, he arranges the collar neatly outside the jacket. He always keeps his hat on in the pub.

Apart from the fact that Caroline Stow-Crat never wears man-made fibres except for stockings, it is far more difficult to tell the difference between her clothes and Mrs Weybridge's, and even more difficult to distinguish Fiona Stow-Crat from Sharon Definitely-Disgusting. Caroline has a good dark fur coat for cold days in London, but would never wear a fur stole, and particularly never call it a 'wrap'. Since sheepskin coats have sunk down the scale, the upper classes of both sexes wear a hideous quilted rubber coat called a 'husky', not unlike Mrs Definitely-Disgusting's dressing gown, except it is nylon and khaki. In the future we have to expect 'husky knickers' to keep out the cold, which sound as though they'd be golden and furry and matted with arctic snow, but turn out to be over-trousers.

Caroline would always tend to underdress. Except for a watch, or a small brooch, 'nothing but pearls before sundown' would be her maxim. Her pearls would have little knots between each pearl. (The world is divided into have-knots, and have-nets.) At night she would wear a lot of very good, inherited jewellery, which would add a lot of light to her face. She would never wear modern jewellery, and particularly never refer to it as 'costume jewellery'. After she'd been through her wild deb stage – and certainly after she was married – she wouldn't show cleavages, or wear miniskirts, whatever the fashion. Nor would she wear see-through shirts. (She thinks the word 'blouse' is very common.)

Caroline would also prefer the expression 'coat and skirt' and although Fiona might say 'suit', neither of them would ever say 'two-piece', or 'costume' or 'skirt suit'. Caroline might wear trousers, but never very tight, and never a trouser suit. Her shoes would be plain, and never too high, or two-tone, or decorated with bows, or with peep toes. Wedge heels and platform heels and coloured boots, particularly drum majorette white boots, would also be out. She used to prefer the word 'frock' to 'dress', but since Samantha Upward's taken up 'frock' as being more old fashioned and Kate Greenaway, Caroline's swinging back to 'dress' again. Other expressions she doesn't use are 'ball gown', 'hostess gown', 'evening gown', 'housecoat', or 'bathrobe' instead of 'dressing gown'. As she has very good legs she doesn't need the flattery of dark stockings, but if she did she'd wear navy blue with blue shoes, rather than black which she thinks are a bit tarty.

Samantha Upward is much more untidy in appearance. She is just emerging from her Third World ethnic phase, and still has a slopppy bra-less, long-straight-haired, intellectual earth mother look. She's not as good at staying on diets, or as naturally thin as Caroline Stow-Crat. She found those kaftans, and peasant dresses almost better than Gideon's sweaters for covering up a multitude of tums.

At dinner parties she's weighed down with ethnic jewellery picked up from various Oxfam, or African project shops (which is the nearest she gets to abroad, now they're so poor). The difference between the upper middle classes and the lower middle, is admirably illustrated by Shirley Williams and Margaret Thatcher. As Rebecca West pointed out to me in an interview: 'Mrs Thatcher has one great disadvantage – she is a daughter of the people and looks trim as a daughter of the people desires to be. Shirley Williams has such an advantage over her because she's a member of the upper middle classes and can achieve that distraught kitchen sink revolutionary look that one cannot get unless one's been to a really good school.' The upper middles tend to be untidy, not only because they're more secure than the lower middles, because they like to look vaguely intellectual, and, because, unlike Caroline Stow-Crat, they don't feel they ought to set an example to anyone.

The middle middles try to dress just like Mrs Thatcher, the Queen and Grace Kelly, very upper classical. Eileen Weybridge shops at Dickins and Jones, Peter Jones or Bentalls of Kingston. She wears velvet jackets over a shirtwaister pleated dress, or a blouse with a pussy cat tie bow and a pleated skirt. When it rains she puts on a scarf decorated with snaffles, and horses' heads which she thinks give it a 'very nice country look'. She wears a camel hair coat with saddle stitching in slightly too dark a shade, and a brown melusine bowler hat for shopping. Her shoes are in slightly too orange a tan, and she spends days and days finding a matching 'handbag'. She rather lets the side down by buying an emerald green trouser suit, with a matching peaked cap for Twickenham. In the evening she wears a polyester floral shirtwaister bang on the knee. She would never show bare arms after thirty-five.

Mrs Nouveau-Richards, coming from working-class origins, likes to dress up whenever she goes out, even to the shops. In the evening, she wears white or silver fox furs and a great deal of very flash modern jewellery, particularly diamonds. On her dresses she has lots of spangles, and sequins, and her figure is as heavily corsetted as her ve-owell sounds but inclined to break out above her stays like an overflowing ice cream cone. She wears long coloured gloves with bracelets outside and invariably very high-heeled shoes with straps round the ankles, and a spangled butterfly or a flower in her hair, which is peroxide blonde (just like Diana Dors). For coffee mornings, she wears a prawn cocktail frock.

Jen Teale, like Bryan lives in drip-dry co-ordinates – little terylene tops which she's always pulling down over the 'derrière' of her terylene slacks, when she is doing anything strenuous. As she hates untidy hair, she puts on one of those scarves with a fitted pleated centre, for tying under the hair. She wears rain hats which match her raincoat, and always carries a plastic transparent concertina hood in her bag in case it rains. Everything is washed after one wearing, and she never buys from jumble sales, until she's 'hand washed' them first. She always wears a bra and a panti-girdle, not only to keep Bryan and others out, but to make her figure as anonymous as possible. She's very keen on capes, because they don't reveal a single outline, and yet look neat. (Mrs Whitehouse wore one recently for probably the same reason, when flying to America, and was described in the *Daily Mirror* as 'The Caped Crusader'.)

If Jen Teale wears a transparent shirt, she always wears a full-length petticoat, and a bra underneath, so all you see is rigging. Even when she relaxes in the evening her primrose brushed nylon house coat is worn over all her underclothes. Although she's not a catholic, she wears a gold cross round her neck to remind people she's a 'nice girl'. For weddings her 'outfit', is a navy crimplene two-piece trimmed with lemon, bought from the Littlewood's catalogue. Her uniform with a summer dress is a long white orlon cardigan.

Mrs Definitely-Disgusting only started wearing trousers a few years ago, when she was cleaning Samantha Upward's house. Like Caroline Stow-Crat she always wears a scarf when she goes out, but hers is in shiny rayon, and made in Hong Kong. Like Jen Teale she buys by mail order, it's the only post she gets, filling in coupons in the *TV Times* while Mrs Definitely-Disgusting watches 'Match of the Day'. When she tries it on in the privacy of her own home, she finds the princess line dress in dusky pink/african violet two-tone floral, in uncrushable polyester 100 per cent washable with figure flattering panels, doesn't look nearly as good as it did in the *Daily Mirror*. Like Harry Stow-Crat, Mrs Definitely-Disgusting has a change coat, in new French navy with a nylon fur collar. She needed it to cheer herself up: her old burgundy barathea used to clash with her 'ot flushes.

Hair

How people wear their hair is an invaluable social litmus with men – less so with women. Although there are exceptions (Lord Weymouth may wear his hair long and in a million pigtails; Lord Lichfield, at least in his photographs, looks like a hairdresser), most of the aristocracy if they're over thirty-five brush their hair backwards, with the parting directly north of the outer corner of the eye, two wings above the ears, and cut just above the collar. Harry Stow-Crat wears his hair very shiny, probably as a result of Nanny's hundred brushes a night. Because he doesn't have much stress worrying about himself like the middle classes, or tend to work so hard, he seldom goes bald. If he did, however, he would never brush his hair forward to cover a receding hair-line, or in strands over a bald patch, or part the hair above the ears, and brush the remaining hair over his bald cranium like anchovies over a hard-boiled egg.

Aristocrats seldom wear their hair over their ears, Mr Heath dropped a class or two visually when instead of brushing his wings back, he trained them forward in two tendrils over his ears. Nor would Harry Stow-Crat cut his hair short in front so it fell in a cowslick like Dr David Owen, or in a serpentine ripple like Lord Mancroft, or in a just breaking fall over wave like the Davids Jay and Steel. His sideboards would stop level with the entrance to the eardrum. Neither he nor Georgie ever comb their hair in public.

Georgie Stow-Crat might well have a fringe – not to hide a receding hairline but because it was trendy. He would, however, start off brushing his hair back, and letting it fall forward, and it would be so well cut, and his features so lean and finely drawn, that the effect would never be like the lacquered thatched roof on top of a cottage-loaf of the spiralist. At the moment there seems to be a trend towards the Edward Fox short-back-and-sides look, (inspired by his television appearance as Edward VIII). So soon, no doubt, Georgie will be looking just like Harry again.

Harry has his hair cut at least once a month at Trumpers when he comes to London. He refers to the man who cut his hair as his 'hairdresser', and asks him to 'wash' never to 'shampoo' his hair. He buys one bottle of Bay Rum each visit, it has a nozzle on it like Angostura bitters in cocktail bars. His hairdresser clips the hair out of his nostrils, but not his ears.

Gideon Upward's hair is still longer and more straggly than Zacharius's (because that used to be trendy in the late sixties). But it's getting shorter. He goes to the barber, when he finds that his shirt collars are getting dirty on both sides. The barber is invariably Cypriot and near the office. After the perfunctory snipping and primping Gideon is asked if he wants 'anything else', which means French letters, always prominently displayed alongside metal combs, razor blades, and various cheap male toiletries. Gideon secretly admires Michael Heseltine who claims only to have his golden mane cut on quarter days. Occasionally in the privacy of his own bathroom Gideon will brush his hair forward like Melvyn Bragg, screw up his eyes, and wonder when he'll ever get an opportunity to use one of those French letters.

The only men clinging to long straggly hair are middle-class left-wing trendies. As a reaction, the right-wing Howard Weybridge, has his hair cut short. So does Mr Nouveau-Richards, but having spent so much of his youth working hard to get to the top, he tries to stay young with Grecian 2000. Jison Richards, now he's a member of the telly-stocracy brushes his blond streaked locks firmly forward to hide any incipient wrinkles across his fawhead, and round the eyes. He has it cut at Smiles, and washes and blow-dries it himself before television appearances, and keeps it in place with all sorts of toiletries. If he is not pulling a bird, he might even sleep in a hair net. He ages ten years in a high wind.

Mr Definitely-Disgusting's hair is seldom cut, and seldom washed. It falls out early, and what remains is coiled in oily strands inside some sort of headdress. He wears it very short.

Dive Definitely-Disgusting has a perm like a footballer. When it's just been done, he looks like a Tory lady – he always combs his hair in public.

Mrs Definitely-Disgusting is also coiffure mad – not only does she help in Mario's salon next to the chip shop on the weekend, but most Fridays goes spangled peroxide blonde and bouffant so that she and Mr Definitely-Disgusting can be seen in all their glory at the pub music night on Friday evening, or the Working Men's club. This bouffant remains till the end of

'Well if you 'aven't got time for the wash, bleach and perm we can just give it a spray of this.'

the week, when it looks like a haystack ravaged by gales. I once heard a hairdresser claim that she has on occasions demolished such edifices only to find them full of a kind of maggots which feed on the lacquer. If Mrs Definitely-Disgusting is not bouffant she wears curlers around the house and in the street, because it's cheaper than drying it by the gas fire and because Mr Definitely-Disgusting's on night shift, and sleeps during the day. This, however, is going out with affluence.

Jen Teale cuts Bryan's hair to save money – likewise that of the kiddies, who are all drenched in Vosene to ward off the dreaded dandruff (Caroline Stow-Crat calls it 'scurf'). Bryan has a shower every day which flattens and brushes his hair forward automatically. If he is a rep and goes to conferences he has a razor cut. Jen wears her hair short because it's more hygienic, and so much cooler in summer. She has a curly fringe halfway down her 'fawhead', and the side bits swept behind her ears, a style Caroline Stow-Crat would think very common. Once a year when she's feeling skittish she scrapes her hair into two bunches above her ears.

Eileen Weybridge has hair exactly like the Queen, so does

her mother, with an additional blue rinse on her grey hair. Samantha's mother has hair like the Queen but slightly looser, more like Mrs Thatcher, and she thinks blue rinses are very vulgar.

Samantha has a fringe on the eybrows, and wears her hair, long, straight and mousy to match her dirndl skirt. She doesn't wash it more than once a week because it would destroy the natural oils. Occasionally she puts on a henna rinse, which Gideon is supposed to admire when she stands under the light. Now she's got bored with the women's movement, she shaves her legs with Gideon's razor, which she leaves clogged in the bedroom. She shaves under the arms too, but smells like a polecat when excited, because she wants to be natural and not use those horrible deodorants.

Caroline Stow-Crat's hair is worn with flick-ups and sometimes an Alice band. Like Harry she has the sort of bone-structures that can take hair worn orf the face – she doesn't need to have a forelock to pull to anyone – but recently she has taken to wearing a quarter fringe on either side, and Harry hasn't grumbled about it. She has her hair done quite often, partly for something to do and partly to catch up on back numbers of *The Tatler* and *Harper's*. Her hair is never in very good condition, as it spends too much time under a headscarf or a hat. A few years ago she would never have dreamt of dying her hair, but streaking looks so natural, and it does mean at least seven hours at the hairdressers looking at *Tatler* and *Harper's*. Her hair often smells of cigarette smoke from going to too many yocktail parties given by the Deputy Lord Lieutenant, Harry. She will go grey suddenly.

Fiona Stow-Crat washes her collar-bone length hair every day, so it always looks slightly untidy, and brushes it back in two wings like Harry. She has been known to dye it extraordinary colours.

On the whole the aristocracy's hair is a sort of light brown, upper-class mouse. If Harry said one of his friends had brought a 'blonde' to a party, the expression would be slightly dismissive because if she were anyone, Harry would know her anyway. He would talk about 'a pretty girl with dark hair', rather than 'an attractive brunette'. And if a girl had red hair, he'd call it red, he wouldn't have any truck with expressions like 'auburn' or 'copper'.

Faces

The upper classes, as has already been pointed out, are tall and thin, and have narrow stoats' heads with very few bumps to them.

Their faces therefore tend to be narrow, with the skin more finely drawn over the nose and jaw bone. Their eyes turn down rather than up at the corners, and although not very large, tend to be bigger than their mouths, which look not unlike the private parts of a female ferret. Often these hang open because they're not ashamed of their teeth. Big rubber tyre mouths, and large rolling eyes, give a face a very plebeian look. Used to very cold houses, and an outdoor life, Harry Stow-Crat has the kind of delicate pink and white skin, which flushes up at parties and in hot restaurants. From lack of stress, he tends to age more slowly than the other classes. Because he has a poker face you are less aware of his wrinkles. At fifty, he may look thirty-five, but when he laughs or gets angry his face suddenly breaks into hundreds of lines like a dried up river bed. Harry and Caroline both have very long thin feet.

As you go down the classes people tend to be bulkier in the face particularly round the jaw and chin. Mrs Definitely-Disgusting's mouth disappears altogether once she's lost her teeth.

15 VOICES

*'The men of Gilead said unto him: "Art thou an Ephramite?"
If he say Nay, then said they unto him: "Say now Shibboleth
and he said Sibboleth, for he could not frame to pronounce it
right. Then they took him and slew him."'*

The Book of Job

When people talk about class barriers, they often mean sound
barriers. The story of the poor Ephramite is one of the saddest
in the Bible, but such a universal one, that the word Shibboleth
has passed into the English language, and has come to mean
among other things the criterion or catchword of a social group.
Thus Jen Teale would have a little eye-meet with Bryan if they
heard Mr Definitely-Disgusting talking about an 'orse, and
Samantha and Gideon Upward would immediately identify a
lower caste if they heard Eileen Weybridge talking about zebras
with a short 'e', or asking for 'a portion of gâteau'.

Your pronunciation and the words you use, are so crucial for
determining your class, that the subject has been already
touched on in numerous occasions throughout the book. For
despite the egalitarian revolution and the embracing of
crypto-working-class accents by some of the upper and middle
classes, a person is still often mocked because of the way he
speaks – this very afternoon, shouting across the road to an old
colonel, I reduced two youths in anoraks to fits of laughter. I
could hear them mimicking me all the way up the street. As
Bernard Shaw said in *Pygmalion*, 'Every time an Englishman
opens his mouth another Englishman despises him.'

Things have certainly improved, however. Thirty years ago
the announcers on the wireless still solemnly put on dinner

jackets every night to read the nine o'clock news, and spoke with an accent called 'B.B.C. English', which was actually upper middle-class (they enunciated far too well to be truly upper-class). Every young actor, who wanted to get on, ironed out his accent and tried to talk just the same. Pitman's agreed with them, so every secretary learning shorthand discovered that 'bath' and 'class' were pronounced with a long 'a', because the squiggles depicting them went on the line rather than above it as they would have done if the 'a' had been flat.

Then came the cultural revolution of the sixties and today, as a result, the English spoken by the B.B.C. (especially on television) has dropped to somewhere between middle and lower middle with dozens of Regional Bosanquets being matey and calling everyone 'luv', and female interviewers with flat accents talking about 'Ufrica' and 'bunk balances'.

What has also happened in the last twenty-five years is that people no longer despise you if you have a strong regional or lower-class accent, so long as you're successful and amusing. Everyone adores Twiggy, and the Campari girl, Zandra Rhodes, and Janet Street Porter are accepted everywhere. This social and cultural change has been described by Geoffrey Gorer as follows: 'The young now like to call themselves upper working-class. Twenty years ago, the bright young of working-class origin with intellectual gifts or talents would have been likely to acquire a B.B.C. accent and pass as upper middle-class. Today they feel no need to hide their accent. They are the new trend setters.'

Maybe. But if these new trend setters were not successful, I doubt if Caroline Stow-Crat, or Samantha Upward, (and certainly Eileen Weybridge) would ask them to dinner. And I suspect that as the country swings back and becomes more reactionary, not only Janet Street Porter and Zandra Rhodes, but all those upper and middle classes with their flat 'a's may begin to sound a bit dated.

In the present climate what people do object to now is the old practice of people changing their accents, as poor Mr Heath learnt to his cost. Everyone thinks politicians are dishonest but when they have 'dishonest' voices they are doubly suspect. Whenever he appeared on television, all classes sat listening to the ironed-out vowel sounds and the slow, low delivery (designed so that every word can be enunciated carefully) and gleefully waited for the first slip. Mr Heath's 'e-out' must have lost him thousands of votes.

But for all of us the whole subject is relative. All English people dismiss upper-class shibboleths they don't use themselves as 'out-dated', or 'snobbish', while still regarding any word they themselves consider vulgar as 'barbarous'. Thus *I* think the word 'luncheon' is pedantic, but the word 'phone' is vulgar. Whereas my children will probably think 'telephone' is pedantic.

Questions of accent are even more elusive. In a recent survey, amongst the English fifty per cent of the people interviewed said they *didn't have any accent*, a statement with which the class above (and very likely the classes below them, too) would have certainly disagreed. In fact everyone has an accent from the Queen downward. It may not be regional, but there is certainly an upper-class, an upper middle and a middle-class accent, which are all quite different.

The trouble with the upper-class is they're inclined to change their vocabulary just to outsmart the lower classes. Now the word 'loo' has sifted down and been taken up by *Daily Mirror* readers, the uppers have reverted to 'lavatory' again. And you could feel the horrified frisson among the upper middles when Princess Anne was suddenly heard to say 'ee-ther' in a television interview. They'd studied *Noblesse Oblige*, they knew the upper classes said 'eye-ther': it was really too bad.

English snobbery about regional accents seems to be based on the proposition that they are O.K. if they're far enough away from London. No one minds Irish, Welsh and Scottish accents half so much as Birmingham or South London ones. West Country and East Anglian are preferred to 'home counties' suburban. If the B.B.C. wants a voice to represent the people, however, they go North and use Colin Welland.

'I seem,' he said recently, 'To have cornered the market in the Common Touch.'

Harry Stow-Crat has a very distinctive accent. Because of his poker face, he only uses vowels that will hardly move his face at all. One opens one's mouth far less if one says 'hice' rather then 'house', and 'aw' rather than the short 'o'. Thus Harry automatically says 'orf', 'corsts', 'gorn', 'clorth' and 'lorst'. This is of course old pronunciation: 'Ride a cock horse, to Banbury Crorse'. Harry also moves his face less by clipping his words:

'If "loo" is out now, there's "bathroom", "gents", "ladies", "convenience", "lav", "water-closet", "WC", "bog", "john", "can", "heads", "latrines", "privy", "little girls' room", "smallest room", "powder room", "khasi", "rears".... There must be *something* we can call it....'

hence 'Lond'ndri', 'mag'str't' and 'Charl't' instead of 'Londonderry', 'mag-istr-ate', and 'Charl-otte'. He often uses a short 'e' for 'ay' like the old man who went into the village shop and asked for some 'pepper'.

'Red pepper or black pepper, sir,' asked the shopkeeper.

'Don't be ridiculous,' snapped the old man 'I mean lavatory pepper.'

The upper-class accent may alter, but they are united in their absence of euphemism or circumlocution. They don't say 'pleased to meet you', because they don't know if they are and wouldn't feel the need to resort to such flattery. They are not arch. They would never talk about 'botties' or the 'little girls' room', or ask, as Howard Weybridge might, if they can go and 'point Percy at the Porcelain'.

Samantha Upward enunciates more clearly than the Stow-Crats. Her features are more mobile, she smiles more, her voice is less clipped. She is also less direct, talking about 'having help' in the house rather than 'servants', and saying 'how's your glass' rather than 'would you like another drink?' Because she is slightly unsure of herself she would probably cling to words

like 'wireless', and 'children' long after the upper classes
were saying 'radio' and 'kids'. On the other hand she would
clip her words far more than Eileen Weybridge – saying
''dmire, ''s'cessful' and 'c'mpete' rather than 'ad-mire', 'suck-
sessful', and 'com-pete'. She wouldn't say 'lorst' or 'corst',
but she would say 'sawlt' and 'awlter'. Dive Definitely-
Disgusting couldn't distinguish Samantha's voice from
Caroline Stow-Crat's, but he would think Caroline sounded
more commanding, and Samantha more hearty and jolly
hockeysticks.

If you met Howard Weybridge you probably wouldn't be
able immediately to tell what part of the world he came from:
his voice would be very careful so as not to slip – a sort of
Colonel Bogus. Mrs Weybridge would articulate far more than
Samantha Upward – she would talk about 'coff-ee' and 'syst-
im', like Mr Healey who is very Weybridge, and probably says
'higgledee-piggledee' between each word. Eileen Weybridge
also says 'act-riss' (the flat 'a' brigade say 'uctress'. Harry
Stow-Crat says 'actr's'). There was one Howard Weybridge
living in Yorkshire who had a marvellously 'haw haw' voice,
but slipped once at a dance when a fat teenager doing the
Dashing White Sergeant with much vigour stepped back on to
his foot and induced him to let out a most uncharacteristic yell
of 'booger'.

Enough has been said about Jen Teale's refinement. All the
main lower middle genteelisms: 'commence', 'pardon', 'serviette', 'perfume', 'gâteau', 'toilet', probably became currency
to show off the speaker's familiarity with the French language.
When it comes to 'o' sounds, though, it is as if the English
language had been deliberately invented to fox the Teales and
the Nouveau-Richards. In fact, I defy anyone to say the following list of words very fast three times without slipping: 'Dolphin, dolt, doldrums, revolving, revolting, involved, holiday,
hold, holly, holm, whole, golf, gold.' Class is a sort of sadistic
'histoire d'O'.

Mr Nouveau-Richards packs Mrs Nouveau-Richards and all
his children off to elocution lessons when he becomes mayor,
and takes a W.E.A. course in 'public speaking'. Mrs Nouveau-
Richards, opening the bring and buy, exhorts everyone to 'give
generously like what I have done'. Mr Nouveau-Richards ticks
Jason off for talking too posh in the factory, it alienates the lads.

'Sorry Daddy,' says Jason. 'You shouldn't have sent me to such a good school.'

Mrs Definitely-Disgusting has a directness of speech not unlike Harry Stow-Crat. She says 'definitely' instead of 'yes'. Harry says 'absolutely'. She speaks in very short unfinished sentences, with a total disregard for syntax, and great use of conjunctions like 'so' and 'but', and 'like I said'. Sentences are often left unfinished, she uses very few subordinate clauses, and punctuates with words like: 'Shame', 'Just fancy,' 'Only natural, isn't it', and 'Do you Mind?' Statement and answer are often the same.

'I told you to hold on tight,' she says.

'Why,' asks Dive.

'I told you to hold on tight, dint I?'

Because the working classes tend to be inarticulate, they also rely very largely on gestures, shrugging their shoulders, waving their hands, rolling their eyes, and winking in the manner of Old Steptoe making faces.

Mrs Definitely-Disgusting is full of malopropisms. She's always wanting to get up a 'partition' or is 'fumigating' with anger. She also uses adjectives instead of adverbs. He cooks lovely, she dresses fantastic.

Because Mrs Definitely-Disgusting has received so many lectures from lefties on the dignity of the individual she's quite keen on the word 'dignified' as the opposite to 'common'. When a working-class girl played truant last April and posed naked on a horse in the middle of Coventry, her mother said afterwards: 'Louise made a very dignified Godiva, we are not ashamed of her showing her breasts, we are liberated parents.'

One would have thought it was more the breasts that were liberated.

16 THE ARTS

The creative writing on the wall.

Of all élite, the two that mix most easily are the aristocracy and the arts: Hamlet and the players – traditionally perhaps because they have the same bohemian disregard for other people's opinion, and the same streak of exhibitionism. In the past, as we shall see later in this chapter, artists have been tragically dependent on the caprice of their rich patrons, but things have changed in the last century. Now successful writers, actors and singers no longer struggle, but are often far richer than the aristocrats.

The Royal family have over the centuries been consistently resistant to the arts. George II hated all 'boets' and 'bainters'. 'Was there ever such stuff as Shakespeare?' asked George III. Although he did have a massive crush on Handel, and even re-wrote one of Dr Burney's reviews of a Handel concert because it wasn't favourable enough.

Queen Mary once wrote in a letter: 'I can't take Mabel about any more, she's too deaf. I ask her "who's that?" and all she says is "What?", so I've told her she can sweep in after me at big functions, but when it's picture galleries and things like that, she can't come.'

Even today one has only to watch the jaws of the Royal family absolutely dislocated with trying not to yawn at Gala performances at Covent Garden. If you go to Buckingham Palace, you find red wallpaper flocked like an Indian Restaurant, pictures that all need cleaning, and a band playing *South Pacific* and gems from *The White Horse Inn*.

The upper classes were traditionally patrons of the arts but because they have had their libraries and old masters, and minstrels in the gallery for so long, like their gardens and houses, they tend to take the arts for granted. Unlike the middle classes – who today make up the audiences at the theatre, ballet and the opera, who tend to regard a knowledge of the arts as a symbol of having got on, and who like to flaunt knowledge.

In the same way, the lower middles who want to rise equate culture with upper-class, and promptly start acquiring books, pictures and records. In the furnishing trade, book-shelves and record cabinets, are actually categorised as 'furniture for the better home'. The more up-market the newspaper or magazine too, the more comprehensive the coverage of the arts.

Art

Put not your trust in prints.

Crossing the threshold of Sotheby's one feels the sacred frisson, that special reverence evoked when great works of art and vast sums of money are changing hands. Of all the arts, painting is the smartest – because it involves the best dressed people and the most money. Private views are far more frequently covered by the glossies, than first nights (which Jen Teale pronounces 'preem*iaīres*'), publishing parties or concerts. This may be because the best galleries are situated around Bond Street and Knightsbridge, only a stone's throw from the offices of *The Tatler* – and because all the elegant aesthetic young men with their greyhound figures and Harvey and Hudson shirts, who work in them look aristocratic, even if they are not.

Caroline Stow-Crat often goes to private views when she's in London, it's nice to have a free drink and meet one's chums after an exhausting day in Harrods, and she likes bumping into all those old school friends of Harry's who in spite of being devastatingly handsome, somehow never got married. The upper classes, too, are very good at looking at paintings, they are able to keep their traps shut and whizz round galleries very fast. (Whereas Samantha Upward brought up to fill gaps with conversation can't repress a stream of 'How lovelies'.)

But what of the social standing of the painter himself? David Hockney is asked to the best parties but, 'Society is so constituted in England,' wrote Samuel Rogers, 'that it is useless for

'"Dejeuner sur l'herbe"? – Looks more like tea and crumpet to me!'

celebrated artists to think of bringing their families into the highest circle when they themselves are only admitted on account of their genius.'

But even genius has to be tempered with charm. No one asked Hogarth to dine: he was the son of a tradesman. Sir Alfred Munnings, too, when he went to paint the Duchess of Westminster, had to eat in the kitchen.

Despite upper-class philistinism, it has always been a status symbol to have one's portrait painted to provide ancestors to be shown off by future generations. Elizabeth I, epitomised royalty's attitude. There is no evidence that she had much taste for painting, said Horace Walpole drily, but she loved portraits of herself. Once a portrait painter became fashionable he went from one stately home to another, sucking up to Duchesses – a sort of Toady at Toad Hall.

'I don't want to become a portrait manufacturer,' sighed Hogarth. While Millais, succumbing to the inevitable tedium, admitted the best bit was putting the shine on his subject's boots.

Harry Stow-Crat doesn't buy paintings – he inherits them, various ancestors were painted by Romney, Gainsborough, Lely and Van Dyck. Norman Hepple, however, has just finished painting Caroline. This was so successful, he will probably do Georgie and Fiona in the holidays. Harry has also commissioned a new painting of the house, taking in the vista of the gorilla island, the flamingo lake and the amusement park.

Mr Nouveau-Richards now thinks it was rather a mistake to commission Francis Bacon to do Tracey-Diane's por-trait (which he rhymes with 'gate', the Stow-Crats say 'portr't') – but at least Mrs Nouveau-Richards has learnt to say 'Trechicorf'.

Ballet

'I do not know anything about ballet, except that in the interval the ballerinas stink like horses,' wrote Chekhov. Ever since then ballet has been prissying itself up, and has become a very lower middle-class art, intensified by all those layers of tulle and the ballerinas walking around on tip toe. Jen Teale loves 'the ballet': all those good tunes, and something undemanding to look at – rather like *Come Dancing*. Except for *Eugene Onegin*, Tchaikovsky is an irredemably lower middle-class composer.

'Have we come for the dancing or the singing?' Mr Nouveau-Richards was overheard saying to his wife as they arrived at Covent Garden on the firm's tickets.

Occasionally Covent Garden have Gala nights, which Jen Teale pronounces 'gay-la', presumably because of the number of homosexuals present. The effeminate appearance of the men puts off Harry Stow-Crat and the Definitely-Disgustings alike. 'Pouffe's Football', Old Steptoe called ballet dismissively.

Actors

Until recently Thespians were not considered respectable. A gentleman might go to bed with an actress and shower her with presents, but he did not make an honest women of her, and, although a few aristocrats married Gaiety Girls, the parental opposition was stiff enough to discourage most Mrs Worthingtons from putting their daughters on the stage.

Since the advent of the talkies, and even more so of television things have changed. Acting is one of the most popular professions for girls from public school, and actors and actressses get lionised out of proportion to any other artists. (When Kurt Jurgens gets half a million for a coffee commercial it's hard to ignore him.)

The upper middle classes who, apart from homosexuals and the coach trade, are the only consistent patrons, tend to go to the theatre for a good sleep, but sometimes they manage to wake up for the last scene. Evidently when Chichester staged *Vivat Regina* some years ago, at the end when Elizabeth and Mary stalk out of opposite corners of the stage, Mary to be beheaded, one Tory lady was heard turning to another, and saying, 'That's exactly what happened to Monica.'

Literature

Like the actor, the professional writer wasn't always socially acceptable. The Elizabethans considered poetry, dancing, and playing an instrument the sort of accomplishment rather like sex, that you did in the privacy of one's own home, but never for money.

Lady Mary Wortley Montagu said that it was contemptible to write for money, and even in the nineteenth century Flaubert attacked the practice – though admittedly from the security of a large private income.

It was only in the middle of the nineteenth century, as Frank Muir has pointed out, that the habit of reading spread down the classes and became wildly fashionable in a very minor way like television today. Another interesting point is that reviewers bitterly opposed to emergent lower middle class writers, savagely attacked Keats for not being a gentleman, and belonging with Leigh Hunt to what was derisively called the 'Cockney' school. 'Cockney' in those days didn't mean working class but 'genteel suburban'. It is hardly surprising that Byron and Shelley, as very nouveau aristocracy (Byron inherited the title from a great uncle, Shelley's grandfather managed to marry two heiresses) should initially attack Keats' poetry, not only because he was beneath them socially, but, more dangerous, he looked suspiciously like a far greater poet. Once Keats was dead he was no more competition, and it was much easier for Byron to leap to his defence in 'Who Killed John Keats', and for Shelley to write his elegy, 'Adonais'.

Recently a reviewer expressed amazement that Thomas Hardy could be simultaneously such a towering genius, and such a raging mean-minded snob. This seems quite logical. Any English novelist, if he is to draw characters with any accuracy must be aware of the minutest social nuance. Most English writers in fact have been frightfully snobbish. All Shakespeare's heros and heroines are upper-class. Any working-class characters were just introduced to provide comic relief. 'It's very tiring playing Shakespeare,' grumbled one actress. 'You only get to sit down if you're a king.'

It is significant that the only English poet to achieve best seller status in the last twenty-five years (apart from the Pam Ayres, Mary Wilson Tea Cosy school of verse) is John Betjeman, who is totally obsessed with class and whose genius is that he can be tender and wickedly funny at the same time about every rung on the social ladder: blue bloodies, civil servants, suburban clerks and cockneys.

Samantha always refers to 'Maupassant', because she

knows saying 'De Maupassant' is considered common in France, and she always talks about 'Willy Maugham' rather than 'Somerset'.

Jen Teale thinks Mrs Definitely-Disgusting's habit of licking her finger so she can turn the page more easily is absolutely 'rev-ollting'. Sharon Definitely-Disgusting reads *Jackie* and *True Romances*, which she calls 'books'.

A Mr Nouveau-Richards rang me the other day.

'Darling,' he said, 'I've just bid a fortune for two first editions.'

'What are they,' I asked.

'I'll just go and look,' he said.

They were Shelley and Keats.

Music

There was one peer who only employed butlers who could play the piano in the Key of C. He didn't give a damn if they could buttle, he merely wanted someone to accompany him when he played on the mouth-organ. He, however, was the exception. Although Harry Stow-Crat sets a good example by singing loudly in church on Sundays, he is actually tone-deaf. His children sometimes learn an instrument at school, which is called 'extras', and grumbled about when it appears on the bill.

In England music was traditionally only respected if it was imported. Italian castrati charged a fortune in the eighteenth century to give concerts to the rich and noble. The middle classes it seems had to make do with a lady from the local opera house.

'I detest these scented rooms,' wrote Coleridge, 'Where to a gaudy throng, the proud harlot heaves her distended breast in intricacies of laborious song.'

Today the upper middle classes, liking their opera sugar coated, regard Glyndeborne as the smart thing to do. They particularly enjoy picnicking with other middle-class people, and writing down the names of the more attractive herbaceous plants in the garden on their programme. There is always a mile long queue for the loo in the interval, while all those Samantha Upwards who pretend to know the opera backwards mug up on the synopsis for the next act.

Mozart, Haydn, Vivaldi and Purcell are upper-class composers, Brahms, Mahler, Schubert and Beethoven are upper middle. Tchaikovsky, Grieg and Mendelssohn are lower middle.

Samantha would simply love to sing in the Bach choir. Her mother adores Gilbert and Sullivan. Howard Weybridge has a few classical records, *Peer Gynt*, the 'Moonlight Sonata' and 'Cav-and-Pack-them-in'. He is also 'very active' in amateur operatics. Jen Teele enjoys *Down your Way* and *Your 100 Best Tunes*.

Mr Nouveau-Richards likes the cuckoo in the Pastoral symphony and claps between movements. Tracey-Diane sways from side to side when she plays 'The Lost Chord' on the pianola. Mrs Definitely-Disgusting likes Mantovani and Ron Goodwin, and thinks Verdi's Requiem is a 'resteront'.

In a recent survey, it was discovered that people who own their houses preferred classical music, but people in rented council houses preferred pop. One suspects the house owners claimed to prefer classical music because they felt they ought to, because it seems more upper classical than pop – after all the announcers do talk in posh voices on Radio 3 while the disc jockeys on Radio 1 and Capital all sound like yobbos.

The Radio 3 voice in fact is not upper-class at all, it is Marghanita Laski sens-it-ive, which involves speaking very slowly, and deliberately to eradicate any trace of a regional accent; with all the vowel sounds particularly the 'os' emphasised: 'vi-oh-lins', and 'pee-ar-noes', 'Vivald-ee' and the 'ball-ay'. The pronunciation of foreign composers and musical terms is also far too good.

The upper classes have frightful accents when they talk in a foreign language. As Harry Stow-Crat's mother once admonished him: 'Speak French fluently, darling, but not like them.'

17 TELEVISION

Why did you choose such a backward time and such such a strange
land,
If you'd come today, you'd have reached a whole nation.
Israel in 4 B.C. had no mass communication.

Jesus Christ Superstar

Light years above everyone else are the Tellys-tocracy. The man
in the street is far more impressed by the doings of Esther
Rantzen, than by those of Princess Anne. 'When I go to the
country,' said Reginald Bosanquet a year or two ago. 'I am
more revered than the Queen.' A couple I know were watching
Angela Rippon read the news one evening, when the wife
admired her dress. 'Why not see if they've got one like it in
Bentalls,' said her husband. So off they went next day and
found a very similar dress.

'Every time Angela appears on television,' confided the sales
girl, 'We get people pouring in here trying to buy what she was
wearing.'

Our own local telly-stocrat David Dimbleby, is particularly
impressive, for with a famous television father, he is second
generation telly and looks like founding a dynasty.

'Once in Royal David's Putney,' sing the children in the
street. Our particular part of Putney is known locally as 'Media
Gulch' because so many television stars, actors, and journalists
live here. You can only keep your end up in fact if you have the
television vans outside your house at least once every two
months, plus a gutted bus where all the crew retire every couple
of hours for something to eat and hordes of men with prema-
turely grey hair and he-tan saying 'Right', are draping plastic
virginia creeper over the porch to give an illusion of spring.

'Oh that reminds me, Bryan. Christine's just had her first under-
stain.'

But apart from creating a new telly-stocracy, the looming
presence of television has done more to change our social habits
than anyone realises. When commercial television appeared in
the sixties, it was hailed by Lord Thomson as the great leveller.
Everyone could afford it. As a new and exciting medium, it
seemed to epitomise the change from a rigid class system. In
fact it has enforced the divisions. Every day twenty-three
million eyes stay glued to the commercial television screen.
Advertising in particular makes people dissatisfied with life, the
initial effect is to encourage them to go out and buy consumer
goods, formerly enjoyed by their social superiors. As they
achieve these, and feel themselves to be going up in the world,
television becomes their social adviser. It tells them where to go
on their holidays, what car they should own, which wines to
order, the appropriate fuel to burn, what furniture to buy.
  Television has also created a new type of plastic family:
smiling squeezy Mums; woolly-hatted Dads playing football
and crumbling Oxo cubes; plastic dogs leaping in the air;
plastic children stuffing baked beans; lovable plastic grans

who are befriended by pretty air-hostesses but never sick. Why aren't we as happy as they are, thinks Mrs Definitely-Disgusting. It isn't fair.

Television increases aspiration, but underlines the differences, and has reinforced a strong Them and Us polarisation, Mr Definitely-Disgusting can pile up goods till he's black and blue in the face, but it's still difficult for him to improve his status, cross the great manual/non-manual divide and join the Martini set.

'You have the highest quality television in the world,' said an American to Professor Halsey, who wrote the recent Reith lectures on class, 'but *I Claudius* would be impossible in midstream America. Nowhere in the Western World does the élite have the confidence both to indulge in its own cultural tastes, and also believe these should be imposed on the masses.'

The report of the Annan Committee on Broadcasting complained that various kinds of upper-class characters – royalty, aristocracy, jet set – occurred in twenty-two per cent of all programmes, almost always in significant roles. Middle-class characters occurred in fifty-six per cent of the programmes and seventy-six per cent of them were significant to the plot. But the working classes only occurred in forty-one per cent programmes and in only seventy-one per cent were significant. In terms of their occurrence, in the population at large the report concludes that middle-class, and even more, upper-class characters are over-represented on television drama, and when they appear, they are likely to appear in important and attractive roles.

It is not just the lower classes who are hooked. The Queen is alleged to watch television to find out about her subjects down the hierarchy. One suspects she's an addict like the rest of us. Evidently, too, the whole Royal family was livid about the spate of royal sagas, particularly *Edward and Mrs Simpson*. Not because the events portrayed were so sensational, but because the actors playing themselves or their relations were, they considered, so common.

Young actors, in particular, have been so brain-washed by the egalitarian revolution, that, according to one casting director, it's impossible to find an actor in his thirties who can convincingly play upper middle to upper-class Englishmen of half a century ago. It's the assurance, the bearing, the tone of voice. Recently a duke's daughter auditioned for a part in Thames Television's dramatisation of a Nancy Mitford novel. Not having a clue who she was, the director passed her over. What was wrong with her, said the producer afterwards. 'She was too middle-class,' replied the director.

Viewing patterns of course vary from class to class. Mr and Mrs Definitely-Disgusting stay plugged into ITV whatever's on. They are such telly junkies, if it breaks down, they nick another one. The only time Mr Definitely-Disgusting switches over is for *Match of the Day* and *Miss World* and for *That's Life* (Esther's so good at getting at Them). They much prefer serials, situation comedy and variety, to current affairs.

Jen Teale enjoys *Come Dancing*, and 'ice skating', as she calls it, but she only watches television if she's sewing or knitting. Bryan Teale grumbles that there's not nearly enough 'motor sport'. He doesn't enjoy current affairs, or general knowledge programmes or even quizzes very much, but he finds it a 'social asset' to have opinions when he talks to colleagues at work.

Eileen Weybridge admires Angela Rippon, and has a soft spot for Julie Andrews, because she comes from nearby Walton-on-Thames. Howard watches *Rugby Special*, and *Panorama*. They are then much less influenced by commercial television than the Definitely-Disgustings.

Samantha insists on watching all the cultural programmes which send poor Gideon asleep. She actively disbelieves everything the ads tell her.

Mrs Nouveau-Richards naturally has a Video tape, 'Hubby and I go out so much, but all our show business friends would be so disappointed if we missed their programmes.'

Harry Stow-Crat turns the television on as soon as he gets home from shooting, and sleeps peacefully through it until the little white dot appears. He might wake up for Anna Ford, whom he prefers to Angela Rippon. So does Mr Callaghan, who has referred to her with typically lower middle caution as 'rather an attractive character'. Harry also watches racing and places bets if he's ever home in the afternoon.

Finally, a brief word about the ads themselves, most of them are deliberately aimed at Mr Definitely-Disgusting because he and Mrs Definitely-Disgusting have more spare cash to spend and are more prepared to splash it around than any of the other classes at the moment. Generally speaking, said an ad man recently, social mobility pulls (which sounds just like *Lady Chatterley's Lover*) don't work on the C.2s which is how the advertising world categorises Mr Definitely-Disgusting. The idea of doing something because Lady X or the vicar does, wouldn't appeal to Mr Definitely-Disgusting, he's read the *News of the World*. He knows about vicars.

Success figures like Twiggy, David Niven, Nyree Dawn Porter, and Frank Muir are therefore used rather than class figures in ads.

According to Charles Plouviez, chairman of Everetts, who has written a brilliant paper on 'Class and Advertising':

'When the Americans are planning a campaign and deciding how to reach the people most likely to buy the product, the main considerations are age and sex. In England they are age, sex and class. The advertisers must not offend class susceptibilities.

'Rural and Scottish accents,' according to Mr Plouviez, are always acceptable, 'but the really rough urban accents are avoided, and "posh" accents which used to be the rule of radio and TV in the days of the B.B.C monopoly – are only used for commercials when they are being sent up. The voice over or unseen voice which delivers the selling message, presents the greatest difficulty because if it is too posh it offends the viewer and if it is too common it offends the client.'

18 SPORTS AND PASTIMES

Oh skipper, my skipper our fearful trip is executed.

In the last fifty years, there has been a complete revolution in sport throughout the world. This is particularly noticeable in England and can be directly attributed to the influence of two world wars, and more generally to the advent of wireless and television. More evenly distributed affluence has created more time for 'leisure', and whilst we have become more a nation of spectators than participators, less fashionable games and pastimes have through their exposure on the media led to a much more varied participating pattern across the classes.

The aristocracy seldom indulged in such games as football, cricket or hockey. Sport to them has always been either closely linked to survival: i.e. hunting, shooting and fishing or to gambling, hence their traditional addiction to racing.

It was left to the middle classes, working through the medium of the public schools, aided and abetted by the church who thought that violent athletic activity took boys' minds off masturbation, to champion the noble art of self-defence and later Rugby football and soccer and often 'organised games'. It should not be forgotten that one of the first football clubs (Association) founded in this country were the Corinthians: a team of gentlemen. They even won the F.A. cup. Team games which emphasised the manly virtues and social solidarity led naturally to the creation of exclusive clubs – almost a defensive movement. This sort of coagulation has always been peculiar to the English – look at the regimental system of the army. Although this goes back much further, the values are the same.

Never let the man next to you see you are afraid, and never let the side down: 'Play up and play the game.' (I have excluded cricket because its social development is much more complicated, and the game is far more deeply rooted in our social history.)

One only needs to go to the University Rugger Match or any home international at Twickenham, 'the last fortress of the Forsyth's' as Christopher Laidlaw called it, to see the English middle classes in all their glory, and to realise that when the crowd howl for England they are really howling for the middle classes and the survival of middle-class values.

Today probably the only really smart game left is real tennis (royal tennis) possibly because there are so few courts. Hunting is no longer smart but bristling with Mr Nouveau-Richards and television stars. The Welsh miner in a red coat is no more an isolated phenomenon.

Fishing is not a sport either, although numbers of the lower classes who indulge in coarse fishing would argue that it was. Harry Stow-Crat has a beat on the Tay, but the fishing on either side is owned by Arabs and stockbrokers. Samantha goes to the fishmongers, the Cousteau-Richards go deep sea fishing off Looe. Mr Definitely-Disgusting sits all day under a green umbrella on the edge of a gravel pit catching inch-long roaches and throwing them back.

Harry Stow-Crat doesn't take much exercise. He plays billiards (not a sport) chemmy, backgammon, (bridge is too difficult) polo, and might have rowed at school. He seldom rows after leaving university, that is left to the working-class clubs such as Poplar and Blackwell, and Thames Tradesmen. He sometimes hunts and takes a packet of pheasant sandwiches. He plays fives at school and perhaps raquets, and occasionally tennis at weekends and croquet (which he pronounces '*cro*aky', not 'cro-*kay*' as Howard Weybridge would). He would never be seen dead on a golf (which he pronounces 'goff') course, and would soon be dead in a squash court. He would never never jog.

Gideon Upward plays squash, tennis, cricket, rugger until he is thirty ('Had to give up because of my knee') – never hockey which he regards as common and only played by minor public schools, Indians and fat-bottomed female clerks from Barclays Bank, and fat-breasted female clerks from Lloyds Bank.

'No we're *not* staying and having a bloody drink with the others. Get the children into the car.'

Howard Weybridge has a 'Support Surrey Rugby' sticker in the back of his car and enjoys 'a few jars' at Esher Rugby Club. He also plays 'gole-f' if he can find room at Sunningdale alongside all the bank managers playing against other bank managers, and spiralists playing with their bosses and letting them win after a tough fight.

Although they now allow the pro to drink in the bar it is evidently quite difficult to get into the Royal Berkshire or Sunningdale Golf Clubs. You have to be proposed and seconded by members who've known you for a considerable time, fill in a form stating your profession and where you went to school, and then get letters of approval from between six and eight members saying you're the right sort of person. At Sunningdale you actually have to play in front of the management committee to prove you're good enough.

'What happens if a nice bricklayer wants to join the club?' I asked the secretary at the Royal Berkshire.

'Well it would be most unlikely,' he said. 'How could he possibly know six of our members?'

Bryan Teale is too busy with 'home improvements' and

tinkering with the Volkswagen to play with anything but himself. His father plays bowls.

Mr Definitely-Disgusting never does anything much out of
doors except kick balls against the factory wall during tea
breaks. He watches television all the time when he's not going
to the dogs or matches on Saturday afternoons or filling in his
football coupons and placing bets. Harry Stow-Crat always
pays his bookie before his tailor because it's a debt of honour.
At the pub, Mr Definitely-Disgusting plays darts, snooker and
dominoes.

Mr Definitely-Disgusting's brother, who's a miner, goes
shooting partridge on top of the coal tips and races pigeons. He
also owns a lurcher called 'Shep'. Coursing in fact has a strong
cloth cap following. When Harold Wilson wanted to give
government backing to a bill banning stag hunting and hare
coursing, Richard Crossman directed his acute political anten-
nae in that direction.

'He (Harold) thinks this is an election winner, and hundreds
and thousands of people who read the *Daily Mirror* will love this
idea. Deer hunting is probably very unpopular, but hare coursing is a very proletarian sport, people in the North enjoy it. I
didn't think we should jump into this without a much more
careful analysis of the minority who oppose it.'

Horses
God save our gracious Quorn.

The horse was one of the first status symbols, like the car, it gave
its owner mobility. Originally the upper classes were the only
people who could afford horses, and many aristocratic titles
come from riding, the French 'Chevalier' for example, the
German 'Ritter', meaning rider, and the English Cavaliers.
Sitting on a horse also enables you to look down on your fellow
men. Horsy people invariably have that deadpan look one
associates with the aristocracy.

Horses have always been a good way up the social ladder, as
Mark Phillips recently showed us. In the nineteenth century
the Rothschilds were accepted into the grandest Victorian
society because the Prince of Wales was at Cambridge with the
Nathaniel Rothschild and shared his interest in racing.

Samantha Upward's father, like many another retired army

Colonel or Brigadier, often finds an interest running the local pony club, and bossing nubile little girls about. Competition is as fierce between the little girls, as it is between the guns out shooting. There was fearsome grumbling at the local Putney show a few years ago, because they all thought the jump in the Working Pony Class had been specially lowered for Princess Alexandra's daughter.

Harry Stow-Crat has his breeches made for him, and pays about £200 for black leather boots, which have a garter strap which attaches to buttons on his breeches, and keeps the boots up and the breeches down. George Stow-Crat however, who's feeling the pinch has brought a pair of rubber boots so well made as to be indistinguishable from leather ones. Even he wouldn't resort to the stretch nylon breeches which show your pants worn by Mr Nouveau-Richards. Georgie wears brown boots for polo and laced boots if he's in the cavalry.

It used to be considered extremely vulgar to have buckles on your reins, they had to be sewn on. But now, except for showing, most people have studs which fasten on the inside. Coloured brow-bands are beyond the pale. It is permissible to wear a white hunting tie or a stock with coloured spots. But Harry Stow-Crat considers it very nouveau to wear a coloured stock with white spots.

When Mr Nouveau-Richards goes out hunting he wears an ordinary white tie, instead of a stock, with his unauthorised red coat – like the show jumpers do on television, and carries his hunting whip upside down without a thong. Tracey-Diane looks like an advertisement in the back pages of a riding magazine. She wears thick eye make-up, dangling earrings, and her loose blonde locks flowing out from her black cap. Mr Nouveau-Richards tells everyone she is 'a marvellous horsewoman'. Harry would say 'a very good rider'. Howard Weybridge calls it 'horse riding' or 'horse-back riding'.

Samantha Upward carefully talks about 'hounds with their "waving sterns", and "pink" coats'. She is rather shocked when Harry refers to 'red' coats. Far too many *nouveaus* have started talk about 'pink', so the upper class have reverted to 'red'. Harry also says his horse is 'lame' whereas Howards Weybridge says his 'mount' is 'limping'. Howard says: 'I was thrown from the horse, which was very frisky.'

Harry says: 'My horse was too fresh and bucked me off/gave me a fall/I fell off.'

Howard says his horse 'jibbed at a hedge'. Harry would say it 'put in a stop' or 'refused at a fence'.

Howard's horse 'gets the bit between the teeth'. Harry would say 'It took off with me', or 'ran away', or 'I was carted'.

Howard's horse 'keeps rearing', Harry's horse 'goes up with him'.

Shooting

'Hunting', wrote Bishop Latimer in 1820 'is a good exercise for a man of rank, but shooting is amusement equally lawful and proper for inferior persons.'

Yet three-quarters of a century later, shooting was the way in which the great landowners entertained their guests throughout the winter months.

The railway helped, as Jonathan Ruffer points out in *The Big Shots*, 'so did technical improvements of the gun. You now combined the opportunities of a Vimy Ridge machine gunner with an infinitely better lunch. And finally, because Edward VII was too fat to hunt, he channelled all his enthusiasms into shooting – and it was natural, that society should exert itself in pursuits which its champion made fashionable.'

Edward VII kept all the clocks half an hour early so he got extra time shooting in the winter. Today people are just as keen. A friend of mine once asked the Macnab of Macnab who's a brilliant shot whether he really needed a secretary three days a week. 'Of course I do,' replied the Macnab indignantly. 'Every day I have to write letters saying: "Dear Charles thank you for asking me to shoot on the fourth, I'm afraid I can't make it," or "Dear Henry, thank you very much for asking me to shoot on the 18th, I should be happy to accept."'

All through the winter in Scotland and the North of England, in anticipation of the coming season, white plumes rise like smoke signals from various hills, where the heather is being burned. It's all anyone talks about at upper-class dinner parties. If you're not careful you can burn a whole moor. (Harry Stow-Crat pronounces it 'maw', the middle classes call in 'maw-er'.)

At Sandringham and Balmoral, Robert Lacey wrote in *Majesty*, day-long shooting sorties take on the character of a military manoevre, with shooting brakes, vans full of beaters drawn by a tractor, and Land-Rovers which you clamber into possibly to find the Queen sitting next to you.

Prince Philip is one of the best shots in the country, which means the world. Prince Charles, it seems, is all set to overtake him.

As soon as people start doing well in business, they take up shooting, and photographs of themselves knee-deep in the bracken beside a grinning labrador with its mouth full of feathers are placed on top of the piano. But the pitfalls are great for the unwary, Mr Nouveau-Richards has no idea what to tip the loader, and keeps shooting his host's grouse, rather like poor Charles Clore asking a neighbouring gun if his loader could join them for lunch.

'Whatever for,' said the gun sarcastically, 'is he teaching you to eat as well?'

It is very smart to drink sloe gin at lunchtime but social death to turn up in gold boots and a shocking pink fun fur and talk throughout every drive, like Mrs Nouveau-Richards.

Despite the Freudian terminology of shooting handbooks – all that talk about 'pricked birds', 'cocks only' days, and 'premature gun mounting' – women are expected to keep very much in the background. Their duty is to provide a good lunch, keep an eye on the dogs and occasionally load. 'After August 12th,' sighed one Edwardian beauty, 'Wives and mistresses don't exist.'

The exception was one Spanish prince who turned up to shoot in Yorkshire with a ravishing mistress, and missed everything he shot at on the first two drives. Bumping along in the Land-Rover to the third drive the keeper heard scufflings and looking round saw the Prince and his mistress humping away on a mattress of slaughtered grouse. After that he shot brilliantly.

19 DOGS

The pooch it was that passed away.

'I can get on perfectly well with the people my children marry,' said one aristocratic old woman, 'What I find difficult is dogs-in-law.' She was talking about the troops of Tibetan spaniels, dachshunds, and fat irascible terriers who join the family circle with a new daughter-in-law.

The upper classes, of course, adore their dogs. In the country they usually have at least five (like Catholics do with issue) and have grilles in the back of the car to stop them being bothered by the children. The dogs coat the furniture with hairs, and wipe their faces on the chair covers, and most of them sleep in the bedroom. (Sir Sacheverell Sitwell's Cavalier King Charles Spaniels have a turquoise drinking bowl to match the bedroom wallpaper.) Their portraits hang under picture lights. Most of them are incontinent but no one seems to mind very much. Randolph Churchill was once heard bawling out his dog for peeing on the sofa: 'Get off, Boycott, you know you're only allowed to do it on the carpet.'

Another old duke was absolutely devoted to a foul terrier called Spot, who was rotund, blind, incontinent, bit everyone and was over twenty. Finally under extreme family pressure the duke agreed to take the dog out and shoot it. Tears pouring down his face, he and Spot set out into the twilight. The family waited in anticipation, and jumped out of their skins when ten minutes later there was a feeble clawing on the door. It was Spot wanting to be let in. At the prospect of having to kill him the duke had had a heart attack. Spot lived on for several more years.

Walk through the gardens of any upper-class garden, and in a quiet shady corner you will find a lot of little crosses marking the dogs' graveyard. One I know in Lancashire includes a favourite parrot buried in a cake tin. A small tombstone in Sandringham bears the inscription 'to the Queen's faithful friend, Susan'.

On the whole the upper classes prefer what they call 'working dogs' – labradors 'to shoot over' (they never shoot 'with' them) – and Jack Russells, Norfolk or Hunt terriers ostensibly to dig 'Charlie' (as they call the fox) out, although they never do. Black labradors are much grander than yellow, and are quite often invited without their owners to shoot in Scotland and travel up quite happily on the train. Another labrador came all the way down to London from Northumberland to be mated. The owner of the bitch booked a room overnight at the Turf Club (presumably in the name of 'Mr and Mrs Smith'). Eight puppies resulted. The owner of a stately home once told me he had terrible trouble when members of the visiting public stretched out asleep on the grass in summer, because his labrador always goes and lifts his leg on any bald head.

King Charles spaniels are very upper-class dogs. So are whippets, springer spaniels, pekes, dachsies, particularly long haired ones. Hounds are never kept as pets, but 'walked' as puppies in the summer. Upper-class dogs often have two addresses on their collars: one for London and another for the country. On the label should be engraved the owners' surname, address and telephone number. It is very vulgar to put the dog's Christian name in inverted commas, and to have anything other than brown leather collars. Tartan collars for scotties or west highland terriers and diamanté for poodles are also out. So are red barrels on the collar or red bows on long haired dogs, or topiary on poodles.

Upper-class dogs only have one meal a day and are therefore quite thin, like their owners. Snipe Stow-Crat is so well trained he doesn't need a collar or lead at all. (Jen Teale would say 'leash'. Mr Definitely-Disgusting uses string, and calls his puppy a 'pup'. He also talks about 'pooches'.)

Upper middle dog owners are almost keener on them than the aristocracy. They don't have so many, so the affection is not divided and they don't keep them for working but to talk to and through. Colonel and Mrs Upward address each other through

'Howard – did you remember to give Petal her pill?'

their dalmatian. Their daughter-in-law, Samantha, has an evening bag lined with congealed fat from bringing home chops and bits of steak for Blucher, her English Setter. Dogs belonging to the upper middle merry-tocracy always reek of garlic from having doggy bag pork chops or Chicken à la Kiev posted through the door to stop them barking and waking the nanny when their owners return home too drunk from restaurants to find their keys.

Dalmatians, English setters, cairns, golden retrievers, are upper middle-class dogs. The upper middles have also recently taken to foreign breeds – weimeraners and rotweillers – because the classes below can't pronounce them. Old English sheepdogs used to be upper middle but have lost caste since they appeared so often on television advertising paint.

Howard Weybridge likes airedales and rough-haired terriers, great danes and Irish wolfhounds. They look so heraldic loping through the pine woods of Surrey. He also likes red setters and cocker spaniels.

Mrs Nouveau-Richards loves Yorkshire terriers, and poodles, and all the show-off dogs like collies and afghans.

Bryan Teale likes dobermanns and boxers because they

don't shed hairs. Jen Teale hates dogs because they're so smelly.

Mr Definitely-Disgusting belongs to the *Daily Mirror* Pets Club and loves all 'pooches'. But he's particularly partial to 'Westies' as he calls West Highlands and alsatians because they're such good guard dogs. And of course you can't beat a good mongrel (though he frequently does). Mongrels (Mr Definitely-Disgusting pronounces the first syllables to rhyme with 'long' and Harry Stow-Crat to rhyme with 'dung') are sometimes called 'street dogs', or 'butcher's dogs', because they used to follow the butcher's van.

On the whole the upper classes don't approve of mongrels. I always pretend mine are lurchers when I go anywhere smart. Caroline Stow-Crat would swallow, then cover up her disapproval by saying: 'But they're supposed to be awfully intelligent and loyal.'

More pointed contempt was shown by a lower middle woman who ran some boarding kennels. I'd sent my mongrel bitch there when she came on heat (Jen Teale would say 'in season') because I didn't want her father whom we also own to get her pregnant. Unfortunately it seemed we were too late. Ten days later the kennel owner rang up: 'It's disgraceful,' she snapped, 'Bringing cross breeds into the world when there aren't enough homes for breed dogs. Why don't you have the father carstrated.' Harry Stow-Crat would never castrate a dog it would be against his male chauvinist principles.

It is pretty unsmart to show your dogs – rather like going in for a beauty contest, and also to enter your guard dog for what are called 'O-bedience' tests.

Recently the paper reported that a Mr Nouveau-Richards paid £100 for what he thought was a pedigree labrador puppy for Tracey-Diane, it turned out to be a hamster.

The upper classes don't like cats as much as dogs, and tend only to keep them in the stables to keep the rats down. The more well bred a cat, usually the more common the owner.

Mrs Definitely-Disgusting refers to her cat as 'Pussy', e.g. 'a neighbour took Pussy when I went on holiday.'

20 CLUBS

If the Englishman's home is his castle, the English gentleman's bolthole is his club. I don't mean the kind of club like Esher R.F.C. or Hurlingham (which is not a club, but a place where foreigners go when Harrods is closed), or the M.C.C. which people join to meet people and play games with their 'own sort', but the kind of club largely based in London, that a man joins to avoid meeting people – not least members of his own club. A club is a useful place to remain incommunicado, particularly from his wife. The porter will always put up a smoke screen.

Although a lot of London clubs have now taken to admitting women, as guests – not as members, this has been done grudgingly. At the Army and Navy there's a separate dining room for them. At the Naval and Military there's a special entrance. At the Garrick they are not allowed to use the main staircase before 7 p.m. and are bundled into a side room at lunchtime, where they are forgotten for long periods by the staff. In the rule book at the Garrick, it says that no lady visitor may be introduced more than ten times within the same year, except members of the family of the member – which presumably keeps mistresses at bay – although any club is the last place to choose for a romantic encounter because of the brilliant overhead lighting.

There used to be a famous ladies' club called the Cowdrey, which described itself rather wildly as a club 'for professional women'. One of the oldest members, a Miss Eardley Wilmot was reputed to have written the words for 'Little Grey Home in the West'. Miss Wilmot once met my father-in-law on the landing (men were allowed to stay with their wives towards the end of the Cowdrey's existence).

'The Stragglers of Asia yes! But not the M.C.C.'

'Oh dear,' she said, 'A man,' and fainted away.

I always like the story about the Atheneum, the august haunt of bishops and dons. It is said that a notice appeared in one of the papers saying: 'The Atheneum re-opened to-day after the annual cleaning, and members were replaced in their original positions.'

Harry Stow-Crat would probably belong to Whites (it took one very grand friend of ours ten years' scheming to get elected) particularly if he was fond of gambling or horses. Even from one's earliest years one must be careful how one behaves. Harry has great delight in permanently blocking the election to his club of a couple of men who once bullied him at school. If not Whites, Boodles, Bucks or the Beefsteak. He would never be seen in the RAC ('The Chauffeur's Arms') or the Junior Carlton. He would have been lunched at the Garrick probably by his lawyer, but never wished to be asked back there because he saw Robin Day in the dining room.

Colonel Upward, Gideon's father, is a member of the Army and Navy, he calls it 'the Rag', and his brother, Commander Upward, goes to the Naval and Military, known as the 'In and Out'.

All but the very smartest of London clubs have allowed the spiralists to join to boost membership, and uneasy-looking goosenecks with brushed-forward hair in high street suiting can be seen there, bewildered by the unfamiliar surroundings, wondering which fork to use and desperately trying to stop their gooseneck guests pulling out sheafs of papers, and discussing work in hand in whining nasal voices. Clubs may not be used for business purposes or used as a business address.

Clubs Harry Stow-Crat would never be seen in include the Savage, the National Liberal, the Farmers Club and the Gresham Club in the city. The Reform is also way down the list now. It is interesting that when Mr Thorpe took Norman Scott there for a drink he used to pretend that Mr Scott was a constituent he was helping with some family problem. He felt Mr Scott was too 'suburban' (his very words) to be introduced as a friend.

Bryan Teale joins the Rotary Club, prompted by Jen who thinks it might advance his career, and belongs to a social club at work. On the other hand Mr and Mrs Definitely-Disgusting go to the working men's clubs on Fridays and have a whale of a time watching high class variety acts and filling themselves with beer. Working men's clubs in fact are the lynch-pin of working-class culture, they started as temperance clubs by a vicar in 1862 to raise the dismal life of the worker. Later Lord Rosebery introduced drinking and smoking. Some of the clubs are colossal. Batley in Yorkshire has 15,000 members and is big enough now to attract stars like Frank Sinatra who might by-pass London on the way. Even Mr Definitely-Disgusting laughs at Charlie Williams the famous black comedian who made his name in men's working clubs. Evidently part of his turn is to mop his face, and say: 'My God, it won't come off. If thee don't laugh, I'll come and live next door to thee.' He deals with problems familiar to the working classes: rents, un-employment, mothers-in-law, class: ('our lodger's such a naice young man').

One of his favourite jokes is Enoch Powell going up to the pearly gates, and a voice says 'Who Dat out Dere?'

'No,' says Knocker. 'Forget it.'

The main thing about all clubs, though, is that they are exclusive. The grand friend who schemed for ten years before he was elected to Whites now drops it into the conversation at every occasion.

There was once a leading financier who wanted to join a smart yacht club. Anxious to find out how his election had gone he despatched a sycophantic minion to find out the result. The minion returned some time later looking uneasy.

'How did it go,' said the financier.

'Pure caviare, I fear,' said the minion.

He had been completely blackballed.

21 THE SERVICES

The origins of most of the oldest families in England are military and feudal. When William the Conqueror wanted to establish himself in this country he offered his henchmen pieces of land if they would provide him with a certain number of soldiers for a specified number of days a year. The henchmen who produced the most men got the most land. By Henry V's reign, things had got a bit out of hand, with everyone calling himself 'knight' or 'esquire', regardless of right. Henry therefore ordered that coats of arms would only be granted to people who had fought at Agincourt, or who could show ancestral right. Even so several hundred people were granted arms in the fifteenth century, and in the sixteenth century many more, an increase that has no parallel in any continental country. It has also always been the practice of monarchs to reward their great soldiers with titles, hence the Dukes of Marlborough and Wellington, and the Viscount Alexander or Lord Montgomery more recently.

Once upon a time the army was very smart. 'An officer,' wrote Lord Stanley, in the nineteenth century, 'shall be the son of a gentleman: a gentleman is understood to mean a man who has plenty of money, and does not exercise any retail trade or any mechanical profession. If you find a horse dealer or a shopkeeper's son, you may be certain that the rule has been relaxed because his father has contrived to ingratiate himself with the class above his own, and not on account of the personal merit of the candidates.'

During the first half of this century, whilst the experience of fighting in two world wars forged many new bonds between Englishmen of different classes, the peacetime professional

'It's quite simple really: the tenth were shiny; the eleventh wore red trousers; the fifth skins wore green trousers; the seventh turn-ups and crossbelts; and all tank men have dirty finger nails'.

army continued to embody the social hierarchies of Victoria's Empire.

Today the army has lost caste, as their numbers are cut, their regiments merged, and the cost of living outstrips their pay. 'Colonels used to impress,' Heather Jenner told me, 'But today there is a completely different attitude to them, it's a devil of a job to get them married.' But although it may no longer be a respository for chinless wonders or second sons of noble houses with nothing better to do, it has, regardless, a rigid social structure.

There are still smart regiments and not-so-smart regiments. Of the Cavalry Regiments, the Blues and Royals, the 17/21st Lancers, or until recently the 10th or 11th Hussars, could claim be the élite, although when the 11th joined the 10th, they claimed to have been dragged down, just as the Blues have been by the Royals. It is smarter to be in armoured cars than tanks, because armoured cars are nearer to horses. The Scots, Welsh and Irish Guards are looked down on by the Coldstream and the Grenadiers, but all except the latter, unite in regarding the Grenadiers as the stupidest.

The Green Jackets (formerly the Rifle Brigade, the Kings

Royal Rifle Corps, and now including the Oxfordshire and
Buckinghamshire Light Infantry) are the most upper-class and
they look down on Regiments of the Line. You can't get much
lower than the Royal Corps of Transport and The Royal Army
Ordnance Corp, unless you are part of an amalgamated regiment like the Royal Anglians. The Army Catering Corps is not
even Royal yet, and there of course is always the WRAC staffed
almost wholly by lesbians and incipient traffic wardens and
lady brigadiers who become dames.

Harry Stow-Crat probably served in the Coldstream during
the war, and many of his family would have served in the same
regiment, his brother was in the Blues. Caroline's brother, on
the other hand, might have been either in the Rifle Brigade (if
he were a Wykehamist or an Old Radleian) or possibly in a
Scottish regiment such as the Royal Scots, both of them great
family regiments. Harry would say 'hurt', rather than
'wounded', he would never talk about 'the C.O.' or 'Mufti'.

Gideon Upward did his National Service in the Royal
Engineers, and remembers all the working-class boys blubbing
on their first night, because they'd never been away from home
before. Later he went to Korea for a year, after what he refers to
as 'hostilities' had ceased.

After National Service in the Signals, Howard Weybridge
joined what he considered was a smart territorial Army Unit
like the H.A.C. and goes away on long drinking weekends on
Salisbury Plain, growing a small clipped moustache. Once in
the Territorials, he would begin by going back to non-
commissioned rank, and have to work his way up. This
mystifies Dive Definitely-Digusting when he too joins the
Reserve Army, and occasionally goes on joint exercises with the
H.A.C. Afterwards he describes Howard and his mob, as 'not a
bad lot of fuckers but why do they talk so funny?' On one
occasion he sidled up to Howard Weybridge saying: 'Tell me
Bombadier, aren't most of your lot, ex-officers?'

'Well quite a few,' Howard admits modestly.

'Well what the 'ell did you get busted for?' asks Dive.

Mr Definitely-Disgusting was a driver in the R.A.S.C. (the
Jam Stealers) during the war, and had a good time getting the
clap twice in Benghazi, and entering Berlin five days after the
end of the war, where he became briefly a black market baron.
He reckons his army days to be the happiest of his life. He is

now a member of the British Legion, because the beer is cheaper.

A last word of warning. Beware of those who use ranks below colonel in civilian life. Colonels and above are usually sound, but it is not safe to ask what they were in. My father-in-law once queried a brigadier too fiercely and finally extracted the information that he had served in the A.R.P. in India in 1939.

Bryan Teale did his national service in the 'Raff'. Socially the Air Force is of little interest – no one knows anyone in it, or rather no one admits to knowing anyone in it. The days of blue-eyed boys with silk scarves, heavy limps and labradors vanished years ago, leaving behind them a flotsam of sub-astronauts with social chips and nothing to do – they don't have any aeroplanes either.

The navy (who call themselves 'the Senior Service') are difficult to categorise socially: they are often away for a long time, presumably at sea. So far as I can discover, there are not many of them left, there must be more retired naval people than there are serving, particularly admirals. However the Navy are a game lot with exquisite manners and a romantic image, probably because one sees them so seldom. Intellectually they are the cream of the armed services. You can't get in unless you have five Os and 3 A-levels.

Harry Stow-Crat had a great great great uncle who fought at Trafalgar, and there is a battered portrait of him in the ballroom, with a hole where some young blood threw a roll at a hunt ball, and there is a rusting sextant, that belonged to another uncle who was in Clippers, in the downstairs lavatory. Harry had an aunt in the Wrens.

Gideon Upward's grandfather fought in Jutland, but no one knows what became of him after the *Queen Mary* sank. It was rumoured that he survived and went to Australia. The Nouveau-Richards' connections with the Navy were restricted to a cruise to Bermuda where they were asked to 'Cocktails' in the Ward Room of H.M.S. something-or-other that was over there showing the flag.

'Is it the only one you've got left?' says Mrs Nouveau-Richards to some frisky first lieutenants.

Wayne Teale succumbs an advertisement in the paper telling him: 'To Join the Royal Fleet – the object is to officer the 34 ships that supply the Royal Navy with fuel, food and ammunition. You'll experience the pride of belonging to a superbly trained élitist unit.' It is very vulgar to classify the navy as the 'royal navy', the upper classes wouldn't be in anything else, and regard the merchant navy as social death.

Occasionally hand-picked officers in the navy are selected to sail in *Britannia*, and keep albums filled with glued-in concert programmes, and photographs of princes in grass skirts being ducked at the Equator to remind them of the trip.

Dive Definitely-Disgusting joined the sea scouts because you could smoke more easily in a whaler or a rusty M.T.B. than you could in a scout hut where you spent most of your time running around trying to avoid the clutches of the scoutmaster.

22 RELIGION

Frequent church-going becomes markedly less likely as one goes down the social scale. The upper classes regard it as a patriotic duty to set an example and go every Sunday, quite often to their own church where they can have their own pew. As Douglas Sutherland has pointed out, the English gentleman knows that God believes in him, it is his duty in return to believe in God. He often reads the lesson, sings loudly but out of tune, and tells the vicar to speak up if he can't hear the sermon. In return his church expects financial support. The Queen always gives £1 to the collection.

Harry would never drive his Rolls-Royce on Sunday, because that day he goes to church. He only takes the Rolls on long journeys.

The church of England is predominantly the church of the upper and middle classes. You find that the middle classes hog all the places on the parish council, act as sidesmen and churchwardens while their wives, with their large well-stocked gardens are responsible for the flowers in church and run fêtes and jumble sales. The working classes feel intimidated and left out.

It's very vulgar to call a vicar 'Vicar' to his face, rather like 'Doctor' and 'Teacher'. You should call him 'Mr Upward' or whatever his surname is. If he's a Canon you could call him 'Canon Stow-Crat'. On letters he should be addressed as 'The Rev Francis Stow-Crat', never 'Rev Francis Stow-Crat', or 'The Rev Stow-Crat'. Despite its apparent social disdain of the working classes, the anglican church, since the introduction of the New English bible, is also getting more folksy and vulgar every day. We now have 'Mother's Day' instead of 'Mothering

'I'm toiling over a hot stove because Mummy prefers faith to works on Sunday mornings.'

Sunday', to get it as far away from a church ritual as possible, and instead of a 'Harvest Festival' we have 'Harvest Home' or 'Harvest Supper'.

Any significance Easter may have had for the masses has disappeared under a mass over overpriced chocolate and Easter Bunny. And nothing can equal the spate of vulgarity which pours forth at Christmas, burying the country under a commercial avalanche of heavenly babes, yule logs, Santa and his reindeer crew, festive robins, jolly cardinals and seasonal cheer.

The Stow-Crats have a real Christmas tree from their moor in Scotland, it touches the ceiling and is decorated with candles and ancient peeling baubles. Snipe has a large mutton bone as a present, and Harry's few remaining tenants and estate servants shuffle in to collect their hams and turkeys and have a drink. In Putney we're lucky, too, because the children of our local telly-stocrat produce a pantomime for us.

Samantha's parents and Gideon's parents take it in turns to go and stay with Samantha and Gideon at Christmas. 'Don't they realise you're working,' Gideon says furiously to Samantha every year. What he really minds about is not being able to drink himself stupid in front of his in-laws, and because

Christmas goes on for so long he won't have a chance to see the secretary he fancies for at least ten days. Christmas staying with in-laws is invariably a nightmare, not enough to drink and Thalia breaks the crib Virgin Mary on Boxing Day. No one fights openly (the Pargeters again) but a muscle is going in both Samantha's and Mrs Upward's face on the last day. Gideon doesn't kick up too much because he knows Samantha's father is going to give him £500 to pay the school fees. (The middle class often use Christmas to hand over money, so the recipient won't feel any loss of independence.) In revenge Colonel and Mrs Upward take Zacharius and Thalia to the pantomime, where all over the theatre you will hear grandparents making cracks against their daughters-in-law.

'You would have had much better seats and been able to see, Thalia darling, if Mummy hadn't been so awfully vague about dates.'

Mrs Nouveau-Richards has a vast silver plastic Christmas tree, groaning with tinsel and flashing lights. Jen Teale insists on a plastic tree too this year, she had to get last year's tree out by Boxing Day because it was moulting pine needles so badly. She hangs the Christmas cards from string across the lounge to avoid dust. Samantha regards Christmas cards as a marvellous excuse not to dust.

Christmas cards are a great class indicator in themselves. The higher classes like simple words inside like: 'With best wishes for Christmas and the New Year', or 'A Merry Christmas and a Happy New Year'. If they have special cards printed, they only put their address at the bottom, and write in their Christian names, or their Christian names and surnames to those they know less well. The Weybridges have 'Howard and Eileen Weybridge' printed as well, and cross out the 'Weybridge' for their 'very good friends'. The Nouveau-Richards have a very large card with a picture of jolly cardinals quaffing indifferent claret in front of roaring fire, and a lovely poem about festive cheer, and 'Hearty Xmas Greetings', plus their name and address in red loopy spangled writing inside. Jason as a member of the telly-stocracy often puts 'Yours Aye', or 'Sincerely Your Jison Richards' on his cards, which are usually of Santa with a red nose. Harry Stow-Crat would write 'Love', particularly if he were writing to a girl. (He would say 'Father Christmas' rather than 'Santa Claus', or 'Santa'.)

The spiralists have a photograph of themselves and their family on the front of their Christmas cards, with a bigger and bigger house in the background as the years go by.

It is extremely vulgar to send your friends a roneo-ed letter bringing them boastfully up to date with all the doings of your family.

Samantha Upward insists on buying cards to support a charity, usually painted with someone's feet. Mrs Definitely-Disgusting only sends cards to relations. She chooses one with 'To a Very Special Daughter' for Sharon, and 'To a Fine Son' for Dive, and inside underlines the bits in the poem which she thinks are applicable. Sharon and Dive club together to send a 'Dearest Nana' card to Mrs Definitely-Disgusting's mother.

Eileen Weybridge thoroughly enjoys the festive season, her house is a picture of 'Yuletide holly rings, whitewashed twigs, and tinsel and ribbon decorations' taken from *Good Housekeeping*. Howard brings home a festive gift box from Bentalls, and a carrier bag full of fancy goods from the fairy grotto as a Special Prize for Cook.

Jen Teale comes into her own at Christmas. Everyone comments on the daintyness of her gifts. She khows that how you wrap a parcel is so much more important than what's in it. Even boxes of chocolates are now smothered in brightly coloured gift-wrap (as she calls wrapping paper) and topped with tasteful concentric circles of coloured ribbon, just like Harrods. She also 'bakes all the Christmas Fayre' without the aid of a deep freeze, and stays looking lovely because she foliows the *Woman's Own* guide for keeping bandbox fresh over the festive season.

The Definitely-Disgustings have a real blow-out. They've contributed 50p a week for a year to the Christmas Club to a fund managed by some busybody, and this year Mrs Definitely-Disgusting is personally going to see that the busybody doesn't abscond with the lot on December 22, like last year's manager who made nine miles on the front of the local paper. Sharon Definitely-Disgusting trails round Woolworths with a list which reads:

Nan: Devon Violets
Mum: Giftpack
Dad: Condor Tobacco
Dive: Brut
Auntie Dot: Thomas and Sarah's brandied peaches

Marlene: Bendy Kermit
Mr Whiskas: Catnip Mouse
Patch: Bumper Xmas Dog Choc Drops

The whole family is glued to I.T.V. over the holiday, except when Mr Definitely-Disgusting, after a surfeit of turkey and all the trimmings, snores his way like a good patriot through the Queen's speech. Patch, having demolished the bumper Xmas Choc Drops, the Catnip mouse, and a stolen turkey bone, is sick.

23 DEATH

Oh happy release where is thy sting?

At last we come to Death the Leveller, who lays his icy hand on Stow-Crats and Definitely-Disgustings alike. Poets over the ages have been haunted by this equalising theme. Shakespeare wrote of golden lads and girls mingling in the dust with chimney sweeps. Hardy wrote of the yokels, William Dewy and Tranter Reuben, lying in Mellstock churchyard beside the Squire and Lady Susan. But even if we are all equal in the moment of death, the living see to it that our departure is celebrated in very different ways.

Once upon a time funerals were occasions for great pomp – with long processions of carriages drawn by horses wearing floor-length ebony velvet, everyone including the children in deepest black, men and boys doffing their hats along the route, and close relations going into mourning for several months. An outward and lavish display was regarded as a measure of the family's affection for the dead. But, like most fashions, it filtered down the classes until today only among the working classes, who are usually much closer to their families, and like any excuse for a party, does the tradition of the splendid funeral linger on.

Attitudes have changed too. In Victorian times, everyone accepted and talked naturally about death – with the rate of infant mortality it would have been impossible even for a child to be shielded from the subject. Sex was the great taboo, with copulation never mentioned, and babies being found under gooseberry bushes. Today everyone talks about sex and birth quite naturally. It is death (like class) that has become taboo. Perhaps it is because most people no longer believe in an after-life, that they cannot face up to the terror of death, and so sweep everything under the carpet. In the old days, a man died surrounded by his family. The Victorian deathbed was one of the great set pieces. Today, according to Geoffrey Gorer's excellent book, *Death, Grief and Mourning*, it is rare in the upper middle and professional classes for a bereaved person to be present at the death (less than one in eight in fact).

The undertaker would pick up the body from the hospital, and none of the family would pay respects to it. In the same way, Samantha Upward or Jen Teale, even if their mother died at three o'clock in the morning, would be on to the undertaker in a flash to get the body out of the house. The Definitely-Disgustings, however, would be much more likely to be present at the death, and to visit the body if they were not. When I worked on a local paper, whenever a working-class person died, I was always invited in for a cup of tea to admire the corpse lying in his coffin in the sitting room. As cremation gets more and more popular, too, the ashes tend to be left with the undertaker, and even a grave to mourn at is disappearing. According to our local undertaker, the middle classes often prefer not to watch that poignant final moment when the coffin disappears through the doors. They specify beforehand that they don't want the coffin to move, and troop out while it's still on its platform.

Fear of expressing unhappiness is also a characteristic of the upper middles – the stiff upper middle lip again. Geoffrey Gorer said his own sister-in-law didn't even go to her husband's funeral, she was so terrified of breaking down in front of all her friends and relations and, wishing to spare the children such a depressing experience, took them for a picnic. Yet as a bereaved person, she found herself shunned like a leper. Only if she acted as though nothing of consequence had happened was she again socially acceptable. Thus, not only death, but overt suffering is taboo. Perhaps this explains the plethora of euphemisms surrounding the subject. Howard Weybridge never 'dies', he 'passes away', or 'passes on', or 'passes over', or 'goes to God' or 'to his rest'. Dean is even described as 'falling asleep'. 'Flowers' become 'floral tributes', even the undertaker prefers to call himself a 'funeral director', and describes a burial as an 'interment'.

Harry Stow-Crat's father, Lord Egliston, would have had a

nice end to his life. He has made everything over to Harry to avoid estate duty, and all the family have been frantically cosseting him to keep him alive the required five years. 'My father's great dread was going senile,' said one aristocrat, apologising for his father who was happily exposing himself in the orangery. 'But now he has, he's enjoying himself enormously.'

Obituary Page, Harry might not bother to pay for an insertion in the deaths column. If he did, it would be simple, saying where his father had died, and where and at what time the funeral would be held. Gideon Upward would also put his mother's death in *The Times*, and he might add her age (Samantha certainly would, out of spite) and the fact that she was the widow of Colonel Upward. Howard Weybridge would use the *Telegraph*. Jen Teale would use the local paper, and add a sentence about 'passing peacefully away' and being 'the loving mother of Bryan and the devoted granny of Wayne and Christine'. The Definitely-Disgustings would probably throw in 'a happy release' and 'a special auntie to Charlene and little Terry', and a 'thank you' to the nurses doctors and district nurses concerned.

When a peer, or peeress in her own right, or a baronet dies, it is customary for letters written to members of his or her family to be addressed by the titles by which they were previously known until after the funeral. Consequently if a friend wrote Harry a letter saying how sorry he was about Lord Egliston, he would address it to the 'Hon. Harry Stow-Crat', and if *The Times* reported the funeral they would describe him in the same way. At the memorial service a fortnight later, he would be called 'Lord Egliston'.

Lord Egliston's funeral would be simple. Harry would wear a dark suit and a black tie, Caroline would dress soberly but not in black. Relations and friends might have to walk across the fields, while the coffin was carried to the family church, which means Gucci shoes sinking into the cowpats. Although it is more upper-class to be buried than cremated it is frightfully smart to *have* to be cremated because your family tomb is so full of your ancestors going back to the year dot that there is no room for you. Lord Egliston might just squeeze into the family mausoleum. The headstone, when it was up, would bear a simple inscription: 'Henry George De Vere Stow-Crat, 5th

Baron Egliston, born April 12 1905, died April 23rd 1979.'
Harry when his time comes, will probably have to be cremated
and put in the family crypt. People would probably send
flowers picked from their own gardens with plain cards, saying
'With love', or 'In memory', in their own writing, not in the
loopy writing of the florist. Being old-fashioned, like the working classes, they might also send wreaths. Afterwards, everyone
would go back to lunch or tea, where depending on the
stuffiness of the family, or on the intensity of the unhappiness, a
certain amount of drink would be consumed.

When very important men die, what diplomats describe as a
'working funeral' takes place, which means that heads of state
from all over the world meet on neutral ground, and while
pretending to admire the wreaths, the Chinese and American
foreign secretaries can discuss matters of moment out of the
corners of their mouths, without appearing to fraternise.

The upper middles would probably drink themselves silly at
the funeral. Although a few years ago this would have been
frowned on. When my husband in the sixties announced that he
intended to leave £200 in his will for a booze-up for his friends,
his lawyer talked him out of it, saying it was in bad taste and
would upset people. The same year his grandmother died, and
after the funeral, recovering from the innate vulgarity of the
cremation service when the gramophone record stuck on 'Abi-
abi-abi-abi-de with me', the whole family trooped home and
discovered some crates of Australian burgundy under the
stairs. A rip-roaring party ensued and soon a lower middle
busybody who lived next door came bustling over to see if
anything was wrong. Whereupon my father-in-law, holding a
glass and seeing her coming up the path uttered the immortal
line: 'Who is this intruding on our grief?'

When Mr Nouveau-Richards dies of a heart attack, Mrs
Nouveau-Richards is worried about how she should arrange
things. They don't report smart funerals in *The Tatler* for her to
copy. She turns up at the church in deepest black with a huge
picture hat and lots of make-up. All Jison's telly-stocratic
friends turn up and keep a weather eye out for photographers
and television cameras. The men wear light-coloured suits and
cry a lot. The girls also wear deepest black and picture hats, but
cry less, in case their mascara runs. Mr Nouveau-Richard's
business colleagues send wreaths, with black-edged funeral

cards, with 'deepest sympathy' printed on them. The flag at the Nouveau-Richards Inc. building flies at half-mast. Mrs Nouveau-Richards insists on the undertakers wearing the full regalia of top hats, pinstripe trousers, and umbrellas.

After he was buried in the cemetery (Caroline Stow-Crat calls it a 'graveyard') Mrs Nouveau-Richards would have a splendid tomb built in strawberry roan marble, and engraved with ornate sentiments about Mr Nouveau-Richards 'crossing the bar to his eternal rest', and being 'the beloved father of Jason and Tracey-Diane'.

The Teales would be very stingy and question the price of everything. Jen thinks death is 'not very naice', and would expect the undertaker to do everything. She wouldn't want the hearse outside the house, she and Bryan would drive the Volks-wagen to the funeral. After all, there's nothing to get upset about: Bryan's mother was 'very elderly' and had been a 'senior citizen' for a long time. There would be no sobbing at the funeral, that's what the Definitely-Disgustings do. And Bryan's mother would probably be cremated, as it's cheaper, although if she did have a grave, Jen wouldn't want the bother of tending it, so instead of earth or grass, the flat bit would be sprinkled with emerald green chips which serve the same function as plastic grass. Floral tributes would be particularly tasteful, and Bryan would probably wear a black armband on his sleeve, or a black diamond sewn on by Jen, for a few weeks afterwards.

The Definitely-Disgustings really push the boat out. 'I'm going to Florrie's funeral tomorrow,' I heard one working-class Yorkshire woman, saying, 'It should be a good do,' a sentiment that would never be admitted by the middle classes.

Mr Definitely-Disgusting even insured for the purpose of being buried right, but alas with the cost of living, the policy seldom comes anywhere near covering the cost of the funeral, which means Mrs Definitely-Disgusting is likely to be left pen-niless and in debt. The problem, said our local undertaker is to stop people overspending in a fit of overemotionalism. Often they get quite annoyed:

'Are you trying to tell me, my missus doesn't deserve the best,' said one man.

One engine driver's widow, who could ill afford it, forked out for six cars, and a very expensive panelled coffin. Afterwards she came and thanked the undertaker, adding that it was worth it, 'Even if I have to go out scrubbing for the rest of my life to pay for it.'

In the old days the streets used to be sanded to deaden the sound of the horses hooves. And even today whole streets in the North and in Wales will show solidarity by drawing every curtain from the moment the hearse leaves the house until the funeral party returns.

The working classes still send funeral cards with poems inside and picture of lilies and purple prayer books on the front, which are displayed on the window sill outside drawn curtains. Often the men go out specially to buy a black suit, and often as many as six cars filled with tearful relations follow the hearse. Frightful rows ensue, too, because someone who thinks he's important enough to travel in the second car, only gets a seat in the third car. Invariably, it's the forty-second cousin once removed who screams and cries the loudest because he's been on the booze since dawn.

Evidently at one cockney gypsy funeral, the dead man had married again after his first wife died. On one side of the grave lined up the first wife's family, on the other the second wife and her family, both glaring across at each other. As the coffin was lowered, the first wife's son shook his fist at the second wife, hissing: 'He's gone to lie with a good woman now.' Whereupon the son of the second wife, nipped round the back and pushed the first wife's son into the grave, and jumped on top of him. A glorious free-for-all resulted, which was only stopped by the arrival of the police.

With the floral tributes, the working classes really come into their own. Once again, because of their diffidence about expressing themselves verbally, they spell it out with flowers. On the hearse are likely to be cushions and pillows with 'Mum' written across, empty chairs saying 'We'll never forget you, Dad'; teddy-bears or favourite dogs for the death of a child; bleeding hearts, harps with a broken string, all made entirely of flowers. Around the Elephant and Castle, people often pay tribute to a man's profession. One East-Ender had a whole market stall full of fruit and vegetables, with all the price tickets, made entirely of different coloured carnations, which took six men to lift on to the hearse. A landlord is often given a glass of foaming beer made entirely of white and brown chrysanthemums, while a bookie might have a floral winning post. One East End boxer had his last fight almost to scale, with a ring, a referee and two boxers – all made of daisies. A florist told me the working classes would consider it insulting to give someone a small posy of spring flowers. If an old age pensioner comes into the shop, and you steer her towards something that looks within her price range, she still insists on buying long-stemmed 'Football Mum's' chrysanthemums at £1 a flower.

The party afterwards will be a terrific booze-up with crates and crates of beer, and masses of stodgy food. One scrap metal merchant even put up a marquee in his garden. Everyone gets plastered and then does song and dance acts. David Storey told me of how he once went to a friend's funeral in Yorkshire. Not knowing the dead man's family, it was only after freezing beside the grave for twenty minutes, that he discovered, on asking one of the mourners, that he was attending the wrong funeral.

'Never mind, lad,' comforted the mourner. 'They'll all be meeting up at the Black Bull same as us afterwards.'

After the funeral Sharon and Dive would club together to buy Mr Definitely-Disgusting a headstone, perhaps inscribed with the words: 'Have a good sleep, Dad.' They would also put another entry in the local paper thanking everyone for their condolences and floral tributes. A year later, it would be considered very remiss if an *In Memoriam* notice didn't appear in the same paper.

'God took Dad home,
It was his will,
But why that way,
We wonder still.
Always in our thoughts, fondest love Doris, Dive, Sharon, Auntie Edna and little Terry.' Quite often there will be additional notices from several other members of the family. Because the working classes tend not to take part in local government and parish affairs, birth, marriage and death, or when one of them gets caught nicking a television, are the only times they get their names in the paper. Howard Weybridge might put an *In Memoriam* to Eileen, or to his brother who was killed in Korea in the *Daily Telegraph*.

*   *   *

But finally our heroes get to the Other Side. How will they fare in the after-life?

Harry Stow-Crat is thoroughly enjoying himself. He is just expressing delight at the prospect of seeing Snipe and Nanny again, when suddenly a beautiful angel flaps past, and Harry can't decide whether to take a pot at her, or ask her out to luncheon. Jen Teale is speechless with admiration at the whiteness of the angel's robe, and wonders if she used a bio wash. Mr Nouveau-Richards having examined the burglar alarm on the pearly gates is boasting to God how much better his own gates on earth were wired up against intruders, and how none of the pearls are as big as the ones he gave Mrs Nouveau-Richards for their silver wedding. Jison Richards is just about to ask Jesus for an in-depth interview. Howard Weybridge is enjoying a round of golf with the Holy Ghost, and Mr Definitely-Disgusting is having a lovely time playing 'Roll Out the Barrel' on the harp, and filling in his football coupon for the match against Limbo this afternoon.

Only Samantha Upward looks perturbed. Who would have thought, she keeps murmuring to herself disconsolately, that God would say 'Pleased to meet you', when we arrived?

REFERENCES

Introduction
Montaigne, *Essais*, II, 12.
Classification of Occupations, H.M.S.O., 1970.
Nancy Mitford, *The Pursuit of Love*, Hamish Hamilton, 1949.
Jonathan Gathorne-Hardy, *The Rise and Fall of the British Nanny*,
    Hodder and Stoughton, 1972.

Chapter 1
Brian Masters, *The Dukes*, Blond and Briggs, 1975.
Shakespeare, *Henry V*, Act V, scene 2.
Jane Austen, *Persuasion*.
Richard Hoggart, *The Uses of Literacy*, Chatto and Windus,
    1957.

Chapter 2
Nancy Mitford (ed.), *Noblesse Oblige*, Hamish Hamilton, 1973.
Harold Acton, *Nancy Mitford*, Hamish Hamilton.
Geoffrey Gorer, *Exploring English Character*, Barrie and Jenkins,
    1955.
Colin Bell, *Middle Class Families*, Routledge & Kegan Paul,
    1969.
Althea, *A Baby in the Family*, Dinosaur.

Chapter 3
Jonathan Gathorne-Hardy, *The Rise and Fall of the British Nanny*,
    Hodder and Stoughton 1972.

Chapter 4
Jonathan Gathorne-Hardy, *The Public School Phenomenon*,
    Hodder and Stoughton, 1977.
Douglas Sutherland, *The English Gentleman*, Debrett's.

Anthony Sampson, *The New Anatomy of Britain*, Hodder and Stoughton.

Ann Thwaite (ed.), *My Oxford*, Robson Books, 1977.

Chapter 5
Ann Thwaite (ed.), *My Oxford*, Robson Books, 1977.

Ronald Hayman (ed.), *My Cambridge*, Robson Books, 1977.

Chapter 6
Peter Wilmott and Michael Young, *Family and Class in a London Suburb*, Routledge & Kegan Paul, 1960.

Jane Austen, *Emma*.

Nancy Mitford (ed.), *Noblesse Oblige*, Hamish Hamilton, 1973.

Harold Acton, *Nancy Mitford*, Hamish Hamilton.

W. S. Auden, *The Dyer's Hand*.

John Betjeman, *Collected Poems*, John Murray, 1970.

Ralf Dahrendorf, *Class and Class Conflict in Industrial Society*, Routledge & Kegan Paul, 1972.

Colin Bell, *Middle Class Families*, Routledge & Kegan Paul, 1969.

J. M. and R. E. Pahl, *Managers and their Wives*, Penguin, 1972.

Chapter 7
Nancy Mitford, *Love in a Cold Climate*, Hamish Hamilton, 1949.

Richard Buckle (ed.), *U and Non U Revisited*, Debrett's.

Geoffrey Gorer, *Sex and Marriage.in England Today*, Nelson, 1971.

Ivan Reid, *Social Class Differences in Britain*, Open Books, 1977.

Chapter 8
Geoffrey Gorer, *Sex and Marriage in England Today*, Nelson, 1971.

Chapter 9
Jane Daverson and Katherine Lindsay, *Voices from the Middle Class*, Hutchinson, 1975.

Lord David Cecil, *Looking Glass Library*, Constable.

V. Sackville-West, *English Country Houses*, William Collins.

Oscar Wilde, *The Importance of Being Earnest*.

John Le Carré, *Call for the Dead*, Penguin, 1975.

Chapter 10
Jane Daverson and Katherine Lindsay, *Voices from the Middle Class*, Hutchinson, 1975.

John Connell, *The End of Tradition*, Routledge & Kegan Paul, 1978.

Chapter 11
Percy Lubbock, *Earlham*, Jonathan Cape.

Chapter 12
Michael Nelson, *Nobs and Snobs*, Gordon Cremonesi, 1976.
Harold Acton, *Nancy Mitford*, Hamish Hamilton.

Chapter 13
Ann Thwaite (ed.), *My Oxford*, Robson Books.

Chapter 14
Richard Buckle (ed.), *U and Non U Revisited*, Debrett's.
Alan S. C. Ross (ed.), *What are U?*, Andre Deutsch, 1969.
Mrs Gaskell, *Wives and Daughters*.
Paul Jennings and John Gorham (ed.), *The English Difference*,
  Aurelia Enterprises, 1974.

Chapter 15
George Bernard Shaw, *Pygmalion*, Preface.
Geoffrey Gorer, *Sex and Marriage in England Today*, Nelson.

Chapter 16
Samuel Rogers, *Table Talk*.
Hogarth, *Autobiographical Sketch*, John Ireland, 1748.
Frank Muir, *The Frank Muir Book*, Heinemann, 1976.

Chapter 17
Report of the Annan Committee on Broadcasting, 1978.

Chapter 18
Richard Crossman, *Diaries of a Cabinet Minister*, Jonathan Cape,
  1977.
J. E. M. Ruffer, *The Big Shots*, Debrett's, 1977.
Robert Lacey, *Majesty*, Hutchinson, 1977.

Chapter 22
Douglas Sutherland, *The English Gentleman*, Debrett's.

Chapter 23
Geoffrey Gorer, *Death, Grief and Mourning*, Cresset Press, 1965.

ADDITIONAL BIBLIOGRAPHY

Robert Bocock, *Ritual in Industrial Society*, Allen and Unwin, 1974.

Burke's Peerage

Debrett's Peerage and Baronetage

D. V. Glass (ed.), *Social Mobility in Britain*, Routledge & Kegan Paul, 1954.

Colin Rosser and Charles Harris, *The Family and Social Change*, Routledge & Kegan Paul, 1965.